M000307187

EUDORA WELTY AND MYSTERY

CRITICAL PERSPECTIVES ON EUDORA WELTY

Harriet Pollack, Series Editor

EUDORA WELTY AND MYSTERY

Hidden in Plain Sight

Edited by Jacob Agner and Harriet Pollack

University Press of Mississippi / Jackson

www.upress.state.ms.us

The University Press of Mississippi is a member
of the Association of University Presses.

Any discriminatory or derogatory language or hate speech regarding race,
ethnicity, religion, sex, gender, class, national origin, age, or disability that
has been retained or appears in elided form is in no way an endorsement
of the use of such language outside a scholarly context.

Copyright © 2023 by University Press of Mississippi
All rights reserved

Welty's unpublished manuscripts "Alterations" and "The Shadow Club" are discussed
and lines reprinted here by permission of the Eudora Welty Collection at the
Mississippi Department of Archives and History and of Russell and Volkening as
agents for the author. Copyright © by Eudora Welty, renewed by Eudora Welty LLC.

The unpublished manuscript of "The Night of the Little House" is discussed
and quoted with the permission of the Manuscripts and Archives Division
of the New York Public Library; Astor, Lenox, and Tilden Foundations;
and of Russell and Volkening as agents for the author.
Copyright © by Eudora Welty, renewed by Eudora Welty LLC.

Two of Eudora Welty's cartoons from "The Great Pinnington Solves a Mystery,"
first published in Mississippi State College for Women's campus journal,
The Spectator (1925), are reprinted with permission of Eudora Welty LLC
and Russell and Volkening as agents for the author.

First printing 2023
∞

Library of Congress Cataloging-in-Publication Data available

LCCN 2022043579
ISBN 9781496842701 (hardcover)
ISBN 9781496842718 (paperback)
ISBN 9781496842725 (epub single)
ISBN 9781496842732 (epub institutional)
ISBN 9781496842749 (pdf single)
ISBN 9781496842756 (pdf institutional)

British Library Cataloging-in-Publication Data available

CONTENTS

EUDORA WELTY AND MYSTERY

UNDERGROUND WOMAN

The Secret History of Eudora Welty and the Mystery Genre

JACOB AGNER AND HARRIET POLLACK

In the work of Eudora Welty, a sense of abiding mystery is key. In "Words into Fiction" (1965), for example—one of her well-known essays on the puzzle of using "language . . . to express human life"—Welty declares, "If this [process] makes fiction sound full of mystery, I think it's fuller than I know how to say. . . . In writing, do we try to solve the mystery? No, I think we take hold of the other end of the stick. In very practical ways, we rediscover the mystery. We even, I might say, take advantage of it" (*Eye* 137). Indeed, throughout her fiction, there is strong and undeniable attention paid to the enigma of language, to finding mystery in the outside world, and to the perplexity of human relationships. Literary critic Ruth M. Vande Kieft in the earliest book-length study on Welty's fiction (1962) would find the term so essential to discussing Welty's fiction that she would dedicate an entire chapter to the subject, titled "The Mysteries of Eudora Welty." And more than three decades later, critic James Olney, in a *New York Times* review of the 1998 Library of America volumes further canonizing Welty's collected works, rang the same bell when discussing her imaginative achievement. "The words mystery and mysterious echo like mantras in Welty's fiction, essays, and memoir," Olney wrote, and the overarching "story" of her literary achievement was "of a pervasive and inexplicable mystery at the heart of human existence and relationship" ("Where the Voice Came From"). Mystery, then, is, and has long been, shorthand for the metaphysical in Welty's imagination.

Now fifty-some years after Vande Kieft's first foray, the talented scholars in this volume address a different, but not ultimately unrelated, aspect, illuminating Welty's deft literary engagements not only with mystery made manifest in language, identity, and relationships, but also through uses of the *mystery genre* itself, its various subcategories and stylistic modes. This turn follows a literary event from 2015, when Suzanne Marrs and Tom Nolan drew attention to a surprisingly rich chapter from the writer's life through their landmark publication of Welty's tender, informing, and widely ranging personal correspondence with the hard-boiled American crime writer Ross Macdonald (aka Kenneth Millar). That cache of letters, clearly revealing Welty as a lifelong fan of the mystery genre, hints at something that has been hidden in plain sight all this time. Indeed, as essay after essay in this collection will make clear, the preeminent southern author from Jackson, Mississippi— "Miss Welty," as so many once lovingly came to call her—very well may have been one of the mystery genre's greatest double agents or, as Macdonald himself might have called her, its "sleeping beauty" and its "underground woman."

These readings reveal Welty as a serious American modernist on the one hand, intersecting her unique talents in genre experimentation and risky obstruction of readers' expectations, and, on the other, as a potentially overlooked contributor to the postmodern turn of the 1960s and 1970s. Through her unpretentious engagement with a seemingly "lowbrow" art form, Welty, despite a public persona based on sheltered literary genius, creatively responded to, complicated, and had her way with a genre so often condescended to in literary studies. And the essays that follow in this collection, while highlighting her remarkable skills as a genre-bending master, her protofeminist energies as a political powerhouse, and her subtly piercing critiques of hegemonic whiteness, draw attention to Welty's studied engagements with the genre.

Welty's personal library, left intact as it stood at her death in what is now a house museum, is full of the evidence of a lifetime of mystery reading. And while of course we often cannot say exactly when (or if) she read all she collected, we can say that her library reflects her wide-ranging awareness of the genre. Reading for entertainment and for pleasure, Eudora Welty provided herself with an extensive education in the genre that, as a literary artist with a penchant for adaptation and innovation, she would frequently draw on. Consider then the history of mystery reflected on her house library shelves.

WELTY WITHIN THE MYSTERY GENRE'S WIDE NET

Welty House Library Holdings: Edgar Allan Poe

As a prolific young reader of her time and place, Welty would have known fellow southerner Edgar Allan Poe's nineteenth-century gothic tales, and, by extension, his creation of the first few detective stories written. Although Poe himself never thought of his stories as such—he called them "tales of ratiocination"—it was Poe nonetheless, with his triptych of stories from the 1840s—"The Murders in the Rue Morgue" (1841), "The Mystery of Marie Rogêt" (1842), and "The Purloined Letter" (1844)—who first established the genre's central traits. Revolving around the subject of violent crimes in modern society and how to solve them, Poe's three stories introduce the first clear instance of that peculiar class of character that would later dominate the genre: C. Auguste Dupin, the archetypal detective figure and his skillful use of logic ("ratiocination") to solve the unsolvable.

Among Dupin's impressive triumphs, "The Murders in the Rue Morgue" chronicles how Dupin solves the mystery of how two women alone in a locked room are violently murdered by an outside party, establishing a sub-genre that would carry on well into the genre's later years: "the locked room mystery" scenario. And in "The Mystery of Marie Rogêt" Dupin again astounds, solving a murder by piecing together crucial information from newspaper reports alone. The last of them, though, arguably tops them all: in "The Purloined Letter," Dupin wins a game of wits with the Minister D, a political criminal who, having stolen a confidential letter, attempts to "hide" it in plain sight, a trick that Dupin, being Dupin, shrewdly anticipates. Thus he brings his defeated double to the mercy of the royal victim whom the Minister had meant to embarrass and control. Poe, turning to other experiments in form, would abandon his ingenious detective and the captivating genre he seemingly invented. But as the course of literary history would reveal, many after him would take up Dupin's mantle to great effect.

Holdings: The Victorians (Charles Dickens, Wilkie Collins, and Sir Arthur Conan Doyle)

We know from Welty's memoir *One Writer's Beginnings* the exceptional importance of her library's set of *The Works of Charles Dickens*. Her mother Chestina (herself no slouch in her love of the mystery genre) had once risked entering a house on fire to salvage the collection that, as Welty would later describe, "had been through fire and water before I was born." Then she would find it lined up in her family's library "waiting for *me*" (846). In Vols. 17 and 18 of that same set, Welty would meet Dickens's *Bleak House* (1852) and in it, Inspector Bucket, who was arguably the first detective incorporated in the novel form. A 1976 letter to Ken Millar would also express Welty's appreciation of Wilkie Collins, the so-called father of the Victorian "sensation novel," whose work she was then rereading as the "perfect antidote" to

"Pulitzer chores" while serving as that year's committee chair. "To go back to 'A Woman in White'" [1859] she wrote,

> it was the form & shape of it, the control, the delicious sensation of seeing the way he unfolds his plot—the suspense of it, which is perfect, is somehow kin to the solidity of it—and the minutiae *counting*— Well, I care about such things and they make me happy—It was like the peace of an ocean voyage to go off on such an excursion." (*Meanwhile* 284)

Welty's comments are apt. Collins's "sensation novels"—a precursor of sorts to the modern "thriller" genre—followed Dickens's *Bleak House* with two early classics, *The Woman in White* (1859) and *The Moonstone* (1868), both in her library. Franklin Blake from *The Moonstone* is often recognized as one of the earliest examples of the gentlemanly detective figure in English literature, and Walter Hartright's story in *The Woman in White* is built around one of the most dazzling plots of the nineteenth century—an ingeniously structured labyrinth of sudden turns, surprises, and spooky encounters. It is interesting to note that, for an author usually more attuned to poetic detail than plot, Welty admired Collins's work. These contributions to the form would also be followed by the fin-de-siècle author, Sir Arthur Conan Doyle, on Welty's bookshelf in the form of *The Casebook of Sherlock Holmes*, a collection of twelve tales featuring the famous detective. And while Holmes made his first appearance in 1887, and was shockingly killed off only six years later by his archenemy, Professor Moriarty, Holmes resuscitated would triumphantly return throughout Welty's childhood in volumes such as *His Last Bow* (1917) and the above *Casebook* (first published in 1927). His legacy in popular culture remains one of the most impactful in the mystery genre.

Holdings: The Golden Age School (Margery Allingham, Agatha Christie, Elizabeth Daly, Ngaio Marsh, S. S. Van Dine)

Poe, Collins, and Doyle, however, were not the only mystery writers available to Welty in her youth. As critic Howard Haycraft would argue in 1941, a "fresher, sharper detective story" would make "bold and rapid strides on its stout legs" both in England and the United States during Welty's childhood years (112). It was Haycraft who labeled 1918–1930 as a "Golden Age" in which the mystery genre took on a literary and commercial artistic maturity.

A series of implied rules began to be associated with the genre's narrative formula. In 1928, for example, American author S. S. Van Dine (Willard

Huntington Wright) extracted and articulated his notion of the genre's conventions and published "Twenty Rules for Writing Detective Stories" in *The American Magazine*. These included the expectations that "a reader must have equal opportunity with the detective for solving the mystery," that "the detective himself . . . should never turn out to be the culprit," that "the culprit must turn out to be a person who has played a more or less prominent part in the story," and that "the method of murder, and the means of detecting it, must be rational and scientific" (189, 190, 191). These and similar rules of the game generated ways of writing: plot types, settings, and subgenres. To help keep readers focused on possible culprits and clues, the convention of sequestering the cast of characters arose. Golden Age mystery authors would contrive a perfectly isolated setting in English life—whether it was a rural manor house in the middle of nowhere (as it is in Agatha Christie's first novel, *The Mysterious Affair at Styles*, 1920) or a moving train (as in her *Murder on the Orient Express*, 1934)—to set the stage for their murder plots, giving rise to informally named subgenres such as "country house" detective tales and "railway mysteries."

The Golden Age was also significant for the way it appeared to cater to both women authors and women readers alike. "To-day a highly respectable proportion of all detective stories," Haycraft wrote in 1941, "including many of the finest, are written by women. This was not always so" (128). Following the early work of pioneering figures such as Anna Katharine Green (1846–1935), Carolyn Wells (1862–1942), and Mary Roberts Rinehart (1876–1958, whose later work, *The Haunted Lady* [1942], is in Welty's collection), women authors would take ownership of the genre in the early 1920s, beginning with the major output of Agatha Christie (1890–1976) and several others—Dorothy L. Sayers (1893–1957), Elizabeth Daly (1878–1967), Ngaio Marsh (1895–1982), and Margery Allingham (1904–1966)—who soon followed. As of late, it also appears that a twenty-first-century version of this gendered "takeover" of the genre has similarly taken place. Following the works of such female crime authors as Gillian Flynn, Megan Abbott, Paula Hawkins, and Laura Lippmann, it not only now seems to many that, as an *Atlantic* article put it in 2016, "Women are Writing the Best Crime Novels," but this new gendered dimension of the genre has also drawn attention to the fact that "[w]omen have been writing books like [these] ever since [the 1940s and 1950s]" (Rafferty). See, for instance, the two-volume Library of America set, *Women Crime Writers* (2015), which highlights eight women authors from that era (including Kenneth Millar's wife, Margaret Millar).

Of these, Christie in particular seems to have been a special figure in Welty's affection. When Welty was eleven in 1920, Christie would bring out an eccentric Belgian detective named Hercule Poirot who stumbles upon a murder mystery set in a remote English countryside manor. With that invention, Christie, a little-known writer at the time, began one of the greatest commercial literary careers in modern publishing. The house library holds nineteen books by the prolific "Queen of Crime"—including, to name a few, *The Mystery of the Blue Train* (1929), *The Tuesday Club Murder* (1932), *Murder in Three Acts* (1935), *Dead Man's Mirror* (1937), *Poirot Loses a Client* (1937), *A Holiday for Murder* (1938), *Ten Little Indians* (1939), and *The Body in the Library* (1942).[1] We can assume these nineteen titles are not a complete record of Welty's familiarity and fandom, considering that she did not own every book she read, but borrowed from both libraries and friends, and that—as we know from her correspondence—she frequently gave books she had just finished and enjoyed to others to read. Note too that while Christie has this place of honor in the extensive Welty House library, several others writers also flaunt numerous titles, such as New Zealand woman crime writer Ngaio Marsh (ten), American authors Elizabeth Daly (fourteen) and Rex Stout (ten), Belgian writer Georges Simenon (sixteen), and British Dick Francis (fourteen). But it is fair to say that Welty first grew up, and then—as this volume will suggest—grew her own art alongside Christie's novels.

Welty herself at the precocious age of sixteen, styled a Golden Age mystery spoof when writing for her college newspaper, *The Spectator* of Mississippi State College for Women. The parody, humorously and grandiosely titled "The Great Pinnington Solves the Mystery" (1925), clearly demonstrates Welty's early awareness of the genre. Welty's send-up shows her knowledge of the form and its tropes, even as it mocks them—with her exuberant youthful mimicry of humorist S. J. Perelman's clever, amusing stylistic flair.

Welty's comedic energy is apparent throughout as she burlesques one of the Golden Age's most well-known tropes: the introduction of the eccentric (and often quite foppishly so) independent detective. In an assertion that is certainly meant to be glib, comic, and silly, her self-reporting narrator deliberates how to properly start her story, *any* story, just to set its plot in motion: "I am going to be a detective with a magnetic eye and a long front name, like Pentington" (83, figs. 1.1 and 1.2). But a problem presents itself; that is, as the Golden Age's immense success suggests, the detective field has already become a quite crowded one. Much about Pinnington immediately reminds us of other "great" detective-eccentrics from that very same era: Christie's Poirot, S. S. Van Dine's Philo Vance, G. K. Chesterton's Father Brown, or even Doyle's Sherlock Holmes. In one particularly clever aside, Welty's narrator realizes that somebody else before her has already claimed her detective's "great" name: Pentington (83). And while it is never made clear from Welty's story, nor evidenced by her house library, Welty's narrator's concern very well may have come from a real place. From 1918 to 1923 (leading up to Welty's story in 1925), the New York author Carolyn Wells (1862–1942), known today for producing up to one hundred and seventy books throughout her lifetime, also published eight novels featuring none other than detective *Pennington* Wise. And thus Welty's narrator deems it "trite" to copy this name too closely—the awkward oversight eventually avoided (comically) by conveniently changing two letters of her detective's name into the vast difference of "Pinnington . . . a noble name" (83) as she so drolly announces.

Moreover, when the narrator—"the hero," even though she is "in real life a Girl" (82)—looks for a murder to investigate, she spoofs one of the bread-and-butter formulas of the genre: the locked-room mystery puzzle so famously engineered by Poe's "Murders in the Rue Morgue" almost a century earlier. The locked-room puzzle ultimately proves itself no match for the ingenuity of young Welty's detective's waggish logic: "I tried the door, but it was locked from the inside. I did not know what to do for a minute, but suddenly I remembered. So I did what I thought of, and it opened the door" (84). Later when she finds a bullet missing from the murder weapon, she repeats that gumshoe logic: "I thought I knew where I could find it. I looked—and there it was" (85). Welty's parodic play—with her detective's name, with speedy and formulaic solutions, and with her own wonderfully silly drawings complementing her story—creates the entertaining dimensions of her early lampoon of the mystery genre.

Fig. 1.1 & 1.2. Two of Welty's cartoons accompanying her early spoof, "The Great Pinnington Solves the Mystery." These illustrations originally appeared in Mississippi State College for Women's campus journal, *The Spectator*, 1925, and were previously reprinted in Patti Carr Black's *Eudora Welty: Early Escapades* (UP of Mississippi, 2005). Reprinted now with permission of Eudora Welty LLC and Russell and Volkening as agents for the author.

What is more, despite its short length and silly tone, much of this youthful production arguably predicts one of Welty's signature strengths as an artist, which the essays of this volume will repeatedly identify: namely, Welty's remarkable ability to innovatively "genre-bend"—in this case, the mystery/ detective/crime-fiction genre(s)—to unpredictable ends. Although this romp from Welty's teen years is not a mature artistic effort, it is both an early indicator of some characteristic creative skills that the adult author would perfect and of the continuing roles that Golden Age mystery fiction would play in Welty's lifetime output.

Holdings: The "Hard-Boiled"/ "Noir" School (Dashiell Hammett, Raymond Chandler, Ross Macdonald, Alfred Hitchcock)

In the same year (1920) when Agatha Christie published her first Poirot novel, another important "first" took place. In April 1920, the inaugural issue of the cheap, gaudy "pulp fiction" magazine *The Black Mask*—printed on pulped ground wood and featuring a bright colored cover—began arriving at dime-store and newsstand counters across the country. Before long *Black Mask* would become an important literary headquarters for a new "hard-boiled" school of ambitious and influential literary stylists. These writers shaped their fictions in reaction, scoffing at "typical laburnum-and-lodge-gate English country house" mysteries, as Raymond Chandler sneeringly painted them in 1944, and jeering too at the women writers who produced them ("The Simple Art of Murder" 6). Critical of "murders scented with magnolia blossoms," the hard-boiled authors "reminded that murder is an act of infinite cruelty" (16). Those views produced longer, darker noir novels such as Dashiell Hammett's *The Maltese Falcon* (1930), James M. Cain's *The Postman Always Rings Twice* (1934), and Chandler's *The Big Sleep* (1939), all of which preceded Welty's 1941 breakthrough onto the literary scene with *A Curtain of Green*. Noir captured a deeply pessimistic American landscape rife with suffocating toxicity. And it introduced obsessive stylistic focus on the symbolic and evocative chiaroscuro of light and shadow, and on the explosive, almost dream-like suddenness of random, all-but-inexplicable violence. These writers too are on the shelves of the house library: Hammett's *The Thin Man* (1934), Chandler's *The Blue Dahlia* (1946), *The Little Sister* (1949), *Trouble Is My Business* (1950), and *Killer in the Rain* (1964)—not to mention numerous titles across Ross Macdonald's career.

It is equally true that Welty knew the techniques of noir—on which the volume shows her frequently drawing—from her movie-going as well as from her reading. Many of Welty's personal letters reveal her interest in mystery films. In her correspondence to Frank Lyell, one of her closest friends, she mentions seeing and reacting to *M* (1931), *I Wake Up Screaming* (1941), *The Glass Key* (1942), *The Lodger* (about Jack the Ripper, 1944), *Laura* (1944), *Three Strangers* (1946), *Mr. Ace* (1946), *Monsieur Verdoux* (1947), *Mystery Street* (1950), *Detective Story* (1951) and *The Thief* (1952).[2] In 1974, she sent Lyell a news clipping about the film version of Agatha Christie's *The Murder on the Orient Express*, and then in 1975, she wrote to tell him about Ken Millar's admiration of Roman Polanski's *Chinatown* (first released in 1974), though she herself was still planning to see it (and perhaps it was only just coming to Jackson theaters).[3]

Much earlier, to John Robinson, she had written about the films of Alfred Hitchcock—in particular, *Secret Agent* (1936), *Suspicion* (1941), and *Rope* (1948).[4] On *Rope*, she commented: "Saw the preview of the new Hitchcock film which was made in two hours' shooting, after rehearsals and never had a break in the time—interesting, fairly. He comes into it (Hitchck [sic]) as a Red neon sign ad flashing on and off in the distance—one scene, like a play—"Rope."[5] And on the "Master of Suspense" himself, she later opined to Bill Ferris:

> I like detective stories, and I don't think in general they make good
> films. They can't do it. But Hitchcock had something you could learn.
> He's a trickster and a magician, but so are writers, in technique. For
> instance, his transitions, which are old hat now, but at the time he
> began them were something new: showing, for instance, a person
> screaming, and all of a sudden that scream turns into a train whistle
> which is the next scene of a train going along. A short story writer
> uses transitions like that in a less obvious way, more in some symbol
> or some detail of observation which becomes a figure in the next
> section. You use something that will transport you from one scene to
> another, even if you don't know it, even if you don't realize it. That's
> like a film. Or else Hitchcock was using short story techniques. I don't
> know who thought of it first. (*Conversations* 169–70)

It is particularly interesting to think about this comment on technique and short stories in the context of noir. Welty's *A Curtain of Green* (1941) came out alongside such classics of the noir era as James M. Cain's *Mildred Pierce*, Hitchcock's *Suspicion*, Orson Welles's *Citizen Kane*, Margaret Millar's (Ross Macdonald's wife) *The Invisible Worm*, and John Huston's film adaptation of Hammett's *The Maltese Falcon*. The closer one looks at several of the stories from this collection, the more one can see connections to the shadowy imagery associated with this particular chapter of the mystery genre's popular legacy. Consider, for example, the first two paragraphs from Welty's story, "The Key" (1941), much of which reads a good deal like many of the menacing noir works from the Depression-era 1930s and postwar 1940s:

> It was quiet in the waiting room of the remote little station, except for the night sound of insects. You could hear their embroidering movements in the weeds outside, which somehow gave the effect of some tenuous voice in the night, telling a story. Or you could listen to the fat thudding of the light bugs and the hoarse rushing of their big wings against the wooden ceiling. Some of the bugs were clinging heavily to the yellow globe, like idiot bees to a senseless smell.
>
> Under this prickly light two rows of people sat in silence, their faces stung, their bodies twisted and quietly uncomfortable, especially so, in ones and twos, not quite asleep. No one seemed impatient, although the train was late. A little girl lay flung back in her mother's lap as though sleep had struck her into a blow. (*CS* 29)

Is this the work of Eudora Welty or Cornell Woolrich? That is, Welty's status as a "southern woman writer" has perhaps prevented us from recognizing the more noirish registers of her voice.

Throughout Welty's formative years as both reader and writer, the mystery genre was itself evolving, moving from its nineteenth-century configurations through those of its "Golden Age," to the transformations of its "hard-boiled" and "noir" eras. And Eudora Welty, amateur sleuth and literary historian, seems to have provided herself with an accidental education in the genre that she then drew on throughout the body of her work.

FUN WITH THE MYSTERY GENRE: ACROSS EUDORA WELTY'S CAREER

In Eudora Welty's signature puzzle-texts—in which a reader needs to find and follow hidden textual clues—it is exactly Welty's innovative play with a reader's competencies with conventions, producing surprised expectations, that makes her a paramount modernist, a woman writer with a most cunning swerve, a short story writer of the first rank, and a remarkable literary innovator. She habitually calls up familiar genres and then delights readers with her transformations and nonfulfillment of expectations. But now we are noting—here and throughout this collection—how often that play is with mystery, crime, and detective fiction genres. Welty evokes the recognizable formulas, inviting readers' expectations, and then has her way with both.[6]

From Welty's *A Curtain of Green*, first consider "The Hitch-Hikers" (a noir fiction, first published in 1939). Thirty-year-old travelling salesman Tom Harris is on the road to Memphis when he stops for two hitchhikers. Before the night is over, one hiker will kill the other in Harris's car. The action is known, but there are discoveries to be made by the reader, hinted at in a fiction that invites curiosity and speculation rather than solution and conviction. At the story's end, Tom Harris's driving on does not restore order, offer resolution, or create peace. The unknowable persists at the story's end, as it often does in Welty's fiction, and yet asks to be understood. That's not to say her puzzles are resistant to careful scrutiny, but beyond first solutions there is almost always another level of mystery, that fissure between what we know of characters and what we do not. It is most helpful to say—as Suzanne Marrs has—that her fictions "reveal, rather than resolve, mystery" (200). Similarly in "Flowers for Marjorie" (first published in 1937), the puzzle we need to solve is not *who* killed Marjorie; we know her husband did it. The official police solution closing the tale resolves nothing for the reader. Rather, the secret is the *why*—suggested to the reader by causes in Depression-era unemployment, in an implied crisis of masculinity, and in the weight of urban anonymity.

Throughout *A Curtain of Green*, there are rumors of murder, abuse, crime, and mystery in tales belonging to other—even comic—genres. In "Power-house" the riddle playfully concerns who killed Gypsy, Powerhouse's wife. In "A Piece of News," the puzzle concerns Ruby Fisher, who reads the newspaper report of another Ruby Fisher violently shot by her husband. It is not only a husband's violence that we discover, but rather, and more mysteriously, Ruby Fisher's imagination as she ponders that plot. In the train station of "The Key," after the noir opener just discussed, the enigma features a red-haired stranger who drops a key that is then picked up by a deaf man, and after observing or imagining the disabled man's relationship with his wife (also deaf), the stranger impishly offers the wife a *second* key. Quite literally then, readers are given keys that lead to other keys, as if the unlocking of one mystery is solely meant to reveal a series of other and *interlocking* mysteries. And this pattern in itself arguably serves as a master key to Welty's signature approach in her puzzle-texts: it is the second-level, secret plot, or plots, that a reader must find.

Put in another way, Welty creates her stories' secrets by both evoking and displacing familiar conventions. Not about restoring order by solving a crime, her story-puzzles characteristically allow mystery to linger and thicken.

This brings the mystery formula to a modernist turn—simple resolution is not to be had.

And Welty's later work continues this use of mystery. The essays in this collection identify and mine the mystery/detective/crime-fiction threads in *A Curtain of Green* (1941), *The Golden Apples* (1949), *The Ponder Heart* (1953), *The Bride of The Innisfallen* (1955), the uncollected 1960s stories "Where Is The Voice Coming From?" (1963) and "The Demonstrators" (1966), *Losing Battles* (1970), *The Optimist's Daughter* (1972), and her late unpublished "The Shadow Club." The stories of *A Wide Net* (1943) are not yet discussed in this collection, but they, too, are full of sleuthing, mystery, and secrets—many are ripe for future work (think of "The Purple Hat").

Welty's familiarities with popular crime and detective fiction, murder mysteries, police procedurals and pulp publications are clear from her play with mystery conventions, from her evocation of familiar plot devices, and from allusions we may hear ringing in her fictions. Her steady consumption of mysteries, evident in her home book collection, is also documented throughout her correspondence to her many friends. And having made friends in particular with the preeminent mystery/suspense editor of her time, Joan Kahn—publishing's Grande Dame of detective stories and the editor of Harper's eleven influential genre anthologies (nine are in the House Library)—Welty wrote blurbs for mystery novels (for example, the 1993 cover of Helen Eustis's *The Horizontal Man* [1946] advertises, "'Stands the hair up vertical. Genuinely scary.' -Eudora Welty"). And she also penned the introduction to Kahn's 1969 collection *Hanging by a Thread*. Then too when Welty wrote book reviews, she knowledgeably discussed the detective in William Faulkner's *Intruder in the Dust* (1949) and in Ross Macdonald's *The Underground Man* (1971), the review that led to her meeting Ken Millar/ Ross Macdonald, to their remarkable friendship, and to her years of consequential correspondence with him.

ROSS MACDONALD AND EUDORA WELTY

Paradoxically after a lifetime interest in writing mystery, in 1970 Welty—at the age of sixty-one—fell into a most significant relationship with a full-time crime writer: Ross Macdonald. As Suzanne Marrs and Tom Nolan tell us in *Meanwhile There Are Letters*, because Welty and Millar physically met on only six occasions, their epistolary infatuation essentially records the entirety of their relationship, with only the gaps of those six face-to-face encounters left for us to imagine (6). Millar had first written Welty in 1970 to praise *Losing*

Battles, and for a year they traded introductory messages. Marrs and Nolan describe how in May 1971, visiting New York City from his home in Santa Barbara, California, Millar "engaged in a . . . real-life . . . stake-out" in the lobby of the Algonquin Hotel, hoping to encounter Welty, who had recently published the *New York Times* review of his novel *The Underground Man* that bolstered his reputation as a writer deserving a literary, as well as popular, following. "His stakeout paid off," they say when depicting the encounter. "As Welty approached the hotel elevator, Millar/Macdonald . . . introduced himself. Abandoning whatever plans she had had, Welty was thrilled to sit and talk" (1). The two writers then carried on their exchange of letters while living across the country from one another, until Alzheimer's disease ended Millar's part of the correspondence in 1980; Welty then, with concern, tenderness, and distress, kept up her side of the conversation solo until Millar's death in 1983. Marrs and Nolan describe the Millar–Welty relationship as friendship moving towards love, not a love affair but clearly a literary intimacy that Welty greatly valued.

Macdonald's Lew Archer series, which spanned eighteen novels over almost thirty years, had established him as a preeminent creator of hard-boiled detective fiction, a member of its so-called "holy trinity" along with Dashiell Hammett and Raymond Chandler (Smith). His work added psychological depth to the genre's solutions as he had developed a compassionate detective, taking the crime novel in new directions. His Archer is a private eye who solves mysteries, but also tries to understand them. And Macdonald's plots repeatedly attend the hidden histories of families, sins of the past shaping the present, and the secret emotional scars of victims and murderers alike.

The two writers' late influence on one another's work is apparent in the record of their exchanged letters. Millar's words seep into Welty's *The Optimist's Daughter* (1972) and Welty's *The Optimist's Daughter* into his *Sleeping Beauty* (1973).[7] Is it happenstance or harmony that in both novels a central character is named Laurel, and in both, an endangered bird becomes a dramatic focus? Moreover, because of this relationship, Welty read and reread mysteries from August 1973 through January 1974, after Millar asks her to help suggest writers and texts for his anthology, *Great Stories of Suspense* (1974). The letters of those months show them swapping judgments on, among others, James M. Cain, John Cheever, Agatha Christie, John Collier, Roald Dahl, Kenneth Fearing, Dick Francis, Graham Greene, Dashiell Hammett, Margaret Millar (Ken's wife), Flannery O'Connor, and Robert Louis Stevenson—all writers who made it into Macdonald's volume. But the two also mention writers who don't—Charlotte Armstrong, Arthur Conan Doyle, Algernon Blackwood, Ray Bradbury, W. R. Burnett, Raymond Chandler, Elizabeth

Daly, Helen Eustis, Michael Gibson, Sheridan Le Fanu, Ngaio Marsh, Patrick O'Brian, William Samson, Julian Symons, Hillary Waugh, and Patrick White. Having read or reread these writers and also the Macdonald Archer novels in this period, Welty began to redraft a crime fiction of her own in 1975, "The Shadow Club," a text discussed in Pollack's 2016 *Eudora Welty's Fiction and Photography* and now by Suzanne Marrs in this collection.[8]

Understanding Welty's relationship with Macdonald has caused readers to think harder about her relationship to the genre in her later years, but our premise in this volume is that Welty was clearly working with the genre across her career. And as a further proof of that assertion, consider the extreme ends of her career: Welty's last short story, "The Alterations," a story Welty worked on in the late 1980s and her first novel, "The Night of the Little House," from the 1930s. And although neither of them were ever published in Welty's lifetime, nor, for that matter, are they likely to ever be published, they each show Welty constructing crime fiction.

WELTY'S LAST STORY AND FIRST NOVEL: CRIME FICTIONS

"The Alterations"[9] (dated by the Mississippi Department of Archives and History as circa 1987) is seemingly the last story that Welty started as her capacity, though not desire, to write gave way to dwindling health. At the story's center are two bodies, one female and abused, and the other, male and very dead. Its layers of drafting make Welty's precomposition process instructively visible. Her jottings on two unlined letter tablets and one unlined notepad are eventually followed by some pages of more fixed and cleaner draft, still handwritten but labeled "to be typed" following her plentiful markings. Throughout the notes, one can see Welty return persistently to her idea, writing it again, varying the dialogue completely, seemingly looking for a best line or version to make itself, and her story, apparent. In her drafting process, she repeatedly rewrites the scene, not culling but exploring the episode anew, producing assorted renderings before settling notes into preliminary form.

Today "The Alterations" is fascinating in part because its topic is unanticipated—especially for a reader who hasn't been following Welty's history with crime plots. With alternate titles—"It's a Lost Art," "A World of Patience Is What It Takes," and (best) "Peau de Soie," the French term referencing silk, literally "silk skin," frequently used in wedding gowns—it is the tale of a dressmaker who kills her long-endured abusive husband by literally undertaking "alterations" to—and on—him. As the character is interviewed by the police, it becomes increasingly clear to the reader that Welty's speaker is a blend of Edna Earle Ponder and the mad narrator from Poe's "The Tell-Tale Heart." As if ripped from the pages of the *National Enquirer*, Welty's plot anticipates Lorena Bobbitt (another woman who would make an extreme alteration to her abusive husband, slicing off his penis with an eight-inch carving knife in 1993 and tossing away the evidence in a roadside field), but more inventive and idiosyncratic in its bizarre depiction of a battered wife's sensational solution to abuse. Welty may possibly have drawn on the news story of a murder committed by a wife who stabbed her husband repeatedly with scissors before covering his wounds with Band-Aids. Her protagonist, alternately named Frieda, Doris, Willy Mae, and Evelyn, but perhaps emerging as Genrose Hopper, is at work over the body of her husband when the police respond to a report of trouble from a client who, expecting to pick up her completed tailoring, has seen a body on the living room floor.

This murder mystery adapts and parodies the police procedural. Procedurals, as critic George Dove comments, are usually about "run-of-the-mill" squad procedures and teamwork that sorts out a crime, rather than a principal detective (118). And they usually focus on the cop story—a convention that Welty in this case jettisons to spotlight her wacky woman murderer. Recalling television's *Dragnet* (and the countless descendants of that series), its prototype of gritty-but-droll detail, its attention to ethical dilemmas in the pursuit of justice, and its enforcers who request but are unable to keep eyewitnesses to "just the facts, ma'am," Welty's officers act as straight men to her quirky wrongdoer.

In Welty's manuscript, the patrolmen, at first bewildered by marks on the victim's skin, interrogate the dressmaker, asking if "something stung him" to make "these ugly risings." In one version, the officers note "fresh superficial needle punctures" that are not drug tracks. Gradually the seamstress identifies her husband's injuries as neat mending she has attempted, after using her stork scissors to repeatedly prick, and then stick, her husband. Grotesquely, but comically, she has repaired the wounds with "invisible darning" and the contents of "a box full of Ouchless 3-inch bandages." "You were sewing on him?" they ask. "'Looks like you been vaccinating him for the smallpox." When the detectives ask if her husband had objected to her darning him to death, she earnestly explains that, drunk, he snored as she worked until, without her at first noticing, he stopped. "Sometimes he puffed out a little sound and once his lips made a little pop, like somebody that's just made a mistake. I stuck my needle back in my collar and my thought turned to Band-Aids. . . . He was bleeding a little faster than my fingers. It was something I hadn't thought of."

Over the pages of these unlined notepads, the couple's history emerges. Saturdays were both the husband's day off and his wife's "busiest day. . . . All her alterations were promised and there was a stream of chattering women and final fittings." The women's activity routinely infuriates Mr. Hopper (alternately named Bud, Floyd, Earl, and Mr. Hobbs). In one version the police note the wife's "black eye." In a few crossed-out lines, the wife reports having asked her husband, "'Did I hit a tender place?' I'd say, 'Well women are tender all over, did you ever think of that?'" The officers then remember a previous incident when "neighbors called us. . . . Sure. You was the one that got hit. He put a wrench to your head and a wonder you ever got up."

On this particular Saturday, sodden with liquor, naked to the waist, and behaving badly, her husband slipped or fell in his stupor: "He was weaving. Waxing. Then he just went over." The police question her role in his fall, asking if she did "more than touch him . . . just a little bit?" Genrose describes it: "I put out my finger, just to shame him, poked him one little push . . . he was ripe to fall. . . . I don't think he knew what hit him . . . it was my hard clean floor." Having left him where he rolled, she comically describes her work on him. "I completely forgot about myself. That's what a wife is good for." Contemplatively she ruminates that "some wives might have kept on once they got started—might have cut on deeper down when they got to where his heart is and cut it out. I never even thought of doing that. I swear I never. That's just when I stopped, and went back and got my soap and water, and my Band-Aids. He looks in good shape, all neat now. Except for his eyes. I'm not responsible for them." Content with her job, she credits herself with his transformation: "how peaceful. . . . I'd made him an angel." The dark comedy of the murderer's self-justifying self-presentation, of her obsessive tendencies and pride in her work, and of her belief in her innocent intention are all underscored. And the possible trigger for her unexpected assault is the wedding dress worn by her dressmaker's dummy: ironically, "just on the other side of the curtain . . . in the shadows" of her parlor, it signals its symbolic outrage "through its glimmer. . . . It was there as if in the wings, as if awaiting its cue to enter on its squeaky little wheels [for its day on center stage]" (Welty's brackets).

Notwithstanding the Welty signatures of unexpected humor, surprise, and homage (here that assured wink toward the situation as well as the voice of Poe's "The Tell-Tale Heart"), and despite her characteristic reflection of and on popular culture through a recognizably feminist lens, it is nonetheless quite the surprise to discover Welty (nearly eighty by then) drafting a comic police procedural uncovering a sensational woman murderer in the ballpark of killer Ed Gein. In her plan for "The Alterations," Welty once again proves herself willing to experiment and evolve as a writer, even after she had, at the age of seventy-eight, perhaps contentedly, or regretfully, surrendered the desire to finish and publish her fiction.

And yet it is also a turn steadily foreshadowed across Welty's career—by the violent abuse scenarios explored not only as early as the stories in *A Curtain of Green*, but even earlier in a 1937 draft of a first novel. This 115-page copy of a manuscript is not currently found in the Mississippi Department of Archives and History—where one would expect to find it alongside her other collected papers—but in the New York Public Library's Russell and Volkening (R&V) historical papers, which were sold to the library by Tim Seldes, Welty's R&V agent, contingent to his selling the agency in 2012.[10]

The common assumption has been that, as a young writer, Welty forcefully resisted market pressure to produce a novel rather than short stories, even though stories were generally judged as scarcely marketable unless supported by a novelist's previous reputation. But this manuscript shows that Welty *had* at first tried to comply with editors' advice. In *Author and Agent*, Michael Kreyling, telling the story of Welty's evolving relationship with her representative Diarmuid Russell, describes both the pressure publishers applied as well as Welty's opposition to it. He also writes that in 1938, Welty had entered a Houghton Mifflin contest for first novels, but she thought even the finalized version of her submission—*The Cheated*—not very good, and accordingly threw that manuscript away after the contest. "The Night of the Little House" is evidently a surviving draft from that project.[11] The Mississippi Department of Archives and History houses about thirty related draft pages titled "The Cheated," but not yet this much longer manuscript. The Welty House has now found the original from which the New York copy was made.

Most surprisingly, the manuscript brings together versions of characters whom we associate with stories not-as-of-yet-written in 1937, when she would have been drafting the novel entry: "Why I Live at the P.O." (1941), "The Whistle" (1938), and "The Key" (1941) as well as characters from 1937's "A Piece of News" and "Lily Daw and the Three Ladies"—two stories published or at least in final process as she drafted "The Night of the Little House." The novella is narrated by a twentysomething woman from New York, Martha Galen, who has come to Victory, Mississippi to paint after she has left her work at a school for the deaf. As it begins, Martha looks for a key to her rental house to reach her by mail, and accordingly her first stop is the town's post office where its postmistress lords over its domain with comic authority—as Sister later will in "Why I Live at the P.O." Then when Martha Galen heads out to paint the landscape and is caught in a sudden storm, she seeks refuge in a nearby cabin. She has been warned that her only neighbors are Clyde Fisher, a moonshiner, and his wife Ruby (characters from "A Piece of News"); it is their house in which she takes refuge.

So this manuscript touches bits of many Welty stories, several not yet written. Eventually Welty would excise and rework nine pages from "The Night of the Little House," next to become the subsequent drafts of "The Cheated," but only published in final form as "The Key" in *Harper's Bazaar* in August 1941. Stripping her text down to nine enigmatic pages, she is both recognizing and claiming as her own the distinctive methods of modernism. And she is affirming the minimalist puzzle-text as her signature story form.

But to glean the full significance of this early novella in the context of Welty's crime-fiction patterns, you also need to know that in it, Clyde and Ruby Fisher have a daughter, Avis, who is abused by Clyde. In a scene recognizable as one of many recurrent flashings of another woman's body reflected on by Welty's sheltered women narrators,[12] Martha Galen—taking Avis as an artist's model—discovers Clyde Fisher's brutality from Avis's nudity:

> I told her quietly and matter-of-factly, "Take off your dress, Avis." Instantly she did. With no questions, [but] with a rapid, mechanical, tired motion, she pulled it off. . . .
> "What made those marks on your back" I asked her finally.
> "Pa beats me . . . But he's been doing that."

Without going into detail on the novella's full cast of characters and their further activities, it suffices to say that Martha seeks to defend and protect Avis with the help of Red Harper—the red-haired stranger from "The Key" whom she first observes in a train station encounter with a deaf couple. Not unlike the occasional team-up of other mixed-gender detective duos, in Martha's ensuing collaboration with Red, repartee and banter echo the screen flirtations of 1930s screwball cinema and, especially, the teamwork of Dashiell Hammett's Nick and Nora Charles in *The Thin Man* (1934). Ultimately their shambling progress towards safeguarding Avis lumbers towards the novella's end in an astonishing Hollywood-style apocalyptic climax where guns are fired and lives are threatened. Martha's rented house burns to the ground, but Red—taking advantage of the chaos to dramatically advance his flirtation with Martha—promises, "We will now spend the rest of the night in my room in the Hotel Constantinople. . . . If Albert Morgan [from the train station] has hung onto the key"—a rollickingly high-spirited line certain to amaze and amuse readers knowing these characters from the later "The Key."

This early manuscript's concern for Avis again draws attention to abuse, a prevalent subject in crime fiction, in plots across Welty's career. Abuse is not only at hand in the crime fictions from *A Curtain of Green*—"Flowers for Marjorie," "The Hitch-Hikers," and "A Piece of News," but in many other of its stories. In "Clytie," suicide, committed by plunging head-first into a rain barrel, is the result of family torment. In "A Curtain of Green," after a tree crushes her husband, Mrs. Larkin, in her grief and rage at insurmountable catastrophe, experimentally aims a potentially maiming hoe at the vulnerable head of her young Black garden helper, "To punish? To protest?" (*CS* 111). In "The Whistle," class abuse is institutionalized in the agricultural system, and in "A Worn Path," institutionalized neglect is expressed in the disappointing response of a clinic nurse ("You mustn't take up our time this way, Aunt Phoenix" [148]). The signal of abuse also applies to comic fictions in the collection. In "Lily Daw" a local girl escaping her father's violence is bullied by the town's droll ladies. Women in "Petrified Man" farcically scheme to enhance their own dominance of their husbands, but face their comeuppance when they contemplate the reality of a rapist. In "Why I Live at the P.O." a daughter uproariously elaborates on the many insults flung by her family. On the other end of Welty's career, the topic is still omnipresent. In *The Golden Apples*, Ran MacLain arguably rapes Maideen Sumrall, triggers her suicide, gets away with it scot-free and is seemingly even rewarded for his notoriety when he becomes town mayor. In "No Place For You, My Love," the story of a travelling woman is understood through a "bruise at her temple" that, when noticed, she felt "come out like an evil star" (*CS* 477). It is possible that Uncle Daniel tickles his wife Bonnie Dee to death in *The Ponder Heart*. And in *Losing Battles*, Lexie Renfro withholds even pencils in her caretaking marriage to the bedridden and dying teacher Julia Mortimer. In *The Optimist's Daughter*, Fay Chisom lays hands on her vulnerable hospitalized husband putting his operated-on eye at risk, and following the trauma, he unexpectedly dies. And in "The Demonstrators," Dr. Strickland administers a lethal sedative in a Jim Crow setting to his Black patient Ruby Gaddy but no hospital care, disturbingly easing her into her death after she has possibly been stabbed by her lover. *Many* Welty fictions are intimate with abuse and domestic violence or have a flirtation with murder about them.

A CRITICAL MYSTERY

Given the consistency of this connection between Welty and the mystery genre, one wonders what delayed its critical recognition? To give credit where credit's due, several contributors to this volume have in their earlier work spotted this relationship: in his 1999 study *Understanding Eudora Welty*,

Michael Kreyling observes the "film noir mentality" of Welty's early stories, especially "The Key" (32). Nolan and Marrs's publication of Welty's and
Macdonald's correspondence is a watershed, revealing and contextualizing
the two authors' relationship and all its implications. Rebecca Mark in 2013
opened the case that Welty's mysterious civil rights story, "The Demonstrators," could, and perhaps *should*, be read as a "detective story," and subsequent
scholarship has agreed, highlighting Welty's racially conscious reworking of
the mystery genre's "shadowy dynamics . . . to shine a light . . . on the darkness
of whiteness" (Agner 190). Most recently Pollack traced "Evolving Secrets:
The Patterns of Eudora Welty's Mysteries" in a 2019 article published in Deborah Barker and Theresa Starkey's consequential volume *Detecting the South
in Fiction, Film, and Television*. The question, however, remains: why has the
full extent of Welty's sport with the genre largely stayed a critical mystery?

Perhaps the most likely culprit for this "crime" concerns what theorists
describe as a "great divide" between high and low culture in the critical imagination.[13] As a great deal of commentary suggests, genre fiction is typically
dismissed as a lesser art form than its "literary" counterpart. In 1973, when
Millar dedicated *Sleeping Beauty* to Eudora Welty, who had recently won the
Pulitzer Prize for literature, a *New York Times* reviewer panned Macdonald's
novel and pointedly brought up the book's dedication, astoundingly asserting it as evidence "that the author has fallen prey to the exuberance of his
critics, and is now writing in the shadow of a self-regard that tends to play
his talent false" (qtd. in Marrs 389). Critical attitudes such as these, avowing
a vast difference between writers of literature and genre fiction and between
the forms themselves, have perhaps dictated the shape of the discussion
surrounding Welty and mystery. Perhaps the actual Eudora Welty—who
was both an on-the-sly admirer of pulp crime fiction and a mystery-fiction-
enthusiast extraordinaire—has been problematically overshadowed by or
even symbolically "killed off" by the demure, refined, and literary persona of
"Miss Welty," the southern lady author with a "sheltered" background? If so,
the set of facts for this game of *Clue* might sound a bit like this: Miss Welty
with the awards statue in the University ballroom.

NEW, IN THIS COLLECTION

We hope to have convincingly shown that Welty was both a pupil to the
mystery genre and a practitioner too. The essays that follow illustrate how
she repeatedly built her specific, varied modernist fictions through innovative

transformations of this genre that she loved and respected. Moreover, their focus on mystery productively shifts attention from characters and plots as they have previously been understood to show new puzzles hidden-in-plain-sight behind those.

In "Eudora Welty and Mystery: Noir Variations," Michael Kreyling extends our introduction's interest in placing Welty in the "history of mystery," while paying particular attention to the gender dynamics shaping the genre's reception. Perhaps unpredictably, he links Welty to the genre's most notorious twentieth-century school: its outrageously appalling noir artists. In the 1970s Welty confessed to Kenneth Millar that she had at last caught up with, and "thoroughly enjoyed," several works by influential noir novelist James M. Cain, especially *The Postman Always Rings Twice* (1934) and *Double Indemnity* (1936). Kreyling, interrogating his unlikely pairing of writers, asks a few questions: "Was Eudora Welty's thorough enjoyment of Cain's hard-boiled and misogynist version of noir an indulgence? . . . Or did she recognize . . . that her imagination had already been there, done that" in her own works? Doesn't Welty's *The Ponder Heart*, for example, contain within it, its own kind of "locked room" murder mystery featuring a Cain-like "feline" woman at the heart of its story? And what about Welty's short story, "No Place For You My Love," which revolves around yet another "Cain gambit"—a man's "predatory gaze" exposing a woman? Kreyling argues that Welty "identified and repurposed the noir vocabulary" instituted by hard-boiled American authors for her own purposes in each of these two stories. "There was a strand in Welty's creative imagination," Kreyling confirms, "that prompted her to identify cultural memes" like noir "and camp them," just "as she had camped the fashion and cosmetics advertisements in *Vogue* and *Harper's Bazaar*."

In "Reading Eudora Welty's 'Petrified Man' and 'Old Mr. Marblehall' as Southern Pulp," Katie Berry Frye attends the pulp publications "strewn throughout" Welty's tales in order to direct readers to their crime-story elements and to their implied critique of problematic white masculinities. She shows Mr. Petrie—a serial rapist on the lam—and Mr. Marblehall—a bigamist with a secret second family on the side—as petrified men leading double lives, products of an era eroding white male control. The pulp magazines that cause Leota and Mrs. Pike to point the finger at Mr. Petrie, and that occupy Mr. Marblehall in bed at night—*Startling G-Man Tales*, *Screen Secrets*, *Terror Tales*, and *Astonishing Stories*—are, as Frye's research on pulp cover art shows, themselves purveyors of fraudulent masculinities. Welty's strategy, Frye senses, is to ironically redeploy these magazines against the very demographic so often lionized by them, patriarchal white men. Frye situates her discussion to emphasize the whiteness of these men: Mr. Petrie's hyperwhiteness ("that white powder all over his face") that defamiliarizes him from his crimes in a region obsessed with fictions about race and rape, and Marblehall's pallid secrets that put him in dialogue with the antebellum histories of unacknowledged Black families shadowing ancestral halls.

Andrew B. Leiter in "Detecting the Forbidden Fruit in Eudora Welty's *The Golden Apples*" shows her Morgana, Mississippi short story cycle to be a mystery about sexual secrets. Reading the 1949 masterpiece as detective fiction intersecting with southern gothic and bildungsroman genres, Leiter attends the children of Morgana as they are left to their own devices to understand sexuality—and come of age. He suggests that multiple characters—Nina Carmichael of "Moon Lake" as well as Loch and Cassie Morrison of "June Recital"—create a composite bildungsroman, rather than one focused on a traditional single protagonist. Turning more fully to "June Recital," Leiter examines the housebound Loch Morrison as a detective figure. The "crime" he has under investigation, however, is not merely Miss Eckhart's attempt to destroy her former residence. Rather, the mystery that beckons him is the chaotic and unspoken realm of sexuality occupying the "abandoned" house next door in various manifestations: premarital sex (Virgie Rainey and her sailor), a history of rape (Miss Eckhart), exhibitionism (Mr. Voight/King MacLain), and gay potentialities (Old Man Moody and Fatty Bowles). Making use of child development research that addresses and elucidates the queerness and fluidity of childhood sexuality, Leiter sketches Loch Morrison's nascent sexual awakening in a provocative reading of both the character and his place in Welty's story cycle.

In "Court's Opened: *The Ponder Heart* and Murderous Women," Rebecca Mark considers Welty's 1953 novella, not typically read as a detective story but clearly fronting a dead body as well as a murder trial. Her reframing of *The Ponder Heart* raises questions about who wants to murder whom, and about the stories of women who kill. Mark argues that, first published in the midst of a "feminine mystique" in the United States, Welty's comedy conceals and reveals female rage against being defined and confined by a certain kind of 1950s womanhood. The women stars of *The Ponder Heart*—Edna Earle, Narciss, and Bonnie Dee—reject their prescribed stereotypes, rebuffing the roles of "the poor spinster . . . the put-upon black servant . . . [and] the suffocated, under-age wife." And Mark breaks ground in the analysis of "domestic noir" by coining them not femme, but "butch fatales," willing to commit murder to defend their right to *have* a story. Each woman could—as in many a murder mystery—be after Uncle Daniel's money, but more significantly they covet his entitlement, his assumed right to tell their stories, his story, and "everyone's stories." Female rage at pontificating, blowhard men—the Uncle Daniels of the world—is what is at stake in *The Ponder Heart*. And each of the women has the motive and the weapons to steal the narrative.

Tom Nolan, biographer of crime novelist Ross Macdonald and seasoned critic of crime fiction for *The Wall Street Journal*, contributes "The Sleuth of Pinehurst Street," contending that Welty and Macdonald (Kenneth Millar) shared an understanding of the crime story's potential. In her astute 1971 *New York Times* review of *The Underground Man*, Welty framed a new assessment of Macdonald, who was quietly transforming "the private-eye novel from a black-and-white casebook of crooks and cops, to a sociologically and psychologically sophisticated chronicle of dysfunctional families and ecological abuse." Her review bridged the high-low literary divide that typically caused crime fiction to be dismissed as undeserving serious attention. And her consequential appreciation helped to propel Macdonald to literary recognition as well as best-seller status. Nolan further contends that the two writers had mutual comprehension of the genre's "shamanistic" potential to treat "the sharpest pains and bitterest moral dilemmas of our society." Nolan supports this claim by examining Welty's 1963 "Where Is the Voice Coming From?" in which an imagined murderer of the real-life civil rights victim Medgar Evers narrates his racist perspective on the tragically bloody encounter. Nolan presents Welty's story as a brilliant realization of the characteristic function of the best detective stories: "to confront us imaginatively with evil, to explain it in the course of a narrative which convinces us of its reality," and in Millar's words, to cast "light and compassion in the dark places where it is very badly needed."

In "Detecting Dr. Strickland: the Author as 'Mindhunter,'" Michael Pickard responds to the trend in recent scholarship concerning Welty's maneuvering of the detective genre in her civil rights era story, "The Demonstrators." These readings have argued that Welty employs the genre's elements to cast a critical light on the story's ambiguous focalizer, the white Mississippi doctor, Richard Strickland. Pickard now calls to reopen and nuance this character's case file, asking "how does a person who has devoted his life to healing others—who had suffered humanizing losses and made personal sacrifices in order to pursue this profession—live with himself, when the system he lives within has turned him into an agent of discrimination and even murder?" Pickard's even-handed answer, which evokes John E. Douglas's pioneering notion of the criminal profiler as "mindhunter," explores the complexity and complicity of Dr. Strickland's position in civil rights era Mississippi. He is, on the one hand, "a doctor of last resort, compromised by wounds of his own that he cannot heal, perseverant, an enemy in the house, better than no doctor at all"; and yet a man possibly aware of—at the same time he tries to resist knowing—his collusion.

In "When a Mystery Leads to Murder: Genre Bending, Hommes Fatals, Thickening Mystery, and the Covert Investigation of Whiteness in *Losing Battles*," Harriet Pollack reads Welty's 1971 novel as monkeying with the crime-fiction form to adapt and question it. The garrulous Renfo-Beecham clan, in its unceasing clamor, undertakes to solve the puzzle of Gloria Short: that is, to identify the clandestine parents of Jack Renfro's bride, a county orphan now married into the family. In droll modification of familiar "country-house mystery" convention, Welty flips the traditionally upper-class British setting by locating this case in a Mississippi "shotgun" homestead. There, no celebrated detective works the puzzle. Instead, the family deems themselves a sort of kith-and-kin investigative team, fully intending to diminish the resented bride to a mystery they have solved. Pollack, in this new reading of a novel that persistently weighs issues of evidence and proof, creates crime-boards on suspect parental pairings, and follows more clues than its reunion members, or previous critics, have thought to use. Moreover, as Welty takes care to thicken rather than resolve the novel's mysteries, all versions of this past stunningly lead to the same startling crime. For a murderer confesses, mid-novel and without consequences, causing Pollack, in due course, to reopen the novel's covert investigation into felonious whiteness.

In "Unsolved Mysteries: Reading Eudora Welty's *The Optimist's Daughter* with Agatha Christie's *The Body in the Library*," Sarah Ford shows Welty referencing and then departing from another enduring woman writer's narrative strategies. Reminding us of Welty's taste for Christie's bestselling mysteries, Ford posits that Welty's novel, with its initial focus on Laurel McKelva's investigation into her father's death and Fay Chisom's involvement in it, borrows from Christie's country house murder mystery formula. Gathering characters and a dead body in a contained space—the McKelva house's library—allows Welty, like Christie, to explore the problematic connections of marriage, class, and property. The library, however, becomes a metafictional space as Welty conducts a genre-bending exercise: "While Laurel initially plays detective by searching for clues in both of her parents' desks, the all-important texts she finds are not . . . purloined objects that only need to be located for the narrative to be complete. Instead, . . . the texts are read, bringing Laurel's parents back to life." Shunning the easy conclusiveness of the classic detective story, Welty's 1972 Pulitzer prize-winning novel moves to explore Laurel's own family relationships, to value "the abiding mysteries of character," and to understand "the question of what and how to read."

Suzanne Marrs's concluding essay, "Confluence: The Fiction of Eudora Welty and Ross Macdonald," examines the autobiographical and textual intersections in the work of the two writers. Highlighting their shared view that distinctions between literary and mystery fiction were artificial and destructive, Marrs further reinforces this belief by assessing these authors side by side. Each felt that the novel of detection was well suited to the complex investigation of heartfelt, autobiographical concerns, perhaps at times more suited than literary fiction, and neither saw it as inevitably escapist in nature. The word "confluence," which Welty believed "exists as a reality and a symbol in one," thus defines a pattern of experience not only for these two intensely devoted friends but also for these two artists (*One Writer's Beginnings* 947). Just as Eudora Welty and Kenneth Millar were united and sustained by the flow of letters written exclusively for themselves, Eudora Welty and Ross Macdonald in their careers jointly realized the power and potential of merging one genre with another, of transforming their personal experience into fiction, and of drawing upon each other's work in doing so. Moreover, Marrs in her reading of Welty's never-published crime fiction "The Shadow Club" suggests that the story's central character—an amnesia victim—"embodies the union of the two writers and the realization that memory"—a resource Millar had lost to Alzheimer's—is itself a treasure "in their lives," key to opening secrets and creating understanding.

Michael Pickard and Victoria Richard finish this volume with a fitting appendix, which will certainly assist future detective-researchers to further develop this volume's topic. "Mysteries on the Shelves in Eudora Welty's House" is a finding aide cataloging the "more than three hundred books belonging or adjacent to the mystery genre, by nearly a hundred different authors and/or editors" that were in the writer's personal library when she died. The inventory, constructed after the contributors of this volume wrote their essays, now helps prove their arguments.

Notes

1. See Appendix in this volume for the full listing of the titles in the Welty House library, by author.

2. The references to these films were gathered from the following unpublished letters held at the Eudora Welty Collection at the Mississippi Department of Archives and History: Welty, Eudora. Letter to Frank Lyell. 4 Mar. 1943, 22 Feb. 1944, 11 Feb. 1945, 25 Mar. 1946, 15 Oct. 1947, 27 Oct. 1947, 17 Nov. 1947, 30 Sept. 1950, 27 Jan. 1952, 22 May 1953, 11 Mar. 1970.

3. Welty, Eudora. Letter to Frank Lyell. 22 Feb. 1975.

4. Welty, Eudora. Letter to John Robinson. 2 Sept. 1936, 27 Jan. 1942, 16 June 1948.

5. Welty, Eudora. Letter to John Robinson. 16 June 1948. These lines are reprinted here by permission of Michael D. Robinson and the Eudora Welty Collection at the Mississippi Department of Archives and History and Russell and Volkening as agents for the author. Copyright © by Eudora Welty, renewed by Eudora Welty LLC.

6. This essay reworks and repurposes sections of Pollack's 2019 essay, "Evolving Secrets: The Patterns of Eudora Welty's Mysteries," with permission of Louisiana State University Press and of Deborah Barker and Theresa Starkey, editors of *Detecting the South in Fiction, Film, and Television*.

7. See Marrs and Nolan (76–77) on *The Optimist's Daughter*.

8. It is difficult to be certain of Welty's composition sequence: archived boxes of "The Shadow Cub" draft seem to mix snips and cuttings from earlier drafts. There are trace elements of its characters in an unpublished 1940s story. These were picked up again in the 1960s, and the race-rape plot perhaps then began as Welty considered devoting a volume to stories about the civil rights era's Mississippi "troubles." That project was eventually scuttled by the decision to include "Where Is the Voice Coming From?" (1963) and "The Demonstrators" (1966) in her *Collected Stories* volume (1980). In 1975, Welty renewed her drafting of "The Shadow Club" and turned to develop its murder-suicide elements.

9. "The Alterations" is discussed and lines reprinted here by permission of the Eudora Welty Collection at the Mississippi Department of Archives and History and of Russell and Volkening as agents for the author. Copyright © by Eudora Welty, renewed by Eudora Welty LLC.

10. Pollack found a photocopy of the unknown manuscript in 2014 in New York as a result of some sleuthing of her own. Confirmation that material was not in the Eudora Welty Collection at the Mississippi Department of Archives and History led to a hunt to find the original manuscript which was eventually located in the Welty house.

11. This manuscript is discussed and quoted with the permission of the Manuscripts and Archives Division of the New York Public Library; Astor, Lenox, and Tilden Foundations; and of Russell and Volkening as agents for the author. Copyright © by Eudora Welty, renewed by Eudora Welty LLC.

12. See Pollack, 2016.

13. For an informing historical overview of this high-low paradigm in twentieth-century modernist analysis, see Robert E. Scholes's 2003 essay, "Exploring the Great Divide: High and Low, Left and Right," which examines both "certain aspects of the divide [that] have never been properly understood [in this context]," and "some of the internal contradictions and other problems" in their analyses, ranging from the work of George Lukács, Clement Greenberg, Allen Tate, Theodor Adorno and Max Horkheimer, and Andreas Huyssen (245).

Works Cited

Agner, Jacob. "Welty's Moonlighting Detective: Whiteness and Eudora Welty's Subversion of the American Noir Tradition in 'The Demonstrators.'" *Essays on Eudora Welty,*

Whiteness, Race, and Class, edited by Harriet Pollack, UP of Mississippi, 2020, pp. 189–213.

Chandler, Raymond. "The Simple Art of Murder." *The Simple Art of Murder*. First Vintage Books Edition, Vintage Crime, 1998, pp. 1–18.

Dove, George N. *The Police Procedural*. Bowling Green University Popular Press, 1982.

Haycraft, Howard. *Murder for Pleasure: The Life and Times of the Detective Story*. Dover Publications, Inc., 2019.

Kreyling, Michael. *Author and Agent: Eudora Welty and Diarmuid Russell*. Farrar, Straus and Giroux, 1991.

Kreyling, Michael. *Understanding Eudora Welty*. U of South Carolina P, 1999.

Macdonald, Ross. *Sleeping Beauty*. Knopf, 1973.

Macdonald, Ross. *The Underground Man*. Knopf, 1971.

Macdonald, Ross, editor. *Great Stories of Suspense*. Knopf, 1974.

Mark, Rebecca. "Ice Picks, Guinea Pigs, and Dead Birds: Dramatic Weltian Possibilities in 'The Demonstrators.'" *Eudora Welty, Whiteness, and Race*, edited by Harriet Pollack, U of Georgia P, 2013, pp. 199–223.

Marrs, Suzanne. *Eudora Welty: A Biography*. Harcourt, 2005.

Marrs, Suzanne, and Tom Nolan, editors. *Meanwhile There Are Letters: The Correspondence of Eudora Welty and Ross Macdonald*. Arcade Publishing, 2015.

Olney, James. "Where the Voice Came From." *New York Times*, 22 Nov. 1998, https://archive.nytimes.com/www.nytimes.com/books/98/11/22/reviews/981122.22olneyt.html.

Pollack, Harriet. *Eudora Welty's Fiction and Photography: The Body of the Other Woman*. U of Georgia P, 2016.

Pollack, Harriet. "Evolving Secrets: The Patterns of Eudora Welty's Mysteries." *Detecting the South in Fiction, Film, and Television*, edited by Deborah Barker and Theresa Starkey, Louisiana State UP, 2019, pp. 142–59.

Rafferty, Terrence. "Women Are Writing the Best Crime Novels." *The Atlantic*, July–Aug. 2016. www.theatlantic.com/magazine/archive/2016/07/women-are-writing-the-best-crime-novels/485576/.

Scholes, Robert E. "Exploring the Great Divide: High and Low, Left and Right." *Narrative*, vol. 11, no. 3, 2003, pp. 245–69.

Smith, Kevin Burton. "Ross Macdonald." *The Thrilling Detective*, 28 Sept. 2018, www.thrillingdetective.com/Trivia.kenmillar.html.

Van Dine, S. S. "Twenty Rules for Writing Detective Stories." *The Art of the Mystery Story*, edited by Howard Haycroft, Vail-Ballou Press, 1946, pp. 189–93.

Vande Kieft, Ruth M. *Eudora Welty*. Twayne Publishers, 1987.

Welty, Eudora. *The Collected Stories of Eudora Welty*. Harcourt Brace Jovanovich, 1980.

Welty, Eudora. *Conversations with Eudora Welty*, edited by Peggy Prenshaw, UP of Mississippi, 1984.

Welty, Eudora. Frank Lyell Correspondence. Eudora Welty Collection, Mississippi Department of Archives and History, Jackson, Mississippi.

Welty, Eudora. "The Great Pinnington Solves the Mystery." *Early Escapades*, edited by Patti Carr Black, UP of Mississippi, 2005, pp. 82–88.

Welty, Eudora. John Robinson Correspondence. Eudora Welty Collection, Mississippi
    Department of Archives and History, Jackson, Mississippi.
Welty, Eudora. *One Writer's Beginnings. Stories, Essays, and Memoir.* Edited by Richard
    Ford and Michael Kreyling. The Library of America, 1998, pp. 831–948.
Welty, Eudora. "Words into Fiction." *The Eye of the Story.* Vintage International Edition,
    Vintage Books, 1990, pp. 134–45.

EUDORA WELTY AND MYSTERY

Noir Variations

MICHAEL KREYLING

Thomas Jefferson (1743–1826), with whom Eudora Welty shares a birthday (April 13), never read a detective novel. He did, however, read almost everything else available; he went into debt buying books by the crate. Since books and reading were at the center of Jefferson's life, he developed some fixed ideas about their influence on character—especially on female character—that are useful as a roundabout introduction to this essay on Welty's attraction to the mystery novel, and in particular her "fun" with noir variations on the form.

In 1783 Jefferson dispatched paternal advice to his daughter Martha (called "Patsy," who was eleven years old at the time) on the content and purpose of her education. He had sent her off to boarding school and could only be an epistolary parent. Drawing, music, and French were his top priorities for an educated young woman. When it came to reading and writing in English, however, Jefferson stressed spelling over anything more adventurous: "It produces great praise to a lady to spell well" (782).[1]

Thirty-five years later Jefferson's ideas had not changed very much. Fellow Virginian patriarch Nathaniel Burwell wrote to Jefferson in 1818 asking for advice on "female education"; the issue was close to home since Burwell had fathered sixteen children by two wives and four of his children were daughters. Jefferson attached a long reading list to his reply, in which novels were only sparingly included. "A great obstacle to good education is the inordinate passion prevalent for novels, and the time lost in that reading which should be instructively employed. . . . The result [of reading novels] is a bloated imagination, sickly judgment, and disgust towards all the real businesses of life" (1411).[2] It is curious to find this note of Calvinist rectitude in a *philosophe* like Jefferson, but the issue of women's access to social power will bring out the patriarch in the most democratic males. When a woman reads, passion and pleasure must be subordinated to instructive employment; novels signal the reappearance of Eden's apple. By nearly all accounts, detective novels had not yet been invented in 1818, but it is not difficult to imagine what Jefferson's estimation of them would have been if he had lived long enough to encounter one.[3] He almost did; the founder of the genre, acknowledged by many, was a fellow Virginian, Edgar Allan Poe (1809–1849), who was nine years old when Jefferson posted his reply to Burwell.

Jefferson's warning against novels in his syllabus for "female education" reminds us that presumably private acts of reading and writing have long been policed for gender segregation in Western literary culture. Only lately, as Sandra Gilbert and Susan Gubar argue in *The Madwoman in the Attic* (1979), have the patriarchy police been compelled to account for their theory and practice of constraining female writers and readers. To restrict reading by gender as Jefferson suggested limits a woman's power to imagine and present her alternative to patriarchal control over "the real businesses of life." Gestation and nursing, as Jefferson pointed out to Burwell, with a tone of stating the obvious, was the central "business" of women (1412). In many cases women's "business" was fatal: one of the contributing causes to the early death of Jefferson's own wife (at age thirty-three) was repeated pregnancy and childbirth. Moreover, "time lost" from instructive employment while reading a novel is a type of employee theft against those who presume to own the reader's labor. Jefferson owned hundreds of slaves during his life; time lost from labor was not a metaphor for him.

In Eudora Welty's lifetime—especially during her professional writing years from the 1930s through the early 1980s—the basic outline of Jefferson's indictment of novels was alleged more stringently against "detective fiction" than against any other subdivision of the capacious category "novel."[4] Most of the policing arguments against indulging in the guilty pleasure of detective fiction warned readers regardless of sex not to expect too much intellectual exercise or aesthetic uplift. Even so, the supply through the "Golden Age" and into the salad days of hard-boiled and noir, increased.[5] Major figures of the Golden Age like Agatha Christie and Dorothy Sayers began publishing in the 1920s when Welty was a teenager. Ngaio Marsh and Margery Allingham debuted in the 1930s when Welty was in college. Dashiell Hammett's *The Maltese Falcon* appeared in 1930, and Raymond Chandler followed with Philip Marlowe novels later in the decade. Kenneth Millar, Welty's particular friend, began his Lew Archer series in 1949. Cultivation of the appetite for, or addiction to, the genre started early in a reader's lifecycle: The Hardy Boys syndicate began in 1927, Nancy Drew's in 1930.

Like her encounter with canonical and high-brow reading, Welty's encounter with the detective genre and its gender and character bylaws was
initiated by her parents, particularly by her mother Chestina Welty. "I can
remember, in the 30's I guess, [Welty wrote to Kenneth Millar in 1975] my
mother, a great mystery reader, saying 'That old James M. Cain! I wouldn't
give you 2 ¢ for all he's written!' (Well, you know the times—she was reading
S. S. Van Dine and Mary Roberts Rinehart along then) and strangely enough I
didn't take her up on it & try for myself. Till now" (*Meanwhile* 236–37). Millar
had sent her a copy of his anthology, *Ross Macdonald Selects Great Stories of
Suspense* (1974) containing a Cain short story, "The Baby in the Icebox."[6] That
appetizer led Welty to *The Postman Always Rings Twice* (1934) and *Double
Indemnity* (1936); unlike her mother, Welty took to Cain (*Letters* 236).[7]

Was Eudora Welty's thorough enjoyment of Cain's hard-boiled and misogynist version of noir an indulgence in or rejection of what Jefferson termed
"inordinate passion"? Was it, for Welty as an author, "time lost" or time off
from the "real businesses" of literature? Did it "bloat" her imagination? Or
did she recognize, reading Cain's noir in the 1970s, that her imagination had
already been there, done that? Was "that old James M. Cain" not really as shock-
ing to her as he had been to her mother?

If Chestina Welty had considered time spent reading Van Dine and Rinehart "instructively employed," and did not value James M. Cain even so much
as a nickel, she was typical of "the times": the Golden Age of the Detective
Novel in the 1920s and 1930s, an age closely identified with women novelists, Christie, Sayers, Ngaio Marsh, et alia, was heavily influenced by sororal
kinship. Mary Roberts Rinehart (1876–1958) preceded her sisters; she was a
member of the generation of G. K. Chesterton (1874–1936) whose "Father
Brown" short stories first appeared in 1910, not long after Arthur Conan Doyle
(1859–1930) brought Holmes back from his watery death at the Reichenbach
Falls in "The Adventure of the Empty House" (1903). Rinehart began her
writing career, as did Louisa May Alcott, when the family fortunes, overseen
by her husband, took a nosedive with a stock market crash in 1903. Rinehart
specialized in the type of genteel mysteries Agatha Christie began to publish
in the 1920s as the foundation of the Golden Age; Rinehart's "Tish" Carberry
novels anticipate Christie's Jane Marple series. Chestina Welty might have
been drawn to Rinehart's Tish, a plucky and ingenious older, single woman
working independently of male police forces and men in general to solve
local mysteries.[8] By the 1920s Rinehart had published dozens of novels and
short stories on this blueprint, many of which had been made into popular
silent films. She kept supplying the mystery and suspense market into the
era of 1950s television.

Mrs. Welty's other favorite author, S. S. Van Dine (né Willard Huntington Wright [1888–1939]), is a different case. Wright began his literary career as a protégé of H. L. Mencken, the scourge of middle-class pretensions to artistic and cultural taste and a confirmed misogynist.[9] Wright was an aficionado of high modernists: Ezra Pound and W. B. Yeats in poetry; impressionists and cubists in painting. His laudatory opinions of German art and culture before and during World War I, however, closed off many outlets for his work. He was caught in a patriotic tsunami of anti-German propaganda, and suffered a breakdown, both nervous and financial. In recovery he began to write his Philo Vance series of detective novels—twelve in all between 1926 and 1939. Embarrassed by what he perceived as his decline from high-brow to middle, Wright assumed the pseudonym S. S. Van Dine. He also made Van Dine a character in the Philo Vance novels, a Watson to Vance's Holmes, recording the genteel and Anglophilic sleuth's refined habits, snobbish opinions of popular culture, and the infallible reasoning that never failed to unravel a tightly wound murder that had flummoxed the police.

Wright, however, has more to add to an understanding of both Weltys (mother and daughter) and their relationships to detective fiction than his dozen novels. He theorized the genre for "the times" and attempted to locate it in a literary tradition, indirectly granting several of Jefferson's allegations against novels in the process. Wright's essay "The Detective Novel" (1926) is an early manifesto in the ongoing defensive campaign in which authors of detective fiction struggle for recognition of the genre and against dismissal by generations of critics who claimed to find, as did Jefferson in novels generally, little or no redeeming social or intellectual value, just misspent time.

Wright's gambit in "The Detective Novel" is simply to create a separate category for detective novels and, thus, slip the critical punch altogether: "Novels of sheer entertainment belong in a different category from those written for purposes of intellectual and aesthetic stimulation; for they are fabricated in a spirit of evanescent diversion, and avoid all deeper concerns of art" (Wright 532). Moreover, Wright's novels of "evanescent diversion" are not to be held answerable to Jefferson's "real businesses of life." Entertainment, shorn of everything else, was, for Wright as he claims it was for Poe (his nominee for founder of the genre), presented in the puzzle that confronted the sleuth: a brain teaser that, in our own time, might be prescribed for staving off dementia. "There is no more stimulating activity," Wright claimed, "than that of the mind; and there is no more exciting adventure than that of the intellect" (Wright 534). "That old James M. Cain!" would soon dissent, opening the genre to something like gritty realism. Crossword puzzles, Wright commented, were stripped-down murder cases. And, indeed, Philo

Vance begins the solution of *The Bishop Murder Case* (1929), the fourth in the series, by translating several physical clues into arcane words ready-made to please an erudite cruciverbalist.

Chestina Welty, then, could feel "cozy" with Rinehart or Van Dine because she would be asked to risk little "passion" or to justify "time lost"; it was in fact time well spent in the exercise of intellectual ingenuity and mental calisthenics. There was no more at stake than a written-over crossword grid—messy, but eventually filled in once the omniscient sleuth revealed who had committed the crime. No wonder, then, that Welty's mother would not spend two cents on James M. Cain, whose novels titillate the reader with adultery, sexual addiction, infanticide (Phyllis Nirdlinger in *Double Indemnity* is alleged to have killed young children for their inheritance), and an electrocuted cat (*The Postman Always Rings Twice*).

Dorothy Sayers, in "The Omnibus of Crime" (1929), follows upon Wright, also staking the beginning of the genre with Poe in the 1840s and bringing it up to her contemporaries Agatha Christie and E. C. Bentley.[10] Like Wright, Sayers wrote as an apologetic advocate for the genre by claiming only subliterary value: "It does not, and by hypothesis never can," Sayers concedes, "attain the loftiest level of literary development. . . . The most successful writers are those who contrive to keep the story running from beginning to end upon the same emotional level, and it is better to err in the direction of too little feeling than too much" (Sayers 376). In the future of the genre, however, Sayers saw a chance of moving up in literary class if the detective genre were to develop "a new and less rigid formula" and ally itself "more closely to the novel of manners" (Sayers 382). Sayers seems to have taken her own advice: in 1930 her next novel with Lord Peter Wimsey was *Strong Poison*, the first of three in which Wimsey's "love interest," Harriet Vane, appears. In the Vane novels Sayers tests Jane Austen's hypothesis that a single man possessed of a fortune must be in want of a wife, as well as a murder they can solve together.[11]

Raymond Chandler (1888–1959) responded to Sayers's "The Omnibus of Crime" with "The Simple Art of Murder" in 1944, voicing the temper of Eudora Welty's "times" rather than those of her mother. Sayers had presided over a large swath of the genre during the Golden Age of the 1920s and 1930s, and of her reign Chandler wrote: "I think what was really gnawing at her mind was the slow realization that her kind of detective story was an arid formula which could not even satisfy its own implications" (394). The new kind of detective story that replaced the Golden Age turned out to be, over time, no less formulaic than a typical Christie or Sayers or Marsh. In 1944, however, it seemed, in Chandler's view, democratic and liberating. It

was also overwhelmingly male. He put Dashiell Hammett (1894–1961) at
the forefront, a male American writer (rather than a British female) who
"gave murder back to the kind of people that commit it for reasons, not just
to provide a corpse; and with the means at hand, not with hand-wrought
dueling pistols, curare, and tropical fish" (Chandler 396). Hammett wrote
in a "realistic" language based on American idioms rather than the *Norton
Anthology of English Literature*. "All language begins with speech," Chandler
explains, "and the speech of common men at that, but when it develops to
the point of becoming a literary medium it only looks like speech" (398).
Hammett's language was "spare, frugal, hardboiled" (Chandler 396). Hammett's heroes the Continental Op and Sam Spade are just as spare, frugal,
and hard-boiled in their emotional lives as in their lingo. Of the hero of the
regendered genre, Chandler was critically frugal as well: "I do not care much
about his private life; he is neither a eunuch nor a satyr; I think he might
seduce a duchess and I am quite sure he would not spoil a virgin" (398). The
shamus is not in want of a wife so much as a one-night stand. It should be
added that, unlike Vance or Wimsey, Chandler's private eye doesn't possess a
fortune. Insofar as the novel of manners of the Jane Austen formula centered
on joining appropriate mates (and their capital), it would have no foothold
in the hard-boiled genre.[12] Neither the Op nor Spade marries. Chandler's
Philip Marlowe, on the other hand, is a late apostate, a bachelor until *Poodle
Springs*, the novel Chandler did not finish before his death in 1959.[13] Ross
Macdonald's Lew Archer is divorced and does not find a woman he thinks of
as more than a one-night stand until the eighteenth and final Archer novel,
The Blue Hammer (1976).

   Chandler's essay is symptomatic of the particularly active discussion of
the genre in the 1940s. In two overtly provocative essays in the *New Yorker*—
"Why Do People Read Detective Stories?" (14 October 1944) and "Who Cares
Who Killed Roger Ackroyd?" (20 January 1945)—Edmund Wilson (whom
Welty chastised in 1949 for condescending to William Faulkner in his review
of *Intruder in the Dust* ["Department" 41–42]) returns to Jefferson's militant,
masculine supervision of reading in general and reading detective stories
in particular. In the first of his two essays, Wilson, like Chandler, scarcely
mentions a female author at all. When he does, he addresses her with the
mock-honorific "Miss" or "Mrs"; Raymond Chandler is simply "Chandler."
Wilson traces the development of the genre along a familiar track from Poe
through Conan Doyle in the nineteenth century, but then ignores Christie
and her sisterhood to arrive at Rex Stout (creator of Nero Wolfe) in the
1920s.[14] From Wolfe's all-male household, Wilson proceeds to Dashiell Hammett and Raymond Chandler in the 1930s. Although Wilson recognizes that

the genre has "grown so prodigiously" during the war years (perhaps anxious readers needed escape from an "all-pervasive feeling of guilt" he surmises), he professes to find no legitimate progress in literary form beyond the "Sherlock Holmes formula": an analytical genius (Wolfe, Holmes) attended by an "admiring stooge, adoring and slightly dense" (Archie Goodwin, John Watson) solves crimes primarily via intellectual acumen ("Why Do People Read" 78). Wolfe almost never leaves his townhouse, his beer, and his orchids. John Dickson Carr's Gideon Fell, whom Welty recommended to readers as always giving "a noble performance" (Polk 393), so bloated he can hardly move at all, repeats the Nero Wolfe pattern. Anything beyond the Holmes formula Wilson denigrates as "padding" ("Why Do People Read" 82). If a detective novelist should insert the question of "which of the two men the heroine will marry," the trace of novel of manners that Sayers thought might elevate the genre, Wilson condemns the move as a "sleight-of-hand" diversion ("Why Do People Read" 82).

"Who Cares Who Killed Roger Ackroyd?" is more provocative in its literary misogyny. Wilson seemed delighted that his first essay, a deliberate poke in the eye to loyal readers of the detective genre, had ignited such opposition that he was deluged with protests; he reported receiving thirty-nine letters (Wilson 59). Women authors, Dorothy Sayers and Ngaio Marsh, were especially recommended to him by his agitated correspondents. But Sayers's *The Nine Tailors* (1934, the ninth novel featuring Lord Peter Wimsey [an "embarrassing name" in Wilson's judgment]) he ranks as "one of the dullest books I have ever encountered in any field," wasting a clever idea for a murder (death by sonic reverberation of church bells) in an "inevitable Sherlock Holmes" formula (59). Of Ngaio Marsh he is even more dismissive, rating her writing ability as "unappetizing sawdust" (60), no better than the "sub-literary" level of the genre as a whole. His final verdict is not so much different from Willard Huntington Wright's in 1926: "My final conclusion is that the reading of detective stories is simply a kind of vice that, for silliness and minor harmfulness, ranks somewhere between smoking and crossword puzzles" (65).[15]

Chestina Welty's daughter, then, had well-worn terrain to deal with when she took up reading detective fiction. By the middle of the 1930s mean city streets were pushing out village byways. As Wilson's *New Yorker* provocations in the 1940s indicate, wartime and postwar gender politics were active in the genre as well. Rehabilitating American masculinity was center stage during and after the war, and the detective was an important exemplar of a type of American manhood that needed reinstatement. Welty was drawn into the controversy not only as a reader; she had a friend in the mystery business. Joan Kahn (1914–1994) took over editorship of "Harper Novels of Suspense" in 1946, sacked many of the list's familiar authors (many of whom were suppliers of "formula" novels) and added new ones—Patricia Highsmith, for example. Welty contributed blurbs and ad copy for a few of Kahn's books: for John Dickson Carr's *The Sleeping Sphinx* (1947) and Jane Langton's *The Transcendental Murder* (1964).[16] Carr (1906–1977), one of the few older authors Kahn kept when she assumed editorship of the "Harper Novels of Suspense," was immensely prolific and wrote under several pen names. He was a master of the "locked room" mystery; a comedic version of which appears in the plot machinery for the "murder" of Bonnie Dee Peacock in *The Ponder Heart* (1953). The death of Bonnie Dee seems to fit Carr's "Type 1": "It is not a murder, but a series of coincidences ending in an accident which looks like murder" (Carr 277).[17]

Welty also wrote the introduction to Kahn's collection of stories of suspense, *Hanging by a Thread* (1969). Kahn's editorial choices—stretching from Tacitus to Dashiell Hammett—implicitly make the argument that stories of crime and detection are woven intricately, like strands of DNA, into the literary consciousness of Western culture and thereby may indirectly claim legitimacy in the canon. Kahn's taste in crime novels veered away from hardboiled and noir. Welty compliments her selection criteria in *Hanging by a Thread* as "gentle" (xix). Harsher voices, like James M. Cain's, Chandler's, and Macdonald's were published at Knopf, seldom at Harper's where Kahn oversaw the list.[18]

Welty finally read her mother's nemesis James M. Cain, then, in the 1970s. Millar had chosen an early Cain short story, "The Baby in the Icebox," for the anthology he sent to Welty. She wrote back that " . . . The Baby in the Icebox' was great fun, so I read *The Postman Always Rings Twice* and *Double Indemnity*—both of which I thoroughly enjoyed" (*Meanwhile* 236). It is not hard to see that "The Baby in the Icebox" would be "fun" to the author of *The Ponder Heart*. Welty saw something in Cain that her mother, reading four decades earlier, probably did not. Noir and screwball farce are genetically related; "The Baby in the Icebox" is the screwball twin of the noir *Postman*, preceding it in the sequence of Cain's work by only a year. Interestingly, by reusing the elements of "The Baby in the Icebox" almost immediately in *Postman*, Cain himself destabilizes his signature tough-guy noir by linking it genetically to screwball parody. The similarity has not been lost on critics: Morris Dickstein has compared *Postman* to Howard Hawks's iconic screwball comedy *Bringing Up Baby* (1938).[19] Some noir habits, however, overtook screwball plot limitations: Cain's tiger in "The Baby in the Icebox," actually kills someone. "Baby" the leopard (and his double) in Howard Hawks's film *Bringing Up Baby* do not eat anybody.

The narrator of "The Baby in the Icebox" tells the tale of Duke and Lura, their filling station/auto camp/lunchroom, and Duke's crackpot scheme to add a wildcat zoo as a roadside attraction. In Cain's noir the road functions as the circulatory system for Depression-era commerce and escape; cars are its blood cells, as likely to carry healthful antibodies as deadly pathogens. Car culture is omnipresent: Walter Huff in *Double Indemnity* sells auto insurance; Mildred Pierce makes a fortune with a drive-in restaurant. When wildcats aren't enough to boost Duke's bottom line, he adds Rajah the tiger. What Duke does not know, and the narrator does, is that while Rajah would gladly eat Duke alive, he purrs like a housecat when Lura enters his cage. All of Cain's women share a certain feral streak, a representation symptomatic of the misogyny-saturated noir. Welty's Bonnie Dee Peacock has a touch of the feline too but toned down from actual caged beast to house pet: "*Yawned* all the time, like cats do" (Welty, *Novels* 359).

A wandering Texas snake wrangler stops at the lunchroom, and before he decamps, is recruited into Lura's bed (where the narrator would dearly love to be), and she becomes pregnant. Duke is initially bursting with pride at the news that he is about to become a father, but eventually suspects that Ron, his "son," is not his own flesh and blood after all. Enraged that he has been cuckolded, Duke plots to kill Lura by setting an unfed Rajah loose in the house. Lura catches on to the plan, pacifies Rajah with raw meat from the icebox where she stashes baby Ron for safe-keeping as she plots to get rid of Duke. When Duke returns to the scene of his botched "crime," he finds Lura alive, Rajah still ravenous, and himself on the menu. Duke shoots Lura, but not fatally. Like Cain's familiar noir male dupes of homicidal women, Duke is no match for the deadly female. In a desperate attempt to repel Rajah he sets his own house afire. Rajah kills Duke before the flames consume them both. When Lura eventually returns to consciousness in her hospital bed, she explains that Ron is still in the icebox—the best place for him, it turns out, as the house had been an inferno. Lura, Ron, and the narrator—a holy family of sorts—take up their lives in the ruins, minus the tiger.

"The Baby in the Icebox," as Welty must have seen, frames noir as a form of farce. Read in close sequence with *Postman* and *Double Indemnity*—as Welty told Millar she had done—a shrewd reader with an eye for farce could see how the darker elements of noir—the fatal sexual triangle, murder, feral women and cuckolded men, the road and the cars and trucks that move us around and loosely define a restless mobile civilization—could be remixed for "fun." About the time Welty finally read traditional noir the remixing had commenced: Robert Altman had remade Chandler's *The Long Goodbye* with Elliott Gould as Marlowe in 1973—three years after Gould had appeared in *M*A*S*H*.[20]

Welty, however, had been there twenty years earlier. *The Ponder Heart*, equipped with a full set of noir accessories, hints that years before she admitted to reading Cain, Welty had absorbed and repurposed the noir vocabulary. There was a strand in Welty's creative imagination that prompted her to identify cultural memes and camp them, as she had camped the fashion and cosmetics advertisements in *Vogue* and *Harper's Bazaar*.[21]

Variations on elements of Cain's brand of noir echo parodically in *The Ponder Heart*.[22] For Duke's roadside menagerie and diner in "The Baby in the Icebox" or "the Greek's" diner and gas station in *Postman* ("nothing but a roadside sandwich joint, like a million others in California"), there is the Beulah Hotel of Clay, Mississippi, and its dining room: assets in disputed ownership as well as tropes in a literary text, as they are in both "The Baby in the Icebox" and *The Postman Always Rings Twice*. Both enterprises suffer from the vicissitudes of automobile traffic. For the fatal love triangle of *Postman*—Cora Smith, the young and feral woman; Nick Papadakis, maybe not old enough to be Cora's "papa" but still too old to satisfy her sexually; and Frank Chambers, the "big and tall and hard" drifter (*Postman* 16)—*The Ponder Heart* substitutes a parody of the triangle's overheated sexuality. Edna Earle, the garrulous spinster in whom logorrhea redirects libido, narrates the tale from beyond its conclusion, in a kind of house arrest in the Beulah Hotel. Uncle Daniel is ersatz husband to Edna Earle; he has married or at least proposed marriage to every other woman and girl he meets. Ovid Springer, Edna Earle's boyfriend, is also, like Cain's Frank Chambers, a drifter (although he does have a job as a wonder-drug salesman). Ovid is, however, the antithesis of "big and tall and hard." The Beulah Hotel and Clay languish like the marooned diner in *Postman*: "Empty house, empty hotel, might as well be an empty town," Edna Earle laments at the end of *The Ponder Heart* (Welty, *Novels* 422). Chambers, readers learn in the final pages of *Postman*, has been writing the story from death row, where he awaits the gas chamber for a crime he did not commit (murdering Cora), although he had murdered her husband Nick and got away with it: a typical case of noir "justice." Edna Earle is condemned to a life of solitary confinement in the Beulah Hotel.

The *Ponder* ménage-a-trois ("in plenty of marriages there's three," Edna Earle insists [Welty, *Novels* 350]) reorients the murderous situation of *Postman* as screwball comedy. The threesome is often crowded into Edna Earle's "trusty Ford": "I passed by the [Ponder] place myself, going for a quick ride

Fig. 2.1. *The Postman Always Rings Twice* (MGM, 1946). Left to right: Cecil Kellaway, John Garfield, Lana Turner at the wheel.

before dark with Mr. Springer when he was tired (so tired I drove) and Uncle Daniel sitting up behind" (Welty, *Novels* 374). The threesome in the MGM film adaptation of *Postman* takes a similar drive (fig. 2.1), with fatal results.[23]

Cain's noir, in particular, is fueled by restless female desire that steams out as adultery, murder, and greed. In *The Ponder Heart* the blend is sublimated in Edna Earle's nonstop talk, Intrepid Elsie Fleming's revving motorcycle engine, and Bonnie Dee's runaway consumerism. It would, however, be too harsh an indictment of Edna Earle to accuse her of Cora's murderous intentions, although the suggestion hangs temptingly in the air. Judge Tip Clanahan, with comic hyperbole, shouts to Edna Earle (and the whole town) from his office window: "What am I going to do with Daniel, skin him? Or are you all going to kill him first?" (Welty, *Novels* 356). The threat is less ambiguous when Bonnie Dee picks up "her little bone razor" ostensibly to shave Daniel: "Edna Earle! Make haste! She's fixing to cut my throat!" Edna Earle answers the call, armed only with a spoon, and Bonnie Dee, "with that razor cocked in her little hand," faces her down (Welty, *Novels* 369). Of course, Uncle Daniel is not killed; Bonnie Dee is—either by a raw form of electrocution (like the house cat in both *Postman* and "The Baby in the Icebox") or by being tickled to death (asphyxiation would probably be the coroner's term).

The typical Cain plot begins with a male gaze that paradoxically prefigures and ensures the male's doom, drawing him into a vortex of desire he cannot escape. "Then I saw her," says Frank Chambers, the drifter of *Postman*, recalling the first step on his path to death row (*Postman* 4). His death row cell (a chamber for Chambers) eerily echoes Virginia Woolf's haven for the woman writer; it truly is "a room of his own," the last but one he will ever inhabit. "Her," in Frank's appropriating gaze, is the fatal woman Cora, feral in her sexuality: "I took her in my arms and mashed my mouth up against hers . . . 'Bite me! Bite me!' I bit her" (*Postman* 111). Later, when together Frank and Cora have consummated the murder of "the Greek," their sex is even rougher.[24] The car with the dead husband's body is scarcely over a cliff before Frank and Cora copulate again. "'Rip me, Frank'" she insists, and he does, tearing her blouse from "throat to belly" (*Postman* 46). Cora became, Cain writes, "like the great grandmother of every whore in the world," complete with black "snaky curls," a cameo by Medusa for added, over-the-top, effect (*Postman* 87).

Sexual attraction in *The Ponder Heart* is never consummated, nor as gaudy as it is in Cain—that is, not in the Ponders' Clay. In Polk, where the Peacocks come from, breeding continues unabated: "Mrs. Peacock was big and fat as a row of pigs" and evidently just as prolific of offspring (Welty, *Novels* 378). Sex in Clay tends to sterility. Uncle Daniel's attractions to a series of women—before he captures Bonnie Dee—are policed by Edna Earle. Evidently, an heir might complicate her title to the hotel. Her own long-term relationship with Ovid Springer, the travelling salesman who is more often on the road than in or near her embrace, is less than physical, composed mainly of car rides or chaste movie dates when "Mr. Springer stays over and makes me go to one of those sad, Monday night movies and never holds my hand at the right places" (Welty, *Novels* 377).[25] Ovid Springer clearly fails to live up to his namesake, the author of *Ars amatoria*.

Welty's parody of noir reveals her understanding of its textual and subtextual schemes, affects, and structuring—and its tendency to parody itself. Texts linked in parodic relationships are, like the couples in noir, related by the pressure of mutual doom. Noir codependencies disclose obscure drives and compulsions thinly covered in normative domestic life, or romances derived from it which are fancied to end happily but (by noir rules) end—for its men—in the gas chamber. Noir is itself parodic—of the standard romance and naïve hope in happiness it so clearly drives to crime, violence, and the unravelling of the institutions and mores of orthodox society. Social and civic norms fail in *The Ponder Heart* as consistently as they do in Cain's noir: asylums incarcerate the wrong inmates; marriages can be "Tom Thumb," trial, annulled, or like Edna Earle's to Mr. Springer, vainly imagined. A murder trial can be interrupted: for dinner (*The Ponder Heart*) or for bribery (*Postman*).

The Ponder Heart is not Welty's only exploitation of noir. She used noir's more solemn misogyny in her short story "No Place for You, My Love," written within a couple of years of *The Ponder Heart* in the early 1950s. "No Place for You, My Love" tracks another Cain noir, *Double Indemnity* (1936). Cain's novel opens with the familiar predatory gaze: "A woman was standing there. I had never seen her before. She was maybe thirty-one or -two, with a sweet face, light blue eyes, and dusty blonde hair. She was small, and had on a suit of blue house pajamas. . . . Under the blue pajamas was a shape to set a man nuts. . . ." (Cain, *Double* 5, 6). Welty's story repeats the Cain gambit, but the short story's opening moment is mitigated by Welty's transfer of the impending sexual transgression from physical to emotional: "The moment he saw her little blunt, fair face, he thought that here was a woman who was having an affair. It was one of those odd meetings when such an impact is felt that it has to be translated at once into some sort of speculation" (Welty, *Stories* 561). The male who inflicts this gaze remains unnamed in Welty's story, the more to emphasize the possessive violence inherent in the entire sex over the individual flaws of one member who is less overtly "nuts." The "impact," at least in the first few lines of Welty's story, is not as ominous as the meeting of Walter and Phyllis in *Double Indemnity*, but it is "felt" by the woman in Welty's story as a reverberation of the male gaze, as "some sort of speculation" that mutates in the direction of physical collision. Looks can kill in Cain's primitive noir; in Welty's version the impact is subtler.[26]

The woman in Welty's story is actually bruised, an injury not disclosed until later in the story; its source—the actual blow and perpetrator—is ambiguous, either the man who picks her up in Galatoire's or her lover back in Ohio. She does, however, like Phyllis Nirdlinger in *Double Indemnity*, present as a woman whose sexual identity cannot be concealed.[27] Phyllis's sexuality is as obvious to Walter as a billboard; the breadth and depth of her rapacity is not uncovered until he is irretrievably stuck in it, like a fly in flypaper. Welty's displaced woman thinks that her privacy has been ransacked by the male gaze too: "It must stick out all over me, she thought, so people think they can love me or hate me just by looking at me. How did it leave us—the old, safe, slow way people used to know of learning how one another feels, and the privilege that went with it of shying away if it seemed best? People

Fig. 2.2. *Double Indemnity* (Paramount, 1944). Barbara Stanwyck, Tom Powers. Fred MacMurray is invisible in the backseat—"In every marriage there's three."

in love like me, I suppose, give away the short cuts to everybody's secrets." (Welty, *Stories* 561) The ambiguity of Welty's "it" doesn't exist in Cain's noir. Nor does the "shying away"; the enforced intimacy of the shared front seat of the automobile abolishes that. The car, in fact, in *Double Indemnity* (fig. 2.2) as in all noir, looms as a major character in the story.

Dark irony is a fixture of noir: Walter had sought to insure Phyllis's husband against physical injury in an automobile accident. And Walter takes his own bullet by driving the wrong car to a rendezvous—a rendezvous at which he plans to kill Phyllis but is shot instead. Welty's day-trippers in "No Place for You, My Love" indulge in no such murderous conduct, and yet the convertible they drive is indispensable as a metaphor for the psychological confinement of their moments together. "I have a car here," says the man from Syracuse not long after he smiles at the Ohio woman "like a villain" (Welty, *Stories* 562). Villain he might be, but the woman has been touched in some way by the fatalistic openness of the noir road and she goes along for the ride. The mystique is tersely stated by Frank Chambers when he tempts Cora to leave with him: " 'Just you and me and the road, Cora' " (*Postman* 29).

As the concrete highway south from New Orleans gives way to a shell road, omens of violence abound in the imagined creatures that inhabit the wetlands (or "primeval mud" [Welty, *Stories* 565]). Mosquitoes attack, and the man driving "struck himself on the forehead" in a futile attempt to mash just one of them; then, in order to escape the swarm, he "increased their speed" (Welty, *Stories* 565). After he and the woman cross the river on a ferry from the east bank to the west, premonitions of violence become more pronounced: "On this side of the river, the road ran beneath the brow of the levee and followed it. Here was a heat that ran deeper and brighter and more intense than all the rest—its nerve" (Welty, *Stories* 568). Both passengers agree that they are in unexplored literal and emotional geography. The woman asks the driver about his wife. "His right hand came up and spread—iron, wooden, manicured. She lifted her eyes to his face. He looked at her like that hand.... Then he lit a cigarette" (Welty, *Stories* 570). The sexual encounter in "No Place for You, My Love" is nowhere near as rough or explicit as Cain's typical conspirators exact of each other—despite the cigarette, a familiar noir accoutrement of sex. But Welty's story knows where it is going.

At Baba's joint, at the end of the road, music strikes up and the man compels the woman to dance: "And suddenly she made a move to slide down from her stool, maybe wishing to walk out into that nowhere down the front steps to be cool a moment. But he had hold of her hand. He got down from his stool, and, patiently, reversing her hand in his own—just as she had had the

Fig. 2.3. *Double Indemnity* (Paramount, 1944). Fred MacMurray, Barbara Stanwyck.

look of being about to give up, faint—began moving her, leading her. They were dancing" (Welty, *Stories* 575). They dance impervious to the collective gaze of the other customers in Baba's. They are not lovers but they are "[l]ike people in love" (Welty, *Stories* 576). And like people in love, they finish their physical intimacy showing signs of bodily effort, "[b]athed in sweat" (Welty, *Stories* 577). The erotic tango of Stanwyck and MacMurray in the supermarket of *Double Indemnity* is no less suggestive (fig. 2.3).

On the road back to New Orleans, the man from Syracuse kisses his captive, but "not knowing ever whether gently or harshly" (Welty, *Stories* 578). "Something that must have been with them all along suddenly, then, was not. In a moment, tall as panic, it rose, cried like a human, and dropped back" (Welty, *Stories* 579). Sexual encounter in traditional noir, however, affords no escape or possibility of gentleness. Someone, usually male, is always dead at the end. Both of Cain's leading men, Frank in *Postman* and Walter in *Double Indemnity*, are doomed the instant they set their respective gazes on the wrong women. The noir woman is always the wrong woman. No one dies at the end of "No Place for You, My Love," but some*thing* does.

Since the publication of *Meanwhile There Are Letters: The Correspondence of Eudora Welty and Ross Macdonald* in 2015, Welty's readers might assume that her engagement with the genre of detective fiction began with her correspondence with Millar, in 1970, and was therefore chaperoned by his literary taste and his modifications to the genre over the course of his Lew Archer novels. The relationships—Welty to Millar, Millar to the genre, Welty to the genre—are, of course, more complicated than that. Welty had been reading in the genre for at least twenty years before she and Millar met as correspondents: "I've been reading your books as they came out since away back when you were John Ross Macdonald," a pseudonym Millar dropped after *Find a Victim*, published in 1954) (*Meanwhile* 2). This was about the same time Welty was writing *The Ponder Heart* and "No Place for You, My Love" and Macdonald was embarked on his Archer series that would significantly change the noir conventions he had inherited from elders like "that old James M. Cain."

Notes

1. Martha Jefferson Randolph (1772–1836) was the only one of Jefferson's white children to survive beyond the age of twenty-five. Even though she was herself the mother of twelve children, Jefferson's daughter often lived in the White House and served unofficially as First Lady when her father was President (1801–1809). Jefferson's wife, Martha Wayles Skelton Jefferson (1748–1782) died at the age of thirty-three; Sally Hemings (1773–1835) was her half-sister.

2. Jefferson to Nathaniel Burwell, 14 Mar. 1818.

3. Nearly, but not by *all* accounts: See "The Death of Agrippina, The Mother of Nero," by Tacitus (CE 56–120). See Kahn *Hanging by a Thread* (417–22). With an Introduction by Eudora Welty, who wryly opined that it could not have been easy for Nero to have his own mother killed (xviii). To be strictly accurate, Kahn classifies the account by Tacitus as "Fact," not fiction, an infiltration by the "true crime" genre (417).

4. A long process of classification and nomenclature is elided here. What I mean by the label "detective novel" is basically what Raymond Chandler meant, but only generally defines, in his essay "The Simple Art of Murder" (1944), which comes up for discussion later in this essay: A plot centering on a murder with the solution of the crime and identification of the criminal left to a private detective, sometimes with but more often without, the assistance of the police.

5. Like the term "detective novel," the period designation "Golden Age" is variously defined. See Julian Symons, "The Golden Age: The Twenties," in his *Bloody Murder: From the Detective Story to the Crime Novel* (104–22). Symons extends the Golden Age into the 1930s, but primarily to describe its decline and replacement by hard-boiled writers. Most critics and historians of the genre follow suit: see Charles J. Rzepka, *Detective Fiction* (2005), *passim*.

6. "The Baby in the Icebox" was first published in 1933.

7. Both Cain novels were made into popular, even cult-status, Hollywood films—*The Postman Always Rings Twice* in 1946 and 1981, and *Double Indemnity* once in 1944 and again for television in 1973. It is altogether possible that Welty saw one or both of the 1940s films. For this essay, I am restricting myself to the written texts of the novels, which differ in many respects from the screenplays. For example, Billy Wilder and Raymond Chandler, who wrote the screenplay for the 1944 *Double Indemnity*, renamed Stanwyck's character Phyllis *Dietrichson* and renamed Walter Huff as Walter *Neff*.

8. Symons sums up Rinehart's novels as having "the air of being written specifically for maiden aunts" (100). Maybe so, but the resourceful woman sleuth has survived. Consider the character of Robin Ellacott in "Robert Galbraith"'s (J. K. Rowling's) *Cormoran Strike* series.

9. Mencken was also, with George Jean Nathan, a founder of the pulp market pioneer *Black Mask*, the incubator of several detective and noir writers. Mencken and Nathan founded *Black Mask* in 1920 but sold it—at a profit—after less than a year.

10. Generational solidarity: Dorothy Sayers (1893–1957), Chestina Andrews Welty (1883–1966), and Agatha Christie (1890–1976). Edmund Clerihew Bentley (1875–1956) was the author of two detective novels, *Trent's Last Case* (1913)—praised by Sayers as nearly perfect—and its late sequel *Trent's Own Case* (1936). He is equally famous for inventing the light verse "clerihew," a short comic poem of two rhyming couplets with lines of unequal length that pokes fun at the multisyllabic name of a famous person.

11. Sayers's fellow crime novelist Ngaio Marsh seems to have taken the cue as well. In *Artists in Crime* (1938) her Scotland Yard detective Roderick Alleyn is smitten with artist Agatha Troy. In the next novel in the series, *Death in a White Tie* (1938), Troy succumbs to his marriage proposal. Welty did not care for the way Marsh handled the courtship and marriage plot (*Meanwhile* 166).

12. For an interesting take on Austen's economic awareness, see Thomas Piketty, *Capital in the Twenty-first Century*, (2014).

13. Chandler wrote the first four chapters of *Poodle Springs* before his death. Robert B. Parker completed the novel and it was published in 1989. Parker (1932–2010) is the author of the *Spenser* series of detective novels (and two other series as well as Western novels). His *Spenser* series has been, in turn, continued by another author since his death.

14. Rex Todhunter Stout (1886–1975) was a prolific writer; his series featuring Nero Wolfe and Archie Goodwin comprises thirty-three novels and thirty-nine novellas published between 1935 and 1975.

15. The debate pro and con is as durable as the genre itself: see for example G. K. Chesterton, "A Defence of Detective Stories" (1901): "Not only is a detective story a perfectly legitimate form of art, but it has certain definite and real advantages as an agent of the public weal. . . . It reminds us that the whole noiseless and unnoticeable police management by which we are ruled and protected is only a successful knight-errantry" (4, 6). Antonio Gramsci (1891–1937) read the "Father Brown" stories in an Italian prison and rated them higher than the Holmes stories of Arthur Conan Doyle. See Gramsci, *Antonio Gramsci: Prison Notebooks, Vol. III*, (1992–1996), p. 399. Also Marjorie Hope Nicholson, "The Professor and the Detective" (1929). Both Chesterton and Nicholson are included in Howard Haycraft, editor, *The Art of the Mystery Story* (Grosset & Dunlap, 1946). See also Wilfrid Sheed, "The Good Word: 'It All Depends On Your Genre," *New York Times Book Review* (5 Sept. 1971, pp. 2 +.) Of Chandler, Sheed opines "his plots and people smell of cheap paper from the pulp magazines where he began. . . . "and Ross Macdonald is just slightly better: "a gifted post-Chandler mannerist" (2).

16. For the ad copy on Carr, see Noel Polk, *Eudora Welty: A Bibliography of Her Work* (1994), p. 393; for the Langton blurb, p. 397.

17. For a treatise on the "locked room" problem, see Carr's *The Three Coffins* (1935), chapter 17. This is excerpted in Haycraft's *The Art of the Mystery Story*, pp. 273–86.

18. The implication of gender bias is imperfect here; at Knopf, Blanche Knopf handled a good deal of the editorial work.

19. See Morris Dickstein's *Dancing in the Dark: A Cultural History of the Great Depression* (2009), where the author compares Howard Hawks' iconic screwball comedy *Bringing Up Baby* (1938) with Cain's *Postman* (402–7).

20. The border separating realism and noir parody has always been permeable. See Mike Davis, *City of Quartz: Excavating the Future in Los Angeles*. Vintage, 1992, pp. 36–46.

21. For Welty's penchant for parody and satire of popular culture, see Eudora Welty, *Photographs*, UP of Mississippi, 1989, pp. xx–xxi; and Suzanne Marrs, *Eudora Welty: A Biography*, Harcourt, 2005, pp. 44–47.

22. The Fields/Chodorov adaptation of the novella for Broadway exaggerated those elements, broadening the comedy as Welty's original text does not. See Joseph Fields and Jerome Chodorov, *The Ponder Heart*, Random House, 1956.

23. In the novel Chambers clubs Nick with a wrench, not a bottle.

24. And, Morris Dickstein adds in *Dancing in the Dark*, "their best sex" (406).

25. The films likely to have played in Clay in the early 1950s include *The Postman Always Rings Twice* (D. Tay Garnett, MGM, 1946); *Where Danger Lives* (D. John Farrow,

RKO, 1950); *Gun Crazy* (D. Joseph H. Lewis, United Artists, 1950); *He Ran All the Way* (D. John Barry, United Artists, 1951). The plots and accoutrements are similar: getaway cars, guns, desperate heterosexual couples. It is tempting to speculate about which "places" in the films Edna Earle deemed "right" for holding hands.

26. Even subtler, perhaps, in Richard Ford's *homage* "Nothing to Declare" in *Sorry for Your Trouble*, Ecco, 2020, pp. 1–23.

27. In the Wilder/Chandler screenplay, Barbara Stanwyck is first seen wearing a towel loosely wrapped over a swimsuit, and she and Walter Neff, the insurance man, pun on her need for more "coverage." Phyllis's famous anklet is an addition by way of the screenplay.

Works Cited

Allen, Dick, and David Chako, editors. *Detective Fiction: Crime and Compromise*. Harcourt Brace Jovanovich, 1974.

Bringing Up Baby. Directed by Howard Hawks, RKO Radio Pictures, 1938.

Cain, James M. "The Baby in the Icebox." *Greatest Stories of Suspense*, edited by Ross Macdonald, Alfred A. Knopf, 1974, pp. 398–411.

Cain, James M. *Double Indemnity*. 1936. Vintage, 1992.

Cain, James M. *The Postman Always Rings Twice*. 1934. Vintage, 1992.

Carr, John Dickinson. "The Locked-Room Lecture." *The Art of the Mystery Story*, edited by Howard Haycraft, Grosset & Dunlap, pp. 273–86.

Chandler, Raymond. "The Simple Art of Murder." Allen and Chacko, pp. 387–99.

Chandler, Raymond and Billy Wilder. Screenplay of *Double Indemnity*. 1944.

Chesterton, G. K. "A Defense of Detective Stories." *The Art of the Mystery Story*, edited by Howard Haycraft, Grosset & Dunlap, pp. 3–6.

Davis, Mike. *City of Quartz: Excavating the Future in Los Angeles*. 1990. Vintage, 1992.

Dickstein, Morris. *Dancing in the Dark: A Cultural History of the Great Depression*. W. W. Norton, 2009.

Double Indemnity. Directed by Billy Wilder, Paramount Pictures, 1944.

Gramsci, Antonio. *Prison Diaries, III*. Translated by Joseph A. Buttigieg. Columbia UP, 2011.

Haycraft, Howard, editor. *The Art of the Mystery Story*. Grosset & Dunlap, 1946.

Jefferson, Thomas. *Jefferson: Writings*. Library of America, 1984.

Kahn, Joan, editor. *Hanging by a Thread: A New Treasury of Fact and Fiction*. Houghton and Mifflin, 1969.

Macdonald, Ross. *Ross Macdonald Selects Great Stories of Suspense*. Knopf, 1974.

Marrs, Suzanne. *Eudora Welty: A Biography*. Harcourt, 2005.

Marrs, Suzanne, and Tom Nolan, editors. *Meanwhile There Are Letters: The Correspondence of Eudora Welty and Ross Macdonald*. Arcade Publishing, 2015.

Marsh, Ngaio. *Artists in Crime*. 1938. Felony & Mayhem Press, 2012.

Nicholson, Marjorie Hope. "The Professor and the Detective." *The Art of the Mystery Story*, edited by Howard Haycraft, Grosset & Dunlap, pp. 110–127.

Piketty, Thomas. *Capital in the Twenty-first Century*. Translated by Arthur Goldhammer. The Belknap Press of Harvard UP, 2014.

Polk, Noel. *Eudora Welty: A Bibliography of Her Work*. UP of Mississippi, 1994.

The Postman Always Rings Twice. Directed by Tay Garnett, MGM, 1946.

Rzepka, Charles. *Detective Fiction*. Polity Press, 2005.

Sayers, Dorothy L. "The Omnibus of Crime." Allen and Chacko, pp. 351–83.

Sheed, Wilfrid. "The Good Word: It All Depends on Your Genre." *New York Times Book Review*, 5 Sept. 1971, 2+.

Symons, Julian. *Bloody Murder: From the Detective Story to the Crime Novel*. Mysterious Press, 1992.

Welty, Eudora. "Department of Amplification." *New Yorker*, 1 Jan. 1949, pp. 41–42.

Welty, Eudora. Introduction. *Hanging by a Thread: A New Treasury of Suspense, Fact and Fiction*, edited by Joan Kahn, Houghton Mifflin, 1969, pp. xv–xix.

Welty, Eudora. *Complete Novels*. Library of America, 1998.

Welty, Eudora. *Photographs*. UP of Mississippi, 1989.

Welty, Eudora. *Stories, Essays, & Memoir*. Library of America, 1998.

Wilson, Edmund. "Why Do People Read Detective Stories?" *New Yorker*, 6 Oct. 1944, pp. 78–84.

Wilson, Edmund. "Who Cares Who Killed Roger Ackroyd?" *New Yorker*, 20 Jan. 1945, pp. 59–66.

Wright, Willard Huntington. "The Detective Novel." *Scribner's*, vol. 79, no. 11, Nov. 1926, pp. 532–39.

READING EUDORA WELTY'S "PETRIFIED MAN" AND "OLD MR. MARBLEHALL" AS SOUTHERN PULP

KATIE BERRY FRYE

A reader looking for clues to the interplay between Eudora Welty's oeuvre and the mystery genre need not look far: a prolific reader in genre fiction, Welty loved mysteries, ghost stories, and the hard-boiled crime story; her early short story "The Great Pinnington Solves the Mystery," not to mention her many reviews of genre fiction for the *New York Times Book Review*, attest to these lifelong literary proclivities. There is also her late-life epistolary friendship with Kenneth Millar, better known to the public as the esteemed detective writer Ross Macdonald. The two authors often shared ideas and suggestions, and Ralph Sipper's *Inward Journey* (1984), a collection of essays in homage to Millar, included a contribution from Welty which the detective writer himself had solicited. Because *Inward Journey* was nominated for a 1985 Edgar Award from the Mystery Writers of America, Welty attended the awards ceremony that year, and although Sippers lost to Jon L. Breen's *Novel Verdicts: A Guide to Courtroom Fiction*, Welty nevertheless took home the Raven Award for Reader of the Year, an award still proudly displayed in her home (Marrs 503). That same year Welty also chose to republish "Old Mr. Marblehall" (first published in the *Southern Review*, 1938) in *Ellery Queen's Mystery Magazine*, a revered crime fiction magazine known for publishing such industry heavyweights as Ruth Rendell, Isaac Asimov, and Peter Lovesey.

Regarding these biographical "clues" involving Welty's love for mystery fiction, perhaps the real mystery is why there has been so little scholarship on the ways in which mystery's many genres informed the author's work, an oversight this collection remedies. And yet it is my contention that the conventions of genre fiction, specifically of mystery, are in part what enabled Welty to tell a particularly southern crime story in two of her earliest stories,

tales about white male anxiety and, by evocation, the legacy of crimes associated with white supremacy. The influence of pulp genre fiction used to evoke
this theme of white supremacy is perceptible in "Petrified Man" and "Old
Mr. Marblehall," twin portraits of white male villainy. In the former, the culprit is a repeat rapist on the run, and in "Old Mr. Marblehall" the titular character is a bigamist whose secret life echoes the slaveholding South's history
of hidden families and mysteries of paternity. Both stories pay tribute to
the mystery genre, appropriating such elements as disappearing acts, doppelgängers, counterfeit identities, and witnesses and informants.

But it is the pulp fiction in particular which the characters themselves read
that offers the most decisive clues as to how to solve each story's mystery. Scattered throughout presumably familiar settings, a small-town beauty parlor
and an "ancestral" hall, are drugstore rental books and magazines, pulp publications popular at the time of Welty's writing. Of course, "pulp" refers both
to the medium and the message. Rising to popularity in the late nineteenth
century, "pulp fiction" took its name from the cheap pulpwood trees used in
the commercial production of these mass-marketed and mass-produced stories, a market which exploded after World War I. Erin A. Smith estimates that
this uptick in readers was somewhere around 10 million by the early 1940s,
the time at which Welty was writing (145). And while early pulp magazines
favored a more generalized hodgepodge of fiction, what quickly emerged in
response to consumer tastes was a bevy of specialized niche genres, including romance, science fiction, and the hard-boiled detective story. The message of these pulp magazines, with their masculine fantasies of conquest
and female subordination, solidly reinforced traditional gender roles. But
although these specialized genres relied on gender in marketing strategies,
the readers themselves crossed boundaries, with women in particular often
dabbling in multiple genres. As Smith notes, "[P]ulp fiction was (and is) a
much bigger and more ambiguously gendered phenomenon. Women wrote
and read pulp fiction in all its varieties—romance, crime stories, science
fiction, tales of lesbian love" (156). The same claim to literary variety could
be said of Welty herself, who not only demonstrated her dexterity at reading
across genres but also in *writing* across them.

Like fingerprints at a crime scene, these textual traces of pulp fiction in
Welty's stories, magazines like the "he-man" *Startling G-Man Tales* and the
weird science of *Terror Tales*, not only help to identify the criminal in each
story but also work to displace more predictable clichés of southernness.
Instead of regional tropes about protected southern ladies and male valor,
Welty's fictions witness a sinister world inhabited by mysterious male double
agents and gossipy beauty salon gumshoes. In reading these texts as ironic

deconstructions of pulp, I suggest that "Petrified Man," on the one hand, rejects the sensationalized racial profiling of Black men as rapists so tenacious in Welty's South and presents something far more disconcerting to her white readers, his uncanny white double. Although the southern rape complex was a hackneyed plot by the time of Welty's writing, it was also a cultural red herring, a case of mistaken identity in which the Black rapist was always the reputed villain. "Petrified Man" corrects this assumption by criminalizing a white man rather than Black. Indeed, it is Mr. Petrie's hyperwhiteness ("that white powder all over his face") that defamiliarizes him from his crimes. And while scholarly analysis of this story has emphasized its satire of the feminine, I argue that "Petrified Man" regenders the whodunit mystery with the women here recast as both the victims and the hard-boiled detectives. The result is a comic if disquieting take on the southern rape complex, one in which the women make the case that men are so ineffectual as to be fossilized. What this double reading of Mr. Petrie ultimately reveals, surprising both the women and the reader, is that Mr. Petrie is actually a white rapist, one whose secret identity as a criminal signals a history of white violence in the South. Similarly, "Old Mr. Marblehall" is also a racial crime story, one in dialogue with the antebellum histories of white men leading double lives. But in Welty's incarnation, this gendered fantasy is exposed as Mr. Marblehall's nightmare, one which minimizes rather than maximizes his power.

What connects both stories are the pulp magazines strewn about, clues that set up the southern historical background, and in turn, the double-life plots of Mr. Petrie and Mr. Marblehall subvert these pulp genres of white male adequacy. Unlike the "he-men" of pulp fiction, these characters are revealed as frauds, and in turn, their emasculation speaks to a pervasive white male anxiety about loss of power. Although southern studies scholars have regarded this cultural fear of male inadequacy as regional, a "crisis of white male sexuality" carried over from the Civil War (Hale 233), this anxiety around white emasculation also references something more systemic in the United States, something more generally about male performance anxiety, female action, and all fearsome "others" outside the prescribed boundaries of Anglo-American heterosexuality. Taking the long view, this ebbing of white male privilege has typically coincided with wartime disruptions of traditional gender roles, from the Civil War to the World Wars. As Megan E. Abbott observes, detective fiction from the World War II era reflects anxieties similar to those from the Civil War, ones indicative of such realities as women assuming breadwinner roles and of "wartime xenophobia" (4–5). Filtering Welty through this lens of crime fiction thus exposes cultural fears about white male inadequacy in a way that situates her work at the crossroads of regional and national, past and present. Considered together, these examples could arguably be described here as "southern pulp," in which Welty pinpoints the Jim Crow South as the cradle of crimes, a place where white men, petrified with fear of being rendered invisible and immobile, are deceitfully unstable.

I. "PETRIFIED MAN"

As a whodunit, "Petrified Man" features a cast of slippery characters which includes several no-count men and a salon full of rowdy women. The focus of the story's criminal investigation is Mr. Petrie, a serial rapist on the lam. As a white rapist, Mr. Petrie's acts imply a cluster of disturbing truths about the slaveholding and Reconstruction South. An inversion of the mythic Black rapist, Mr. Petrie functions as an uncanny double that reminds the reader of the very real history of white violence. Like Mrs. Pike, the reader can't quite remember how they know him, although he puts them "in mind of somebody" (27). But who is he and what about him is familiar? In order to evade authorities, Mr. Petrie moonlights as an attraction in a traveling freak show, and his sideshow performance of masculinity is both exaggerated—he is rock hard and hard-boiled—and diminished, paralyzed, ossified. In fact all the story's men suggest caricatures of male inadequacy, particularly as they are perceived by the women. From Mr. Petrie's slow paralysis ("He's turning to stone," 22) to Fred and Mr. Pike, the slacker husbands who would rather fish than look for work, who "lay around the house like a rug" (22), these men have no jobs and no viable ambitions. Fred and Mr. Pike can be seen as synecdoche for a general white male emasculation, perhaps even foretelling the decline of white America. In another generation, they too will be petrified men, ossified monuments to ideological stasis. As Leota speculates about her husband, "I wouldn't be surprised if he woke up some day and couldn't move" (22).

Even three-year-old Billy Boy does not escape being emasculated by the women. Within the world of the text, a childcare crisis plays out on the sidelines: while Leota chats up each customer, Billy Boy is quite literally underfoot, "making tents with aluminum wave pinchers on the floor under the sink" (19). When Mrs. Fletcher snips, "I never saw him before" (19), Leota clarifies that she is merely babysitting the little boy as a favor for a friend. This favor indicates a matrix of childcare complications, one that includes over-extended working mothers, communal parenting, and corporal punishment. It also foregrounds the unemployed Mr. Pike as a deadbeat dad. Although he reportedly has the time to watch his own son while his wife holds down a job—as Leota notes repeatedly, neither her husband nor Mr. Pike "has got a job to his name" (26)—he does not, leaving the working women in the text to cobble together childcare as best they can. On this point the text again suggests the male anxiety associated with female financial independence. Working class women who put in long shifts, Leota and Mrs. Pike are the family providers, and the husbands' ongoing resistance to gainful employment speaks to a male cultural disempowerment and consequent fear of female action. Leota's exultant paddling of Billy Boy underscores this anxiety: he represents both the threat of a reinstated patriarchy, one capable of "penetrat[ing] and fill[ing] the whole curious beauty parlor," as well as its possible downfall (28). The text ends with Billy Boy's expulsion from the female homosocial world of the salon. Shamed by his spanking, he kicks and stomps his way out the door.

In "Petrified Man," this male fear of being perceived as inadequate should be read in dialogue with the southern rape complex. As decades of scholarship attests, the threat of rape, whether as a real or imagined act, pervades southern literature. The perceived threat was the Black man, ostensibly made bestial by the charms of white women, and this perception justified decades of lynchings of Black men by angry whites. But this version of the race-rape narrative has been challenged by feminist scholars, among them Jacquelyn Dowd Hall, Kathryn Lee Seidel, and Grace Hale. These cultural historians have asserted that the southern rape complex was in reality a conspiracy theory, an elaborate performance intended to preserve the racial hierarchy while releasing the violent impulses of white men, not Black. In "The Mind That Burns in Each Body," Hall argues that the private acts of rape and the public spectacle of lynchings worked together to reinvigorate white supremacy after the Civil War (333). Thus the reality of sexualized violence against women was perpetuated by white men, although as enacted on generations of enslaved women, difficult to prove. Referencing Hall's work on suffragist Jesse Daniel Ames, Seidel notes that the rape complex was also a convenient "focus or displacement" for the chaos and disappointment of the Reconstruction (139). This "chaos" would have included an unsettling of gender roles, created in part during the war by the white women who took on male roles in the men's absence (Hale 233). Subsequently inverting the narrative, shifting the blame for rape to Black men, allowed white men the illusion of regaining their manhood through the act of protecting white women against the invented threat of a supercharged Black masculinity.

Uncannily similar to the ideological function of pulp fiction, this battle cry to protect white women sets up the southern rape complex as its own kind of southern protopulp fiction, one which the women themselves safeguard, however unwittingly. Arguably, the women in Leota's salon see themselves as empowered rather than as enslaved, comforting themselves that their lazy men do not control them, not really. As Mrs. Fletcher chastises, "Women have to stand up for themselves, or there's just no telling" (25). And yet the women are unable to escape entirely the socially prescribed roles of marriage and motherhood. In the world of the beauty parlor, childbearing and rearing are frequent topics and unwelcome tasks, with pregnancy in particular being regarded as undesirable, as being "far gone" (18). After Mrs. Fletcher shrugs off Leota's endorsement of the traveling freak show ("I don't like freaks," 20), Leota compares Mrs. Fletcher's unborn child to one of its attractions: "Well, honey, talkin' about bein' pregnant an' all, you ought to see those twins in a bottle" (20), which she later describes as "[k]inda pathetic" (21). The only stay-at-home wife in the cast, Mrs. Fletcher perhaps best captures the anxiety around race and gender for white women. Long revered as the gatekeepers of lineage, white women had the responsibility of keeping up the business of white reproduction, a role fraught with limitations and unwanted responsibilities. Mrs. Fletcher's attitude towards compulsory procreation reflects this ambivalence: noting that she "don't like children that much," she muses about having an abortion, "I'm almost tempted not to have this one" (19) and later adds, "If a certain party hadn't found it out and spread it around, it wouldn't be too late even now" (24).[1] And yet as a financial dependent, Mrs. Fletcher is also somehow outside of this conversation on female autonomy as she is ultimately powerless to stave off her destined role as a mother. Inside the protected female homosocial world of the salon, she exaggerates her options and her freedom, but in the outside world, she knows her place. In the end, it is she who joyfully disciplines Billy Boy, admitting, "I guess I better learn how to spank" (28).

But if the women are victims in this cultural conspiracy, they are also the hard-boiled detectives, finding clues where they least expect them. When *Startling G-Man Tales* publishes Mr. Petrie's wanted photograph, the pulp magazine itself becomes a clue in the capture of Petrie for it is only after Mrs. Pike sees his image that she solves the mystery of the rapist's identity.[2] *Startling G-Man Tales* is itself suggestive of pulp magazines like *Strange Stories* (fig. 3.1) and *Startling Stories* (fig. 3.2), both beginning publication in the late 1930s. Sharing the tagline of "A Thrilling Publication," both magazines famously featured the cover art of Earle K. Bergey, who favored bullet-bra heroines clad in fetish wear, usually variations of brass, chains, and gauze, getups which are eerily evocative of the Medusaesque "wild-haired ladies" who frequent Leota's salon (28).[3]

Fig. 3.1. Earle K. Bergey cover for *Strange Stories*, December 1939.

Within "Petrified Man," these pulp primers on heterosexism function as clues to crimes of gender discrimination and misogyny, depicting the white women as willing participants in the sadomasochistic beauty standards that enslave them. Not unlike Mr. Petrie's self-imposed freakery, these women's sideshow bodies are being prepped to perform the rites and rituals of patriarchy. Pulsing with girl-on-girl violence, the salon is such that technicians with "strong red-nailed fingers" (17) like to yank, choke, pin, and "cook" their customers who return week after week for their shampoo-and-sets. In describing Mrs. Montjoy's last-minute hair appointment before giving birth to a "seb'm-pound sound," Leota recalls that her customer "yelled bloody

Fig. 3.2. Earle K. Bergey cover for *Startling Stories*, fall 1944.

murder" during the permanent process, her howls from Leota's hair-pulling
intermixed with howls from her labor pangs. When the pregnant Mrs. Fletcher notes that Mrs. Montjoy "must have been crazy" to undergo such treatment while in active labor, Leota quips, "Just wanted to look pretty while she
was havin' her baby" (24). In this culture, the transition from maiden to
matron is treacherous, and these women have the scalp burns to prove it.

Mr. Petrie's four rape victims thus literalize the voluntary victimization
playing out daily in Leota's salon. However, just as they have become inured
to their own participation in the misogyny complicit with the southern rape
complex, so too are these detectives unable initially to see beyond Mr. Petrie's

disguise. His theatrical makeup is a cosmetic whiteout that disorients Mrs. Pike, not to mention the reader; the white powder throws the reader as well as the women off his trail, suggesting that Mr. Petrie's crimes have repeatedly been overlooked precisely because he has been too white. When Leota interrogates Mrs. Pike on her failure earlier to identify the rapist, Mrs. Pike insists, "I didn't recognize him with *that white powder* all over his face. He just looked familiar [. . .] and lots of people look familiar" (27; my emphasis). And yet this raced brutality, what bell hooks names as white terrorism,[4] is the open secret Welty's fiction uncovers: if the fantasy of white supremacy hinged on helpless white women and bestial Black rapists, the reality had more to do with white thugs, less a homogenized community of white defenders and one increasingly divided along lines of gender and class.

A forensics examination of the white powder thus establishes its centrality to the mystery. Reminiscent of the white dusting powder once used at crime scenes, Mr. Petrie's camouflage becomes another example of what Patricia Yaeger calls "scattered whiteness," imagery that thematizes "white southerners' racial blindness" (xii). As such, it functions as a kind of red herring, blinding Welty's readers to the white man's true identity and reframing the text as a case of mistaken identity and false suspects. But in this instance, the mistake is not in falsely accusing the suspect but in inferring his innocence from his skin color. It is not until Mrs. Pike peruses Leota's copy of *Startling G-Man Tales* and sees the "reward-offered" photograph of Mr. Petrie, ostensibly without his makeup, that she connects his two identities, identities that blend and blur the performative with the normative. Without the pulp magazines and their peddling of masculine fantasies (including the capture of a wanted criminal), the women were poised to have lost the trail.

Worth emphasizing is the metatextuality of *Startling G-Man Tales* as a clue. As Smith notes, hard-boiled detective stories often used consumer goods as "object lessons in how power, social class and status were displayed for others to read" (149), and reading Leota's magazine as such a commodity complicates the ways in which the text plays on class and gender. After Mrs. Pike solves the mystery, what seems most to bother Leota is not Mr. Petrie's sexual crimes against women but her missed opportunity for financial and social gain. As she reiterates, the magazine was "*mine*, mind you, I'd bought it myself. . . . And *my* magazine, right next door to *my* beauty parlor" (26–27; my emphases). Leota's purchase of a pulp magazine marketed to male readers thus underscores her assumption of masculine agency, first as a breadwinner and then as a consumer. In the heterosexist world of the salon, she's content to push Hollywood fan magazines à la *Screen Secrets* on her patrons, but in the privacy of her own home, she transgresses boundaries.

Here too I should call attention to the titular difference between *Startling G-Man Tales* and real-world publications like *Startling Stories*. Whereas the latter is of classic science fiction ilk, Welty's addition of "G-Man," slang for "government man," heightens the appeal to a gendered audience. In her 1978 interview with *New Orleans Review*, Welty disavowed any symbolism in her use of the pulp magazines in Leota's salon, insisting, "It's just what they would be reading" (Prenshaw 27). And yet, despite the author's disclaimers, it is difficult not to read *Startling G-Man Tales* as part of a triple intrusion of masculine culture into this female world: first the military machismo celebrated by the magazine title, then Mr. Petrie's acts of sexual terrorism, and finally Billy Boy's persistent meddling. These intrusions signal an antifeminist patriarchy that, not unlike the cover art of *Startling Stories* and *Strange Stories* with their near-nude models paired with variations on monstrous masculinity, has the women in its clutches.

Furthermore, reading the text as a mystery plays on crime fiction's uneasy relationship with racial tension. Just as Bergey's covers for these pulp magazines also bring to mind the perceived "repulsive" racial threat of other "species" from which white women needed protection, so Mr. Petrie's white camouflage can be interpreted as a racialized metaphor for otherness.[5] Writing of the films noir based on these same pulp narratives, Eric Lott claims that it perpetuates "a sort of whiteface dream-work of social anxieties with explicitly racial sources, condensed on film into the criminal undertakings of abjected whites" (551), and when applied to crime fiction more generally, Lott's observation reframes Mr. Petrie's disguise. In this context, his whiteface shores up a painful history of racial performativity and cultural appropriation, one that uses a sensationalized whiteness to cover up his wrongdoing. Moreover, his whiteface exposes the villain in the southern rape plot as not belonging to the mythic Black rapist but to a society of insecure and power-crazed white male supremacists. In this sense, Mr. Petrie's portrayal of heightened whiteness as an example of racial performativity both uses and displaces blackface minstrelsy. Rather than crossing lines of color, Mr. Petrie overplays both his racial complexion and his masculinity, his petrified "hardness" becoming an absurd literalization of the white hard-boiled male. Worth noting is that many white hard-boiled men from pulp fiction "put on" these tough-guy personas only by appropriating Black masculinity. In *Hard-Boiled Masculinities* (2005), Christopher Breu argues that well-known white protagonists like Carroll John Daly's *Race* Williams were engendered by a kind of "surreptitious racial borrowing" (35), and the platform that first brought these protagonists to the public was the publication aptly entitled *Black Mask*. If we locate Mr. Petrie on this continuum of white machismo, then his performance of freakshow masculinity points to a kind of internalized blackface, one that seeks to "mask" his criminal activities through a zealous application of white face powder.[6]

Mr. Petrie's phenotype thus serves as both his crime and his alibi; it is the very thing which makes him both familiar and universal and at the same time, strange and invisible. He personifies an ongoing crisis of whiteness: embodied, he is unchecked, barbarous male sexuality; disembodied, he is just like everyone else, pandemic and invisible, the ubiquitous white male able to slip from town to town unnoticed. This crisis alludes to Richard Dyer's theory on the catch-22 of whiteness and sexuality: "Whites must reproduce themselves, yet they must also control and transcend their bodies. Only by (impossibly) doing both can they be white" (30). Mr. Petrie's double life captures this catch-22 of being both universal signifier and no one in particular, and his manipulation of whiteness becomes a reminder of the crimes of the South, the legacy of paralysis and freakery imposed on generations of Black bodies. But rather than exonerating another white man of his crimes, "Petrified Man" becomes its own startling story, one in which the female detectives solve the mystery and the white man gets caught in his own freak show.

II. "OLD MR. MARBLEHALL"

Both "Petrified Man" and "Old Mr. Marblehall" foreground male conquests for more—more women, more power, and in the case of Mr. Marblehall, more property and more progeny. But whereas the former offers an inverted case of mistaken identity, one in which the detectives presume the villain's innocence, "Old Mr. Marblehall" emerges as a race and gender crime story, one that intimates the slaveholding South's troubled past of promiscuous paternity. Embroiled in a double life worthy of the pulps he likes to read, Mr. Marblehall seems to use his alias Mr. Bird to enliven his staid life as a member of the Natchez noblesse, but his secret identity brings him no furtive pleasures.

Both Mr. Petrie and Mr. Marblehall are petrified men, the former ossifying while the other, "insultingly and precariously well-preserved" (93), slowly mummifies with "one foot in the grave" (91).[7] Like Mr. Petrie, Mr. Marblehall leads a double life, one populated with dual residences and families, "two totally different lives, with completely different families, two sons instead of one" (96). In this duplicity, the Marblehall home is shrouded in secrecy, everything "draped and hooded and shaded" (92). And like Mr. Petrie, Mr. Marblehall is a performer. Not only does he descend from a stage actor, but he stages his dual existence, the first as Mr. Marblehall, his "real" life, and the second as Mr. Bird. This mysterious double life, however, yields no opportunities for sideshow amusement. The vacation house is shabby ("Nobody ever looks to see who is living in a house like that," 94), the second wife resembles "funny furniture" and is "really worse than the other one" (94), and the young sons have "long little wilted fingers" (92), both legitimate heir and bastard son denounced as "cunning little jugglers" prone to "sudden fits and tantrums that frighten their mothers and Mr. Marblehall to death" (95). If double lives often articulate male fantasies about sex as power, the reader cannot quite discern the benefits of Mr. Marblehall's dirty little secret. His theatrical stint as Mr. Bird does not free him. On the contrary, it ensnares him further in a "violently small" version of domesticity (95), one sluggish with banality.

The nexus between both lives is Mr. Marblehall's nightly reading material, *Terror Tales* and *Astonishing Stories*. Just as Leota's hard-earned copy of *Startling G-Man Tales* helps to solve the mystery of Mr. Petrie, Mr. Marblehall's creepy pulp fiction about "horrible and fantastic things happening to nude women and scientists" (95) provides compelling clues on how to read our protagonist. Because pulps would soon be eclipsed by mass-market paperbacks in popularity, causing the former to fade within American culture, Mr. Marblehall, insofar as he represents a dying breed of southern patriarch, is unsurprisingly immersed in a dying breed of media, one that promises a virile resilience even as its cheaply produced, thin pages are already disintegrating. Furthermore, these dark fantasies and lurid tales hint at Mr. Marblehall's desire to be read as a libidinous villain not unlike the shadowy male figures who emblazon the covers of *Terror Tales*—that is, not as an old man but as one "quaintly secretive and prepared for anything" (91). And similar to Bergey's hyperbolic representations of gender on the covers of *Strange Stories* and *Startling Stories*, John Newton Howitt's cover art for *Terror Tales* favored a macabre masculinity with predators in pursuit of distressed damsels (fig. 3.3). Noting the influence of the "weird tale" pulp genre on this story, Mitch Frye asserts that Mr. Marblehall "uses his enjoyment of the fantastic as a means of envisioning resistance to the restrictions of Southern social life" (89). I would elaborate on Frye's analysis to emphasize that although Mr. Marblehall tries to appropriate the sinister machismo depicted in his pulps, he fails. When Mrs. Bird confesses what her husband "does in bed" (95), her admission is not about his sexual prowess but about his inability to perform: instead of enacting a nightly ritual of sexual domination, Mr. Marblehall gets in bed and reads "stretched out with his clothes on and don't have one word to say" (94). Mr. Marblehall is a voyeur, not a vanquisher.

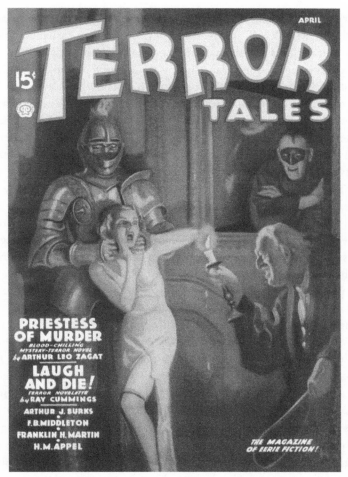

Fig. 3.3. John Newton Howitt's cover for *Terror Tales*, April 1936. © Steeger Properties, LLC.
All rights reserved.

In sifting through these clues, the story's setting emerges as a crime scene.
Mr. Marblehall's drama plays out in a town steeped in the history of slavery,
from its proximity to the Mississippi River to his four-columned home as
a signifier of the antebellum mansions amassed by wealthy Natchez plant-
ers and slaveholders. Moreover, the Marblehalls can trace their relationship
with the city of Natchez back to 1818, one year after Mississippi was admitted to the Union (Polk 168–69). In calling attention to the story's setting,
I find it instructive to compare the 1941 story with its earlier incarnation.
First published in 1938 as "Old Mr. Grenada" in the *Southern Review*, the story

underwent significant revisions before Welty republished it three years later as "Old Mr. Marblehall" in *A Curtain of Green*. Even a casual comparison of the two versions reveals that the changes further emphasized the story's debt to a specific time and place: there is the addition of "the United Daughters of the Confederacy" to the roster of Mrs. Marblehall's socialite obligations as well as its semantic swapping of "big new house" (Chengges 3) with "ancestral home" (Welty 92). Consider too in "Old Mr. Marblehall" the sons are ranked, his legitimate son now deemed "the first one" (95) rather than simply "the other" (Chengges 5) and perhaps most tellingly, the narrator observes that Mr. Marblehall's fastidious appearance is deserving of "a little black boy" to attend him (93).[8] These revisions speak volumes, not only about the text's awareness of raced and classed hierarchy in the Jim Crow South but also about the narrator's more explicit communication with the reader. In the 1941 iteration, the narrator's frequent use of direct address magnifies the assumption of shared values between the narrator and Welty's reader, thereby making both complicit in Mr. Marblehall's open secret. As Noel Polk observes, the entire town possesses "an almost preternatural consciousness" of Mr. Marblehall's double life (170).

The open secret of Mr. Marblehall's life connects the story's regional context with the antebellum South's history of white men leading mysterious double lives, from Thomas Jefferson and Sally Hemings in Virginia to the pervasive practice of *plaçage* in New Orleans. Of the latter example, Kenneth Aslakson writes of this practice of white men having secret or secondary families with women of color as being akin more to "common law marriages than concubinage," with the white fathers sometimes adopting their illegitimate children (718). A handful of Welty scholars have noted this racial undercurrent in Mr. Marblehall's double life, with Michael Kreyling observing "a hint" of miscegenation lurking about the text (23–24). In my reading of "Old Mr. Marblehall," the protagonist's gleeful duplicity, his pursuit of "two totally different lives, with completely different families" (96) cannot and should not be read in a vacuum. There is about his second life a whiff of chicanery, something evocative of Mary Boykin Chesnut's "a thing we can't name" in her indictment of white supremacy and miscegenation laws (29). Consider the second son's imagined tracking of his father Mr. Bird "across town" to the Marblehall address: there the reader foresees the boy's shock after learning of his father's more entitled family, one safely ensconced behind a "wrought-iron gate" in the ancestral home with its "rosy lamps," its garden with fountains and stone "pigtailed courtier mounted on the goat" (96). Mindful of Lott's assertion of "the raced double lives of noir protagonists," I would argue that the text never articulates the racial origins of Mrs. Bird and her son because it does not need to—within the one-drop world of the text, there is no burden of proof. Rather, if "Old Mr. Marblehall" plays to the mystery genre, the mystery here is less about the threat of blackness and racial ambiguity than it is about our protagonist's motivation. Although it is a deeply gendered fantasy he pursues, one pulsing with bigamy and obsessed with property and patrilineal inheritance, the text reminds us again and again that Mr. Marblehall is not getting a deal: both sons "frighten their mothers" (94); his second wife is not a limber sex object but is "so static she scarcely moves" (94). So why then pursue the doubling? Why double his discontent? The answer is that after sixty years of having "never done anything" (94), Mr. Marblehall wants to feel alive, to "store up life" (96), and so he proceeds with a kind of Rube Goldberg strategy to "multipl[y] his life by deception," one which he hopes to conclude in "some glorious finish" (96–97).

But his efforts to double himself bungle the fantasy. As it turns out, having two families is double the trouble, and there is no ejaculatory finish, no "great explosion of revelations" as he had hoped (97). Simply put, his acquisition of people and property engenders neither privilege nor power. Rather, in Welty's comic riff on white masculinity, "Nobody cares" (96): there are no devastated wives with whom to contend, no children reeling from their father's emotional fraud. There is also no outraged community to hold him accountable, and herein lies an important distinction between Mr. Marblehall and the heritage of white male privilege which he unwittingly represents: unlike his predecessors, Mr. Marblehall wants to be found out as he supposes such an "astonishing, unbelievable, electrifying" discovery would somehow validate his existence (96). But in the absence of any accountability, Mr. Marblehall ends where he began, leading a life of no consequence. The punch line lands: Mr. Marblehall's grand plans ironically reduce him to nothingness, solidify his insignificance, replicate his immateriality. In the battle between stasis and mobility, the former wins, rendering him a flightless suburbanite, not a bird but a stone, another petrified man daily being rendered more and more immobile and invisible, a marble tombstone for white male puissance. His doubling becomes a disappearing act.

In conclusion, both "Petrified Man" and "Old Mr. Marblehall" dally with the mystery genre, deploying such stratagems as double lives, disappearing acts, and doppelgängers. These crime-story elements convey white male anxiety in an era that was eroding white male control, and the felonies of rape and bigamy are presented within the context of this anxiety. Furthermore, they evoke historical backgrounds that reverberate of American racial crimes. As throwbacks to the slaveholding South, their settings should thus be read as crime scenes, as sites of racial turmoil wherein the double lives of white men were not mere pulp fiction but a painful historical reality. Considered together, these examples of southern pulp capture what Patricia Yaeger called a "constant uneasiness about the meaning of whiteness" (20), and it is Welty's interrogation of hegemonic notions of whiteness that leaves the reader to consider the residual trauma from the South's history of toxic white masculinity. In summary, Mr. Marblehall and all such men believe they can win only by taking rather than giving and in this misguided belief they choose deceit over transparency, ruthless acquisition over concession, the pursuit of property over the pursuit of life and liberty. One of the most enduring and destructive pulp fictions of white supremacy has always been that more begets more, when in fact it often leaves you with less.

Notes

1. Harriet Pollack notes that in fiction by Welty's peers, Mrs. Fletcher's reticence towards pregnancy and interest in abortion are unique because she is "a conventionally married woman making this choice for reasons of controlling the body that has been culturally constructed as a woman's instrument for controlling men" (147). See Pollack, "Was Welty a Feminist?" in Pollack, *Eudora Welty's Fiction and Photography: The Body of the Other Woman*. U of Georgia P, 2016, pp. 133–60.

2. In more ways than one is *Startling G-Man Tales* a clue. Welty originally published "Petrified Man" in the spring 1939 *Southern Review*, and in this earlier version Leota's magazine was fittingly titled *Startlin' Detective*. This magazine, perhaps in reference to the pulp *Startling Detective Adventures* then in publication, underscores Leota's and the women's roles as private eyes sleuthing for clues. Two years later in her revision for *A Curtain of Green*, Welty renamed the telltale magazine *Startling G-Man Tales*, and the timing of this revision suggests that *Startling Stories*, a science fiction pulp beginning publication in January of 1939, can be read as a possible real-world antecedent for *Startling G-Man Tales*.

3. It is rumored that Bergey's cover models inspired such fetish-wear icons as Princess Leia's metal "slave" bikini in the 1983 film *Return of the Jedi* as well as Madonna's cone bra popularized in her 1989 video "Express Yourself."

4. See "Representations of Whiteness in the Black Imagination" in bell hooks, *Black Looks: Race and Representation*, South End Press, 1992, pp. 165–78.

5. Many thanks to Jo Ellyn Clarey for her suggestion that Mr. Petrie's "white powder" references the history of blackface.

6. Coincidentally, Race Williams made his first appearance in "Knights of the Open Palm," a short story in the 1923 "special issue" of *Black Mask* which took as its topic the resurgent Ku Klux Klan. While Daly's story features his protagonist at odds with the racist ideology of the Klan, some of the issue's stories are complicit while the issue's cover foregrounds a Klansman clutching a smoking cross. See Sean McCann, "Constructing

Race Williams: The Klan and the Making of Hard-Boiled Crime Fiction." *American Quarterly*, vol. 49, no. 4, 1997, pp. 677–716.

7. Noel Polk was perhaps the first to write about Mr. Marblehall as a petrified man, noting "his name is almost a palindrome, at the center of which is 'Mr. Marble.'" See Polk, "The Landscape of Alienation in 'Old Mr. Marblehall.'" *Faulkner and Welty and the Southern Literary Tradition*, UP of Mississippi, 2008, p. 173.

8. For a more comprehensive assessment of differences between the two texts, see Catherine H. Chengges, "Textual Variants in 'Old Mr. Grenada'/'Old Mr. Marblehall.'" *Eudora Welty Newsletter*, vol. 10, no. 2, 1986, pp. 1–6.

Works Cited

Abbott, Megan E. *The Street Was Mine: White Masculinity in Hardboiled Fiction and Film Noir*. Palgrave Macmillan, 2002.

Aslakson, Kenneth. "The 'Quadroon-Plaçage' Myth of Antebellum New Orleans: Anglo-American (Mis)Interpretations of a French-Caribbean Phenomenon." *Journal of Social History*, vol. 45, no. 3, 2012, pp. 709–34.

Breu, Christopher. *Hard-Boiled Masculinities*. U of Minnesota P, 2005.

Chengges, Catherine H. "Textual Variants in 'Old Mr. Grenada'/'Old Mr. Marblehall.'" *Eudora Welty Newsletter*, vol. 10, no. 2, 1986, pp. 1–6.

Chesnut, Mary Boykin Miller. *Mary Chesnut's Civil War*. Edited by C. V. Woodward, Yale UP, 1981.

Dyer, Richard. *White*. Routledge, 1997.

Frye, Mitch. "Astonishing Stories: Eudora Welty and the Weird Tale." *Eudora Welty Review*, vol. 5, spring 2013, pp. 75–93.

Hale, Grace Elizabeth. *Making Whiteness: The Culture of Segregation in the South, 1890–1940*. Pantheon, 1998.

Hall, Jacquelyn Dowd. "'The Mind That Burns in Each Body': Women, Rape, and Racial Violence." *Powers of Desire: The Politics of Sexuality*, edited by Ann Barr Snitow et al., Monthly Review Press, 1983, pp. 328–49.

hooks, bell. *Black Looks: Race and Representation*. South End Press, 1992.

Howitt, John. Cover. *Terror Tales*, April 1936.

Kreyling, Michael. *Understanding Eudora Welty*. U of South Carolina P, 1999.

Lott, Eric. "The Whiteness of Film Noir." *American Literary History*, vol. 9, no. 3, 1997, pp. 542–66.

Marrs, Suzanne. *Eudora Welty: A Biography*. Harcourt, 2005.

Polk, Noel. "The Landscape of Alienation in 'Old Mr. Marblehall.'" *Faulkner and Welty and the Southern Literary Tradition*, UP of Mississippi, 2008. *Open WorldCat*, http://api .overdrive.com/v1/collections/v1L2BowAAAE0PAAA1a/products/f7cea024-407f-41db -b0cc-105e186d5b60.

Pollack, Harriet. *Eudora Welty's Fiction and Photography: The Body of the Other Woman*. U of Georgia P, 2016.

Prenshaw, Peggy Whitman, editor. *More Conversations with Eudora Welty*. UP of Mississippi, 1996.

Seidel, Kathryn Lee. *The Southern Belle in the American Novel.* U of South Florida P, 1985.

Smith, Erin A. "Pulp Sensations." *The Cambridge Companion to Popular Fiction*, edited by David Glover and Scott McCracken, Cambridge UP, 2012, pp. 141–58.

Welty, Eudora. *The Collected Stories of Eudora Welty.* Harcourt, 1982.

Welty, Eudora. "The Great Pinnington Solves the Mystery." *Early Escapades*, edited by Patti Carr Black, UP of Mississippi, 2005, pp. 82–88.

Yaeger, Patricia. *Dirt and Desire: Reconstructing Southern Women's Writing, 1930–1990.* U of Chicago P, 2000.

DETECTING THE FORBIDDEN FRUIT IN EUDORA WELTY'S *THE GOLDEN APPLES*

ANDREW B. LEITER

Eudora Welty's mythically infused modernist masterpiece, *The Golden Apples* (1949), defies easy categorization. The short story cycle, which Welty point-edly asserted, "isn't a novel" (*Conversations* 43), features a cast of characters who reappear in various stories, all but one of which are set in fictional Morgana, Mississippi. The book's nebulous position between short story col-lection and novel invited relatively early critical assessments, such as those by Thomas L. McHaney, Michael Kreyling, and Danièle Pitavy-Souques, that address the unity of the work in terms of mythical allusion.[1] Subsequent critical considerations, like Rebecca Mark's *The Dragon's Blood: Feminist Intertextuality in Eudora Welty's "The Golden Apples"* (1994), continued to engage the collection's mythical framework while also advancing in virtually every cultural and literary studies area including the work's intersections with various genres. Patricia Yaeger and Ruth Weston have illustrated the con-nections of *The Golden Apples* to (southern) gothic/grotesque traditions, with Yaeger demonstrating that Welty's gargantuan female (Miss Eckhart) speaks to the racial and sexual hierarchies of southern society and Weston addressing the gothic elements that emerge from the tension between the community and the assimilation of the individual.[2] Other critics have exam-ined the bildungsroman elements in "June Recital" and "Moon Lake," more specifically. Leslie Kathleen Hankins, for example, has correlated those ele-ments with Welty to argue that the book might be understood as an artist's coming of age story: "If we read the text as a revisionist female *Künstlerroman* of relating, Cassie, Virgie, and Miss Eckhart form a powerful triad of shifting relations, a constellation of women artist figures relating to each other and to the community" (404). Likewise, Harriet Pollack has argued that Welty's girl

stories, including "June Recital," "can also be read against the generic conventions of the 'portrait of the artist as a young woman'" conjoining a "sexual
awakening and an artistic awakening" (*Eudora* 24).[3] In this essay, I seek to
complicate these considerations by suggesting yet another genre intersection
in *The Golden Apples*' coming-of-age stories. More specifically, I contend
that Loch Morrison, Cassie's younger brother, should be considered part
of the composite bildungsroman and that his perspective brings elements
of detective fiction to the cycle, a genre in full bloom during the respective
time periods of "June Recital" and "Moon Lake." In my consideration of "June
Recital" as detective fiction intersecting with southern gothic and bildungsroman genres, I argue that Welty positions sexuality and sexual knowledge as
mysteries or crimes that individuals must investigate as a problematic but
unavoidable focal point of maturation.

The conjunction of sexuality with gothic childhoods and imaginations
is not unusual in twentieth-century southern letters as the works of William Faulkner, Truman Capote, Dorothy Allison, and others demonstrate,
and Welty's contemporary Lillian Smith, in her autobiography *Killers of the
Dream* (published the same year as *The Golden Apples*), illustrates how the
taboos around sexuality as well as race in her southern upbringing gave "our
emotions their Gothic curves" (85). In *One Writer's Beginnings* (1983), Welty
recalls a disturbing memory that illustrates this connection in her own life.
As a child, she repeatedly asked her mother where babies came from, but
she never received a direct answer. The silence cloaking sexuality was the
norm for her community, "I doubt that any child I knew ever was told by her
mother any more than I was about babies," and in Welty's case, the secrecy
about sex becomes conflated and confused with other silences: "Not being
able to bring herself to open that door to reveal its secret, one of those days,
she opened another door" (18). Specifically, the evasion became mixed with
her mother's tragic secret, the infantile death of Welty's older brother: "She'd
told me the wrong secret—not how babies could come but how they could
die, how they could be forgotten about" (19). The secret is revealed when the
young Welty discovers, among her mother's things, two coins that were used
to cover the dead baby's eyes. Sally Wolff has studied this recollection in *One
Writer's Beginnings* as the genesis for the widespread thematic attention to
dead babies and endangered mothers in Welty's fiction; however, I am more
interested here in how the silence about sexuality, as opposed to the death of
her sibling, interacts with the gothic elements of childhood imagination as
Welty presents it. As she explains in summary of the troubling memory, "The
future story writer in the child I was must have taken unconscious note and
stored it away then: one secret is liable to be revealed in the place of another

that is harder to tell, and the substitute secret when nakedly exposed is often the more appalling" (19).

Similar to her memoir, Welty's short story cycle conflates sex with gothic elements from children's perspectives. Left to their own devices to understand sexuality, the children of *The Golden Apples* contribute to a composite bildungsroman that features multiple characters—Nina Carmichael of "Moon Lake" and Loch and Cassie Morrison of "June Recital"—instead of a traditional single protagonist. The silence surrounding sexuality leads to the characters' imaginative association of sex with danger, the unknown, and death in "Moon Lake," and with criminality and madness in "June Recital." The secrecy regarding sexuality—and the attendant "gothic curves"—act as the mysterious focal point of the characters' coming of age. In "June Recital," Welty engages detective fiction to frame sexual knowledge as the mystery/ crime under investigation. Specifically, I read the housebound Loch Morrison as a detective who witnesses a crime through his telescope, and I examine how the narrative employs aspects of detective fiction such as the abandoned house as the site of the mystery, investigative work, bumbling law enforcement, and last-minute intervention.

"June Recital" and "Moon Lake" are the two overt coming-of-age stories in *The Golden Apples*. The former story alternates between the perspectives of the bed-ridden, malarial Loch Morrison and his older sister Cassie as they contemplate the visitors to the abandoned old MacLain house next door and, in Cassie's case, the memories of her relationship to her former piano teacher Miss Eckhart and Virgie Rainey, Cassie's poorer but more musically talented and independent-minded classmate. The latter story addresses the experiences and friendship of three girls at summer camp near Moon Lake and is largely related from the perspective of Nina Carmichael, who is fascinated with Easter, an independent and toughened orphan who drowns but is resuscitated by (the now teen-aged) Loch Morrison. The stories share a joint coming-of-age interest in the mysteries of life—a grand and abstract clearinghouse for the intersections of personal growth, interpersonal and familial relationships, societal conventions and pressures, sexual knowledge, racial and class identity, gender restrictions, mortality, and so on. Consequently, the stories have been most commonly compared in terms of Cassie's and Nina's development through their relationships with their lower-class peers. Pollack offers the clearest summation of this paradigm in the two stories: "Nina, attracted to Easter just as Cassie is to both Virgie Rainey and Miss Eckhart—that is, as a proxy and alter ego entered imaginatively to explore behaviors otherwise forbidden or inaccessible—contemplates this other and secret way to live, bridging differences in imaginative acts that also open breathing space and provide escape from her own confined and protected identity" (*Eudora* 15).[4]

As the girls contemplate their identities and respective relationships, their attempts to penetrate the shroud of mystery surrounding life become narrative focal points. In Cassie's case this appears often as contemplative interrogatives. When she tries to make sense of Miss Eckhart's decline and increased ostracism from the community, for example, her attention shifts to an ephemeral and symbolic hummingbird: "Metallic and misty together, tangible and intangible, splendid and fairy-like, the haze of his invisible wings mysterious, like the ring around the moon—had anyone ever tried to catch him?" (67). Similar imagery and questioning appear throughout the story and highlight the abstract and elusive nature of knowledge at the heart of Cassie's development. Likewise, Nina's perspective in "Moon Lake" engages the intangible mysteries of life whether it is the temporality of existence considered through the prism of a ripe pear, the erotic intrusion of a personified night into Nina's tent, or the conflation of sex and death in the powerful scene of Easter's drowning and revival while the other girls watch.

The latter scene in particular illuminates a sexualized world that is fundamental to the characters' coming of age. Loch Morrison pulls Easter from the lake where she has stopped breathing, places her on a picnic table, and performs lengthy and violent CPR in a manner resembling sexual intercourse: "He lifted up, screwed his toes, and with a groan of his own fell upon her and drove up and down upon her, into her" (145). At the culmination of this traumatic scene, Nina reflects on its meaning as she and other girls aid the resuscitated Easter: "In that passionate instant, when they reached Easter and took her up, many feelings returned to Nina, some joining and some conflicting. At least what had happened to Easter was out in the world, like the table itself. There it remained—mystery, if only for being hard and cruel and, by something Nina felt inside her body, murderous" (154). This epiphanic moment speaks to Nina's evolving perspective on mortality, sexuality, gender, and, perhaps, gendered violence, while simultaneously acknowledging the remaining mystery surrounding these seemingly intertwined aspects of life.

In a parallel scene in "June Recital," Cassie's contemplation of her relationship with Miss Eckhart and Virgie Rainey becomes mixed with Virgie's sexual precociousness as she and Kewpie Moffit emerge from a tryst in the old MacLain house, and while I agree with Pollack's assertion that the "fascination of middle-class daughters with their freer counterparts is not simply or primarily about sexual freedom" (*Eudora* 16), overt and subtextual references to a variety of sexualities permeate the stories in which Cassie and Nina come of age. Both "June Recital" and "Moon Lake" attest to Annette

Trefzer's contention that Welty attended to a multitude of sexual themes and orientations in her work: "In addition to her life-long interest in exploring themes of sexual initiation, especially threshold experiences of young women . . . Welty creates a fictional world marked by libidinal currents that flow often directly against normative heterosexuality" (85). Loch's graphically sexualized revival of Easter and Virgie's copulation with Kewpie offer presumptively vicarious moments of (hetero)sexual knowledge or maturation for Nina and Cassie respectively; however, these two moments also coexist with and—to some extent—mute a variety of nonnormative sexualities that comprise the mysteriously erotic and violent gothic spaces of Moon Lake and the MacLain house.

These two respective sites take on their gothic dimensions through the conjunction of sex and the unknown, in part, because the children are left to their own devices to navigate the mysterious realm of sexuality.[5] Welty emphasizes these silences in "June Recital" at various points. Loch's description of sex between Virgie and Kewpie Moffit, for example, suggests that he has no base of knowledge on which to draw and that he lacks the vocabulary to describe what he sees: "like the paper dolls sprung back together, they folded close. . . . Like a big grasshopper lighting, all their legs and arms drew in to one small body, deadlike, with protective coloring" (30). Likewise, when Cassie recalls that Miss Eckhart was once raped, her description substitutes a threat of death for the sexual violence: "One time, at nine o'clock at night, a crazy n----r had jumped out of the school hedge and got Miss Eckhart, had pulled her down and threatened to kill her" (57). While these two descriptions speak to an evasive vocabulary that suggests a broader communal aversion to discussing the details of sexuality, an incident involving Cassie and her parents emphasizes the enforced nature of such silence. During the children's piano practices with Miss Eckhart, a fellow boarder at the MacLain house interrupts the lessons by exposing himself to the children: "While Miss Eckhart listened to a pupil, Mr. Voight would walk over their heads and come down to the turn of the stairs, open his bathrobe, and flap the skirts like an old turkey gobbler. . . . When he flapped his maroon-colored bathrobe, he wore no clothes at all underneath" (47). Miss Eckhart threatens to beat the children if they talk about Mr. Voight's terrifying routine, and when Cassie tells her parents anyway, her father dismisses the tale and threatens her with "no picture show money" if she repeats it (48). The clear lesson—that some subjects should not be broached—extends, as Cassie understands it, from both a lack of words as well as audience: "And for what Mr. Voight did there were no ready words—what would you call it? . . . Some performances of people stayed partly untold for lack of a name, Cassie believed, as well as for lack of believers" (49). The realm of sexuality may be unaddressed in the communal and family circles, yet it exists nonetheless in what might best be understood as the psychic fringes of the community embodied in the marginal gothic spaces of Morgana Woods, Moon Lake, and, in "June Recital," the old MacLain house.

Considerations of "June Recital" as a coming-of-age story have concentrated more fully on Cassie than on her younger brother Loch; however, his investigation of events in the MacLain house are as suggestive of threshold events for him, arguably, as the more explicit threshold experiences of Cassie. The alternating perspectives of Loch and Cassie have led some critics to read them as at odds with each other thematically or to value one higher in Welty's schema of characters, but my reading of the dual perspectives is more in line with Jacob Agner who argues that "its contrapuntal montage between Loch and Cassie's minds instructs readers to thread together all of the separate-but-connected perspectives of *The Golden Apples*" (56).[6] I specifically view their perspectives as complementary illustrations of a shared movement toward adulthood in a mysteriously sexualized world. Agner and others, including Jason Dupuy, Dina Smith, Leslie A. Kaplansky, and David McWhirter, have demonstrated the influence of film on "June Recital" and contend that Loch's framing/viewing of the events next door is cinematic in nature. These filmic readings suggest intersections of Loch's perspective with silent film, Keystone Kops, adventure film, and thrillers.[7] In addition to these cinematic intersections, however, Loch's chapters similarly correspond with elements of detective fiction with Loch as the investigative figure. His detective work reveals a pronounced sexual subtext seminal to his development, and it offers a metanarrative for investigative reading of "June Recital."

This volume has already extensively contextualized Welty's engagement with popular fiction trends from the Golden Age of detective fiction, the era defined by Howard Haycraft as beginning in 1918, coinciding both with Loch's youth in "June Recital" and with Welty's own. It is important now to add that the subgenre of youth detective fiction emerged between the events of "June Recital" and Welty's composition of *The Golden Apples*. At the end of Haycraft's Golden Age—and likely inspired by the commercial success of mystery novels in the era—the Hardy Boys series was inaugurated in 1927 and was followed three years later by the Nancy Drew series. Welty was an adult when these series began, but their popularity would not likely have been lost on a bibliophile like her; furthermore, she clearly had an interest in the intersection of youth detectives and more aesthetically complex modernist fiction. Specifically, she praised Faulkner's detective bildungsroman, *Intruder in the Dust* (1948). In a review, published the same year as *The Golden Apples*,

Welty describes *Intruder* as "a double and delightful feat, because the mystery of the detective-story plot is being raveled out while the mystery of Faulkner's prose is being spun and woven before our eyes" ("In Yoknapatawpha" 598), a description that is equally apropos of Welty's prose and Loch's sections of "June Recital."

The opening chapter features Loch Morrison—and the reader by extension—as detective voyeurs, peering through Loch's bedroom window via telescope at the former MacLain residence. The plot, to this extent, resembles Alfred Hitchcock's thriller *Rear Window* (1954), and while "June Recital" predates the movie by several years, Welty could have read the short story on which the film was based; "It Had to Be Murder" by Cornell Woolrich appeared in *Dime Detective* in 1942 and as "Rear Window" two years later in Woolrich's short story collection *After-Dinner Story*.[8] At any rate, Loch's sections of "June Recital" reflect staples of detective/crime fiction beginning with the purportedly abandoned house as the scene of criminal activity, a trope that bridges the gothic and detective elements of the novel. Houses, of course, feature prominently in the detective fiction tradition—in addition to the abandoned houses, we might include English country manors as mystery sites, locked-room mysteries, and so on. Haunted, mysterious, or abandoned houses, however, are also staples of gothic fiction such as Charlotte Brontë's *Jane Eyre* (1847), Charlotte Perkins Gilman's "The Yellow Wall-paper" (1892), and Shirley Jackson's *The Haunting of Hill House* (1959), and of southern gothic fiction, more specifically, like Edgar Allan Poe's "The Fall of the House of Usher" (1839), Capote's *Other Voices, Other Rooms* (1948), and Faulkner's *Sanctuary* (1931) and *Absalom, Absalom!* (1936). Although hardly exclusive to southern versions of the gothic tradition, sexualized fears particularly permeate the gothic spaces of "haunted" houses in southern literature: in the four works listed above, for example, we find incest, homosexuality, rape, and miscegenation shaping the gothic contours of the respective texts and houses. While Welty resisted the label of southern gothic writer, in "June Recital" Loch brings his investigative eye to the similarly sexualized gothic house next door.[9] The "vacant" structure is in fact simultaneously occupied by the sleeping Booney Holifield (the night watchman at the gin) as well as Virgie Rainey and Kewpie Moffitt; meanwhile, the house is visited by Miss Eckhart, Old Man Moody, Fatty Bowles, and King MacLain, whom Loch mistakes for Mr. Voight, the flasher and former boarder in the home. Loch studies the house as two "crimes" unfold. Virgie and Kewpie's relationship represents a premarital transgression against communal sexual norms that is policed by the women returning from cards, and Miss Eckhart's crime of arson is interrupted by Old Man Moody and Fatty Bowles.

In the traditional ratiocinative detective fashion of Poe's Dupin, Doyle's Holmes, and early versions of Christie's Poirot, Loch observes the actions and appearance of those in the house to piece together evidence and draw conclusions about what is happening. With Miss Eckhart's arrival he notes, "Here came an old lady. No, she was an old woman." He draws this class distinction based on the evidence that she has "nothing in her hands, no reticule or fan." Furthermore, he assumes from her "unsteady-looking" appearance that she evidently walked a long way and "must have walked in from out in the country" (28). His conclusions are not always correct, but they are based on reasonable assessments of the evidence at hand. He mistakenly supposes that, because Miss Eckhart has come from somewhere besides town, she "might be the sailor's mother come after her son," since "the sailor didn't belong in Morgana anyhow" (28). As Miss Eckhart places newspaper around the house, Loch draws a comparison to his mother's habits: "And from her gestures of eating crumbs or pulling bits of fluff from her bosom, Loch recognized that mother-habit: she had pins there" (30). Based on what he presumably knows about his own mother, he mistakenly thinks that Miss Eckhart is decorating the house instead of planning to burn it down. Continuing to watch her actions and process their implications, however, Loch will arrive at the correct conclusion that she has arson in mind. This realization will lead him to misinterpret Miss Eckhart's metronome which Loch first views as "a new and mysterious object in her hands" and then as "a small brown wooden box, shaped like the Obelisk" (33). Watching Miss Eckhart intent on burning down the house, Loch hears the ticking of the metronome and concludes that the object is part of her destructive plans: "the box is where she has the dynamite" (34). Easily dismissed as childish imagination, Loch's conclusion that the metronome is a bomb is not absurd considering Miss Eckhart's actions, and Loch, as I discuss below, reevaluates the metronome in a manner that places it at the heart of his symbolic maturation.

With Loch's detective work of surveilling the house, processing evidence, and drawing conclusions, Welty frames the scene in the house as investigative detective fiction, and the ensuing action within the house similarly invokes generic conventions of crime fiction. For example, law enforcement arrives at the crime scene in the form of Fatty Bowles and Old Man Moody, who serves as the town Marshall. Their entrance to the house and the novel functions as a last-minute intervention and prevention of the crime: "caught in the act!" they shout at Miss Eckhart (81). In their apprehension of Miss Eckhart, they simultaneously resemble the comic relief of bumbling law enforcement officers. Loch has already noted that Virgie and Kewpie resemble a Keystone Kop routine as they chase each other in a bedroom upstairs: "around and around like the policeman and Charlie Chaplin, both intending to fall down" (30). When Moody and Bowles attempt to put out the fire, similar slapstick re-emerges: "Old Man Moody and Mr. Fatty, exchanging murderous looks, ran hopping about the parlor, clapping their hats at the skittering flames, working in a team mad at itself, the way two people try to head off chickens in a yard. They jumped up and knocked at the same flame. They kicked and rubbed under their feet a spark they found by themselves, sometimes imaginary" (82). As the scene continues, King MacLain—freshly returned to his former home after one of his long perambulations—dismisses them as "clowns" (83). They knock over furniture and break a chair rushing toward the metronome which they mistake by sound for a rattlesnake and then by sight as a potential bomb before throwing it out the window to be safe. They do stop the crime by extinguishing the fires, and they then place Miss Eckhart under arrest, escorting her between them out of the house and down the street as a prisoner with the admonition: "It don't signify nothing what your name is now, or what you intended, old woman. . . . We know where you belong at, and that's Jackson" (87). The seemingly authoritative assessment of a crime attempted and averted, as well as a criminal apprehended and headed to Jackson to be processed as criminally insane, may well represent the objective reality of the immediate events in the house and reflect standard parameters of a crime thriller with order restored at the end. Such a summation and tidy ending, however, leaves unaddressed the multifaceted nuances of what has transpired in the house, particularly when we consider what Loch's investigative work reveals in terms of the sexualized gothic space of the house.

In Loch's first mention of the house, he notes, "His family would all be glad if it burned down; he wrapped it with the summer's love" (20). The foreshadowing of Miss Eckhart's attempted arson is clear, but Loch's subsequent and fantastically associative description of the house is equally suggestive: "He let his eyes rest or go flickering along it, as over something very well known indeed. Its left-alone contour, its careless stretching away into that deep backyard he knew by heart. The house's side was like a person's, if a person or a giant would lie sleeping there, always sleeping" (20). Loch's personification of the house suggests a latent and unspoken or sleeping enormity that—both in its imaginative phrasing and in Loch's manner of viewing—represents a counternarrative of sorts to his more ratiocinative investigations of events in the house. Welty positions the Morrison household (Loch excepted) as antagonistic toward the old MacLain home which has already been established in "Shower of Gold" as the site of a broken marriage with King MacLain's philandering as the source of the familial collapse. Loch's "love" for the house thus sets him immediately at odds with his family's perspective on the house and its association with illicit sexuality. Loch again emphasizes the mysterious and forbidden secrets associated with the house when he notes the "small stair window shaped like a keyhole—one made never to open" (21). While the story establishes a historical tangential link to sexuality, the house quickly emerges as a continuing revelatory site for the unspoken realm of sexuality in Morgana when Virgie and Kewpie dash into the house to have sex in one of the bedrooms. Tellingly, Loch views the affair via his father's telescope, a scientific tool of observation and an unmistakably phallic lens through which the family views aberrant events such as lunar eclipses of the sun or the unsettled gender behavior of a female aviator passing overhead. In the latter instance, Loch remembers the telescope as "gripped in his father's hand like a big stick, some kind of protective weapon for what was to come" (23). The transfer of the telescope from father to son marks an apparent (if unwitting) passing on of a patriarchal, presumably objective, and phallically inscribed device, used by Loch to investigate the secret world of sexuality as he watches Virgie and Kewpie. We might even understand Loch's investigative voyeurism as tacitly condoned heteronormative indoctrination in a community that lionizes King MacLain's philandering and elects his son mayor, in part, for having "taken advantage of a country girl who had died a suicide" (238). Loch's vicarious sexual education, however, when considered in conjunction with the other visitors Loch observes, bring to mind Welty's notion in *One Writer's Beginnings* that the attempt to uncover a secret often reveals a different secret "harder to tell" and "often more appalling."

The overt sexual relationship between Virgie and Kewpie receives the fullest critical attention, particularly in terms of Virgie's independent precociousness, "It was she that had showed the sailor the house to begin with, she that started him coming" (24), and in terms of how Virgie's character thus relates to Cassie Morrison's coming of age. This heterosexual union—considered mildly problematic by the community because it is premarital—masks a panoply of other implied and more problematic sexualities that converge in the MacLain house and highlight other unspoken elements of sexual violence, bizarreness, and queerness that exist beneath the veneer of heteronormative Morgana. Miss Eckhart's arrival on the scene, for example, not only brings her madness to the house but also her history of rape and the white-segregation-era fears of miscegenation that contribute to her ostracism and eventual madness: "When Dr. Loomis made her well, people were surprised that she and her mother did not move away. They wished she had moved away" (57). Likewise, when Loch watches King MacLain's arrival and mistakes him for Mr. Voight, the confusion brings Voight's history of exposing himself to children back to the house. Although Loch does not explicitly detail Mr. Voight exposing himself, he remembers Voight most clearly as "foam[ing] at the mouth" (84), a description that resembles Cassie's memory of the terrifying look on Voight's face when he exposed himself as "belligerent," with "bared . . . teeth," and "frantic" (49). Additionally, Welty brings a queer subtext to the scene. Critics such as Suzan Harrison have noted the homoerotic aspects of Cassie's relationship with Virgie, but I turn here to the arguably homoerotic nature of Old Man Moody and Fatty Bowles's relationship as revealed from Loch's perspective and how it might complicate our understanding of Loch's initiation into sexual knowledge.[10]

Welty's implementation of detective fiction elements is particularly well-suited to Loch's investigations into the sexualized world of Morgana, Mississippi. Welty indicates, as I have already discussed, that deliberate avoidance of sexual subject matter places the onus on children to acquire such knowledge on their own, and in Loch's case, his detective work does exactly this. Furthermore, as Gill Plain has demonstrated in *Twentieth-Century Crime Fiction: Gender, Sexuality and the Body*, the detective genre comprises an important part of the gender and sexual politics of popular culture in Welty's contemporary society and does so in ways that are more complicated than the heteronormative veneer traditionally associated with the genre. Hardboiled detective fiction, despite its well-earned hypermasculine reputation and its objectification of women, at times exhibits homoerotic tensions beneath the tough-guy surface. John T. Irwin, for example, has argued that the aforementioned Cornell Woolrich "was extremely conflicted about his homosexuality" and this contributed to "the persecutory aspect of cosmic Fate" that permeates his fiction (154). Meanwhile, Plain has studied the ambiguous sexuality of Raymond Chandler's iconic detective, Philip Marlowe. Plain reads Chandler's "novels as idealising the homosocial at the expense of the heterosexual" and contends that "within the tough-guy framework of the genre, Marlowe's homoerotic intimacy can pass unnoticed" (65, 75). I would like to suggest that something similar is occurring in the MacLain house with the obvious heterosexual relationship between Virgie and Kewpie masking a potentially homoerotic relationship between the representatives of the law as unveiled by Loch's extralegal detective work.

Critical interpretations of "June Recital" have positioned Old Man Moody and Fatty Bowles's arrival on the scene at the MacLain house as a patriarchal, if comical, intrusion on Miss Eckhart's attempt to incinerate her failed alternative and feminine artistic life. Rebecca Mark, for example, argues that their appearance marks the "moment the masculine world intrudes" and that the men "increase their fertility and their virility by putting out this old woman's fire" (88). While such readings illuminate the gendered obstacles inhibiting feminine imagination, they are, perhaps, too quick in reading Moody and Bowles as traditionally masculine, considering the many peculiar aspects of the men's characterization.

Loch, with his investigative eye processes many of the details he sees, particularly regarding Miss Eckhart, but he also records a variety of details concerning Moody and Bowles that he does not decipher for the reader. In a move that implies the limitations of a patriarchal heteronormative perspective, Loch sets aside his father's telescope and literally climbs from his bedroom window onto a limb for a closer observation with his own eyes. Welty offers the reader-voyeur the textual evidence from Loch's observations that are necessary to fill in the gaps in his interpretation. As Loch watches from his tree, "Here down the street came Old Man Moody, the marshal, and Mr. Fatty Bowles with him. They had taken the day off to go fishing in Moon Lake and came carrying their old fishing canes but no fish" (78). Moon Lake, like Morgana Woods, serves as a site in the broader story cycle where individuals test the strictures on human relationships and sexual identity, and while the description of the phallic "old cane poles but no fish" might indicate a poor day of fishing there, they might also suggest that fishing was never exactly the priority of the day for the two. Furthermore, hanging upside down in the tree, Loch associates the two men with Virgie and the sailor lying on their backs in the house. By emphasizing Loch's inverted position, Welty offers a pointedly subjective perspective, one that quite literally flips the implied ratiocinative objectivity of Loch's telescopic investigations on its head *and*, perhaps, the presumed heteronormativity of his voyeurism. The lovers upstairs, whose intimacy in Loch's mind is associated with their legs (like an "M," "paper dolls," and a "grasshopper" [29–30]), resonates with his perception of the men: "In his special vision he saw that they could easily be lying on their backs in the blue sky and waving their legs pleasantly around, having nothing to do with law and order" (78). When Loch pairs the two couples in this manner, it suggests that he possibly perceives the relationships to be similar in nature. Immediately following this image of waving legs, the two men invoke a superstitious charm against division that is more suggestive of an intimate couple than of typical friends: "Old Man Moody and Mr. Fatty Bowles divided at the pecan stump, telling a joke, joined, said 'Bread and butter,' and then clogged up the steps" (78–79). Passing on either side of a severed phallic tree, the two men reaffirm their relationship as close as "bread and butter" before dance-stepping on the stairs to the house.

Readers might understand such details as evidence of a fairly standard, albeit oddly described, homosocial fishing trip, but the sexually charged imagery accumulates in ways difficult to reconcile with heteronormativity.

For example, in a nod toward Faulkner's *The Sound and the Fury*—specifically Caddy's muddy undergarments and all of their sexually symbolic weight as she climbs the tree to spy through the window at the scene of Damuddy's deathbed—Loch notes from his tree that, as the men peer through the window at the scene of Miss Eckhart's rage, "There were round muddy spots on the seats of their pants" (79). An avid Faulkner reader, Welty here seems to reimagine one of the most familiar scenes of symbolic sexual knowledge in American modernism with Loch's perspective on the men's soiled backsides. As Moody and Bowles watch the attempted arson unfold, they remain in oddly intimate positions, and with Loch hanging directly over them, he "could have dropped a caterpillar down onto either of their heads, which rubbed together like mother's and child's" (80). Fatty Bowles then "lifted his arm, that had been hugging Old Man Moody's shoulders, and transferred to his own back pocket a slap that would have cracked Old Man Moody's bones" (80). Moments later, Fatty Bowles gestures with his "old fishing knife" and when Loch shouts at them that "the house is on fire," they react "a little as if they were insulted, [and] they raised up, [and] moved their fishing poles along" (80). Is their "insulted" reaction to Loch's detective work a response to his doing their job for them, or his startling intrusion on their intimate familiarity? Notably, the text's emphasis is not on the relocation of the men but rather on their adjustment of "their fishing poles," and Loch's warning links the men and their poles to the fire smoldering between them, around which they comically dance in their attempt to extinguish it.

The fire, like so many images and events of *The Golden Apples*, is multivalent, and it should be understood for its association with artistry and passion—the allusion being to Yeats's poem "Song of the Wandering Aengus" which Cassie returns to at various points, and thus to sexuality and to the polyvalent triangulation of Cassie, Virgie, and Miss Eckhart. As such, the scene attests to Trefzer's contention that, like other high modernists, Welty was "interested in the connection between erotic power and the life of the mind" (89). Moody and Bowles might thus be understood as stifling feminine aspirations and transgressive potential as they put out Miss Eckhart's fire, but Loch seems to also witness a simultaneous stifling of queer desire with the arrival of King MacLain (Mr. Voight in Loch's mind). Morgana's mythic fornicator brings an authoritative heterosexual gaze and mocking laughter to the other men's effort to extinguish the flames: "Mr. Voight shook all over. He was laughing, Loch discovered. Now he watched the room like a show. 'That's it! That's it!' he said" (82). In response to MacLain's ridicule, Moody and Bowles redouble their efforts to douse the fire: "So they put the fire out, every spark, even the matting, which twinkled all over time and again before it went out for good. When a little tongue of flame started up for the last time, they quenched it together; and with a whistle and one more stamp each, they dared it, and it stayed out" (82–83). The subtext of this scene as a whole suggests a homoerotic "fire" between Moody and Bowles that, when interrupted by MacLain, reverts to a heteronormative performance intent on masking their relationship by extinguishing—with compensatory enthusiasm—Miss Eckhart's fire as it literally flares between them.

I would like to shift here from what Loch sees transpiring in the MacLain house to a consideration of how the events and his reactions might inform our understanding of Loch in ways that run counter to readings of him as a heteronormative and even aggressively patriarchal figure in the subsequent "Moon Lake." The occurrences in the MacLain house, as I read them, stress some particularly queer moments in the central scene of Loch's childhood. I use "queer" in the same sense as Steven Bruhm and Natasha Hurley, editors of *Curiouser: On the Queerness of Children*, use it: as a "spacious" term that "indicate[s] a deviation from the 'normal'" and that "derives also from its association with specifically sexual alterity" (x). The essays in that collection address the multifaceted dynamics of childhood queerness in terms of identity formation, and I am particularly interested in Kathryn Bond Stockton's essay "Growing Sideways, or Versions of the Queer Child" in which she writes: "The child, from the standpoint of 'normal' adults, is always queer: either 'homosexual' (an interesting problem in itself) or 'not-yet-straight,' merely approaching the official destination of straight couplehood (and therefore estranged from what it 'should' approach)" (283). Stockton offers an alternative model of growth—the "growing sideways" of her title—that allows for the queer childhood identities that run counter to adult efforts to categorize. Her study speaks to the complexities of childhood sexuality and its fluidity, while her point that certain childhood sexualities can "braid, one with another," speaks to simultaneously existing sexual potentialities—that is what seems to be happening to Loch in "June Recital" (310).

As the action in the MacLain house unfolds from Loch's investigative perspective, I would argue that we witness a moment of simultaneous sexualities and fluidity as the child investigator observes both a heterosexual unveiling in the upstairs bedroom and a queer revelation downstairs. Critics have assumed that Loch is too young to understand what he sees transpiring in the house, but while he may not understand every detail and implication of his observations, the text presents consistent evidence that the scene is, at least, a symbolic if not literal sexual awakening for him—and that awakening is as textually attentive to Bowles and Moody as it is to Virgie and Kewpie. It is easy to misconstrue Loch's awakening as heterosexual because

the scene opens with his observation of Virgie and Kewpie, yet his vicarious identification is not with their physical consummation but rather with
his own phallic consumption: "he would love, himself, to lie, on a slant and
naked, to let the little cottony tufts annoy him and to feel the mattress like
billows bouncing beneath, and to eat pickles lying on his back" (29). Likewise,
although Loch views the tryst through the seemingly patriarchal, phallic
telescope—the "protective weapon" given to him by his father—it is hardly
a convincing symbol of masculine heterosexuality considering Loch closes
the eye on the "cool telescope" and bemoans, "Poor old Telescope" (30), suggesting, perhaps, sexual uncertainty in response to the heterosexual scene he
observes. In fact, when Loch leaves behind this patriarchally inscribed lens
and escapes his confinement by climbing out on the extending branch in
order to get an unmediated closer look at events, Loch's branch emerges as
equally phallic as the telescope during his observation of Moody and Bowles.
It is while Loch watches the men—rather than while he watches Virgie and
Kewpie—that his actions become symbolically if not overtly masturbatory.
As the two men approach the house in the queer manner detailed above
and Loch warns them of the fire, he is described as "riding his limb up and
down" (80). He subsequently resents MacLain's intrusion on Bowles and
Moody because "to tell the truth he made one too many" (82), and as Bowles
and Moody extinguish the fire with MacLain watching, Loch is "riding the
tree, his branch in both fists" (83). Welty's arrangement of the subtextual
nuances in this scene associate Loch and his metaphoric masturbation with
the simultaneous relationships, queer and heteronormative, revealed before
they are both contained by MacLain's arrival.

Understanding Welty's attention to the homoerotic in "June Recital" opens
a new perspective on Loch and his fascination with the enigmatic and potentially explosive (as he imagines it) metronome. The metronome links Loch
to Bowles and Moody as Loch recovers the device after Bowles—also fearing
its explosiveness—throws it out of a window, an action that elicits Moody's
concern about "flinging evidence" (86). The metronome, however, is not part
of Miss Eckhart's plans for immolation; rather, the device suggests Welty's
attention to the limitations of traditionally masculine, ratiocinative investigation and her return to a counternarrative emphasizing the imaginative
and associative psychological realms that shroud the greater mysteries of
sexuality and identity throughout *The Golden Apples*. The obelisk-shaped
metronome, too, has its phallic resonance that becomes more pronounced
as Loch examines the mysterious object: "When he examined it, he saw the
beating stick to be a pendulum that instead of hanging down stuck upwards.
He touched it and stopped it with his finger. . . . He released the stick, and it

went on beating" (87–88). Welty signals the correlation between the metronome and the secrets of the house when Loch discovers "a little key in the
side of the box . . . that controlled it" (88). Loch turns off the metronome
and stores the key inside the device in a manner that brings to mind his
description of the key-shaped window in the MacLain house "made never
to open." Arguably, a symbolic attempt to contain the homoerotic, turning
off the metronome suggests the broader communal disapprobation and
silence regarding homosexuality as well, perhaps, as Loch's first movement
toward repression. Loch's action, however, is far from a definitive closure
considering he keeps the metronome in his bedroom and thinks, "All by
itself, of its own accord, it might let fly its little door and start up" (95). The
looming threat resonates with Hitchcock's famous "bomb theory" in which
he distinguished suspense from surprise, although in this case not only is
the reading audience aware of the "explosive" device, Loch, too, senses the
impending danger. Not surprisingly, his sleep is deeply troubled in wake of
the day's events: "Even floating, he felt the pressure of his frown and heard
his growling voice and the gnashing of his teeth. He dreamed close to the
surface, and his dreams were filled with a color and a fury that the daytime
that summer never held" (96).

To be clear, I am not arguing here that Welty characterizes Loch as definitively gay in "June Recital," nor am I arguing that he has witnessed homosexual congress between Bowles and Moody. I am arguing, however, that
Loch witnesses a textually unconsummated homoerotic encounter that he
imaginatively associates with the physically consummated heterosexual relationship upstairs and to which he responds in a symbolically and ambiguously masturbatory fashion while closeting that knowledge in the form of
the potentially eruptive metronome. As such, Loch's interaction with Moody
and Bowles (and Virgie and Kewpie) associates his investigation of the gothic
space next door with a broader panorama of sexualities than mere heterosexual indoctrination, and Welty's attention to the possibility of male homosexuality here is consonant with her attention to the same elsewhere in her
oeuvre and in *The Golden Apples*. Critics have delineated, for example, Welty's
sensitivity to the difficulties faced by gay men in the mid-twentieth century
as well as the prevalence of same sex desire in various works, including "The
Hitch-Hikers" (1941), *Delta Wedding* (1946), and *The Optimist's Daughter*
(1972).[11] Specific to *The Golden Apples*, critics such as Rebecca Mark and
Alison Graham-Bertolini have analyzed the homoerotic subtext permeating
"Music from Spain" and Eugene MacLain's day spent with the Spanish musi-
cian. It is fair to say that Bowles, Moody, and Loch have plenty of company
in Welty's sexualized imaginative landscape.

If we recognize Loch's perspective and symbolic interaction with queerness as a seminal event in his characterization and maturation, this moment of "growing sideways," to borrow Stockton's term, not only reshapes "June Recital" as a composite bildungsroman that includes the gendered communal pressures on Cassie paired with the communal heteronormative pressures on Loch, but it also significantly complicates Loch's character in "Moon Lake." "Moon Lake," perhaps even more so than "June Recital," is a sexualized, gothic coming-of-age story. As numerous critics have noted, the story is rife with clitoral, vaginal, and phallic imagery that establishes a highly eroticized landscape and maturation experience for Nina and the other campers.[12] This eroticism suggests both heterosexual and non-heteronormative sexualities, while the lake and its environs simultaneously reflect a psychic landscape attuned to the unknown, the imaginative, the dangerous as expressed in the gothic imagery of snakes, swamps, sex and death, rape and resuscitation. Loch, as he appears in this story, has been considered primarily as a masculine figure adjunctive to the girls' development, particularly as he relates to the unknown and frightening threshold of sexual maturity. Yaeger, for example, reads Loch as a symbol of masculine, phallic aggression whose role is to reduce Easter to "'feminine' passivity" through symbolic rape ("The Case" 438). Furthermore, she argues that "While Loch Morrison's masculine 'ordeal'—a week on Moon Lake with girls—becomes a fairly painless source of initiation upward into the world of male power, Easter's ordeal is an initiation downward—into the nether world of feminine sexuality as it has been patriarchally inscribed and maligned" (440). Critics have disagreed with and/ or complicated Yaeger's assessment of Loch's resuscitation of Easter, but such appraisals of Loch continue to assess him from the girls' perspective with the emphasis on what he means for their development.

Rather than merely a masculine figure imposing a violent heterosexual lesson on the female campers, might Loch too be better understood as yet another victim of proscribed heterosexual gender roles? If we understand his childhood investigations of the MacLain house as a prescriptive heterosexual education interrupted and undermined by a suggestively homoerotic identification, might Loch's apparent hypermasculinity in "Moon Lake" also be masking a counter sexual narrative? *The Golden Apples* is Welty's most subjective and correspondingly multivalent work, a work which fully embraces indeterminacies of genre, structure, and voice, as well as character, identity, and sexuality. It is a mistake to conceive of Loch in "Moon Lake" as somehow exempt from these dimensions of Welty's complex artistic vision. His name, after all, means "lake," and Welty thus intentionally associates him with Moon Lake, the very site of myriad sexual mysteries and partial unveilings.

Loch's development in "Moon Lake" is marked by his antipathy for the job
and the female campers. He is a "martyred presence" enduring "the ordeal of
a week's camp on Moon Lake with girls" forced upon him "by his mother"
(112–13). Welty has written that she loosely based aspects of the story on her
brother's experience as a girls' camp lifeguard,[13] but family associations aside,
is Loch's apparent distaste for the job of lifeguard at a girls' camp perhaps
less indicative of patriarchal contempt for femininity than it is potentially
indicative of a distaste for the traditional masculine role of protector into
which he is being forced? Homosexual youths are not, of course, innately
antagonistic toward females, but a youth with uncertain or conflicted sexual
orientation might reasonably resent the gendered assumptions associated
with Loch's job at the camp. Furthermore, his disinterest in females is not
limited to the younger girls of the camp but instead encompasses all females:
"all girls, orphans and Morgana girls alike, were the same thing to Loch;
maybe he threw in the two councilors too. He was hating every day of the
seven" (112). Loch's repetitive diving into the lake suggests a phallic penetration that illuminates his presumed masculine presence relative to the girls'
burgeoning sexual awareness, but he only "dived alone when the lake was
clear of girls" (113). In fact, he avoids the girls altogether—a pattern the text
indicates will be definitive for him: "That way, he seemed able to bear it; that
would be his life" (113). Even his imaginative phallic play pointedly excludes
the girls. When he fires "an imaginary gun," he is sure to aim "at something
far out, where they never were" (112).

To reiterate, the textual evidence suggests that perhaps the animosity the
girls feel emanating from Loch might not be masculine contempt for infe-
rior femininity so much as a teenager struggling within the enforced role
of masculine protector of the feminine. In this sense Loch shares much in
common with Easter whom he brings back to life with metaphoric copulation. They are paired in that disturbing scene as joint victims of compulsory
heteronormativity. Nina and Jinny may imagine Loch "pounding his chest"
and "bragging" in the wake of the resuscitation but what they actually see is
quite different: "Nevertheless, standing there with the tent slanting over him
and his arm knobby as it reached up and his head bent a little, he looked
rather at loose ends" (156). The last we see of Loch Morrison in "Moon Lake,"
then, is not an embodiment of triumphant heterosexual masculinity; we
are left, rather, with the image of an adolescent boy struggling to hold himself together.

This final image, however, is not the last word on Loch Morrison. Welty
provides one additional brief piece of news about Loch in the last story
of the collection—a seemingly minor comment that, in fact, reverberates

with Loch's investigation of the MacLain house in "June Recital" and that underscores the limitations of patriarchal assertions of objective and prescriptive truth. Cassie explains to Randall MacLain in "The Wanderers" that Loch moved away: "Ran, don't you remember he's in New York City? Likes it there. He writes us" (261). The comment, while directed to Ran, also evokes the image of Loch fleeing or running from his hometown to a place where he is now happy. Loch's flight from Morgana associates him to some extent with the wandering King MacLain through whom Welty reintroduces the masculine detective motifs in "The Wanderers." Snowdie MacLain reveals that she sank her family resources in failed investigations of his mysterious disappearances: "Virgie, I spent all Mama and Papa had tracing after him. The Jupiter Detective Agency in Jackson. I never told. They never found or went after the right one" (260). Named for the divine Roman paterfamilias, the Jupiter Detective agency speaks not only to the assumed patriarchal masculinity of the detective role but also simultaneously emphasizes the failure of the investigations and their misguided trajectories. By highlighting this patriarchally inscribed investigation gone askew, Welty invites readers to recall the limits of Loch's telescopic investigation of heterosexuality and the redirection toward still more secretive and expansive realms of sexuality contained in the MacLain house—an investigation revealing Morgana as unfit for marginalized queerness and ironically highlighting his ambiguous sexuality and eventual preference for New York.

Cassie's update on Loch enjoying New York is an admittedly undeveloped aside in a highly complex story, yet it is a loaded comment that might be understood as a reflection on the stifling small town environment for homosexuals. Despite efforts to suppress homosexuality in New York in the first half of the twentieth century, "gay men . . . forge[d] a collective social world in the face of that opposition" (Chauncey 24), and the city would certainly have been less stultifying for a gay man than Morgana, Mississippi. As Donnie McMahand and Kevin Murphy have noted in their study of Welty's engagement with homosexuality, "To queer sons and daughters of the South . . . flight . . . remain[s] an all too common and immediately recognizable element of southern queer life dictated by the demands of the closet" (79). Welty was no stranger to the difficulties of homosexual life for men in the South, and according to Trefzer: "Spending a lot of time in the company of gay men, including her close friend [Hubert] Creekmore with whom she collaborated on photography exhibits, theater productions, and script writing, certainly made Welty privy to the queer side of her hometown" (85). Furthermore, her intimate relationship with John Robinson may have also contributed to her interest in the struggles of homosexual men. Welty spent several months with Robinson in San Francisco in 1947 and wrote parts of *The Golden Apples* while there. In Pollack's essay, "Reading John Robinson," she explores Welty's relationship with Robinson during this period in conjunction with Creekmore's novel *The Welcome* to understand the possible social pressures on Robinson as he was seemingly beginning to accept his homosexuality. Subsequent scholars have also documented this biographical thread. Suzanne Marrs, for example, argues that Welty was discontented with life in San Francisco and supposes that her discontentment was tied to Robinson's sexual orientation: "The trouble Welty experienced seems likely to have been trouble in her relationship with Robinson. Perhaps she and Robinson both were beginning to realize that he needed a man, not a woman, to share his life" (107). Robinson subsequently moved to Europe and "would settle into a lifelong relationship with a man" (109). The evidence indicates that while writing *The Golden Apples* Welty may have become aware of the pressures gay men faced while she was personally invested in these issues. Loch's departure from Morgana connects him to the other "wanderers" who spiritually and/or geographically move beyond the restrictive confines of the community, but his development throughout *The Golden Apples* suggests that his move to New York City might be more specifically a departure from the heteronormative pressures of Morgana. Perhaps in New York queerness is not unspoken and confined to the detested gothic house next door; perhaps Loch might there unlock the mystery of the metronome without fear of explosive consequences.

Notes

1. McHaney studies the mythical allusions and argues that "One way Miss Welty has achieved this effect of completeness is by using themes and variations based on Celtic and Graeco-Roman mythology" (589), while Kreyling contends that Welty achieves "unity" through "the fixed cast of characters" and "the network of mythological and literary allusions" (*Eudora Welty's* 77). Danièle Pitavy-Souques attends more specifically to the Perseus-Medusa mythology as the unifying thematic element.

2. In "Beyond the Hummingbird," Yaeger contends, "In depicting the explosive body of a giant woman, Eudora Welty is exposing the southern power structure and its pervasive influence—the ways in which sexual and racial boundaries are enforced by white children as well as white men" (301), while Weston writes, "One result of such carefully controlled assimilation is its frustration of those it subsumes, whose resultant behavior often takes the form of eruptions. . . . To be lost in the family wilderness or caught in the network of the carceral community is, in Welty's fiction, to be faced with the ultimate danger to individual human identity" (131).

3. Additionally, David McWhirter argues "that we might also read Welty's great story sequence as a kind of southern *kunstlerroman*, a portrait of the regional artist as a young woman" (84).

4. For related comparative readings of "June Recital and "Moon Lake," see also, Suzan Harrison's "Playing with Fire," Carol Ann Johnston's "Sex and the Southern Girl," and Imola Bulgozdi's "Girls in Search of a Viable Identity in Eudora Welty's *The Golden Apples*."

5. In his recent essay "So Easy Even a Child Could Do It: William Faulkner's Southern Gothicizers," Jay Watson addresses "That Evening Sun" and the Compson children's internalization and reproduction of gothic tropes to navigate the realms of racialized and sexualized violence: "Faulkner's story, then, reveals the seemingly inevitable way in which southern terror takes on racialized, sexualized contours at the outset of the twentieth century. It offers, as it also dramatizes, a crash course in Southern Gothic, showing how early southern children learn to recognize and experiment with the genre, to construct and manipulate terror in culturally shaped (indeed sanctioned) ways" (16).

6. For a couple of the critical arguments prioritizing Loch, see Susan V. Donaldson's "Recovering Otherness in *The Golden Apples*" and Kreyling's *Understanding Eudora Welty*. Donaldson compares Loch's perspective and his "standards of adventure and magic" to Cassie's communally defined perspective and asserts, "That Cassie, like so many residents of Morgana, accepts the role of audience and community member and the borders between insiders and outsiders as 'natural' and inevitable is one of the tragedies of *The Golden Apples*" (498–99). Kreyling argues that "Loch is clearly on the side of pleasure, as is Virgie. [. . .] In the other camp, those who police physical pleasure, is Loch's sister, Cassie" (121). For two Cassie-centric readings of "June Recital," see Pollack's "Story-making in *The Golden Apples*" and *Eudora Welty's Fiction and Photography*.

7. On cinematic framing, see Agner (61), Dupuy (520), Smith (92), Kaplansky (587), and McWhirter (7). On the thematic intersections, Agner writes, "Loch's cinematic design steadily zooms in on what he thinks will make for a great adventure story, full of intrigue and action" (69); Dupuy argues that it is "as if Virgie is 'starring' in Loch's silent film" (520), and that the apprehension of Miss Eckhart "ends chaotically in a manner reminiscent of the Keystone Cops films" (522); McWhirter studies the influence of cinematic eroticism in the silent film era (*passim*); and Smith argues that "Welty thus calls attention to generic expectations—moving from a male thriller to a female melodrama—through these differing point-of-view narratives of the same scene" (97).

8. *After-Dinner Story* was published pseudonymously under the name William Irish in 1944. The relationship between Woolrich's story, Welty's story, and the Hitchcock film is particularly interesting in light of Welty's admiration for Hitchcock as "a trickster and a magician" whose cinematic transitions resemble the techniques of the short story writer: "You use something that will transport you from one scene to another, even if you don't know it, even if you don't realize it. That's like a film. Or else Hitchcock was using short story techniques. I don't know who thought of it first. It's been there forever" (*Conversations* 169–70).

9. Welty invoked Poe's "The Fall of the House of Usher," specifically, when she dismissed the notion of herself as a southern gothic writer: "When I hear the word [gothic] I see

in my mind a Gustave Dore illustration for 'The Fall of the House of Usher.' Anyway it sounds as if it has nothing to do with real life, and I feel that my work has something to do with real life. At least I hope it has" (*Conversations* 138).

10. Harrison argues "Both 'June Recital' and 'Moon Lake' are coming-of-age stories in which homoeroticism opens the imagination and creative possibilities, while heterosexuality closes them" (303).

11. See Axel Nissen's "Queer Welty, Camp Welty" on "The Hitch-Hikers"; Trefzer's "'Something Inarticulate'" on *Delta Wedding*; and Donnie McMahand and Kevin Murphy's "'*Remember* right'" on *The Optimist's Daughter*.

12. For readings of the sexual imagery in "Moon Lake," see among others, Price Caldwell's "Sexual Politics in Welty's 'Moon Lake' and 'Petrified Man,'" Brannon Costello's "Swimming Free of the Matriarchy," Harrison's "Playing with Fire," Johnston's "Sex and the Southern Girl," Mark's *The Dragon's Blood*, Noel Polk's "Water, Wanderers, and Weddings," Michael Scott's "Easter as Sexual Pathfinder in Eudora Welty's *Moon Lake*," and Yaeger's "The Case of the Dangling Signifier.'"

13. Welty wrote in 1988: "Like Loch exactly, I remembered, when Edward was at a stage where he could hardly endure the presence of girls, he lived surrounded by them, more or less at their mercy. Whatever happened at that camp, he was on hand, dwelling in boredom and disgust, but as a Boy Scout, *prepared*" (Afterword 151). These biographical intersections might suggest that Loch's characterization in "Moon Lake" thus merely reflects Edward at that age, but such an assessment would ignore the artistic filter all authors bring to their characters when reality merges into fiction. In the case of Loch specifically, a casual biographical dismissal of his character ignores the sexualized resuscitation scene—which Welty noted was her invention—not to mention the many lesser details that provide thematic and aesthetic continuity with Loch's character in "June Recital" (151).

Works Cited

Agner, Jacob. "A Collision of Visions: Montage and the Concept of Collision in Eudora Welty's 'June Recital.'" *Eudora Welty Review*, vol. 5, 2013, pp. 55–73.

Bruhm, Steven, and Natasha Hurley. Introduction. *Curiouser: On the Queerness of Children*, edited by Bruhm and Hurley, U of Minnesota P, 2004, pp. ix–xxxviii.

Bulgozdi, Imola. "Girls in Search of a Viable Identity in Eudora Welty's *The Golden Apples*." *Critical Insights: American Short Story*, edited by Michael Cocciarale and Scott D. Emmert, Salem Press, 2015, pp. 160–74.

Caldwell, Price. "Sexual Politics in Welty's 'Moon Lake' and 'Petrified Man.'" *Studies in American Fiction*, vol. 18, no. 2, 1990, pp. 171–81.

Chauncey, George. *Gay New York: Gender, Urban Culture, and the Making of the Gay Male World, 1890–1940*. Basic Books, 1994.

Costello, Brannon. "Swimming Free of the Matriarchy: Sexual Baptism and Feminine Individuality in Eudora Welty's *The Golden Apples*." *Southern Literary Journal*, vol. 33, no.1, 2000, pp. 82–93.

Donaldson, Susan V. "Recovering Otherness in *The Golden Apples*." *American Literature*, vol. 63, no. 3, 1991, pp. 489–506.

Dupuy, Jason. "'The Piano Player at the Picture Show': Virgie Rainey and Navigating High and Low in *The Golden Apples*." *Mississippi Quarterly*, vol. 65, no. 4, 2012, pp. 517–31.

Graham-Bertolini, Alison. "Finding the Extraordinary in Welty's 'Music from Spain.'" *Eudora Welty Review*, vol. 7, 2015, pp. 79–92.

Hankins, Leslie Kathleen. "Alas, Alack! Or A Lass, a Lack? Quarrels of Gender and Genre in the Revisionist *Künstlerroman*: Eudora Welty's *The Golden Apples*." *Mississippi Quarterly*, vol. 44, no. 4, 1991, pp. 391–409.

Harrison, Suzan. "Playing with Fire: Women's Sexuality and Artistry in Virginia Woolf's *Mrs. Dalloway* and Eudora Welty's *The Golden Apples*." *Mississippi Quarterly*, vol. 56, no. 2, 2003, pp. 289–313.

Haycraft, Howard. *Murder for Pleasure: The Life and Times of the Detective Story*. 1941. Dover, 2019.

Irwin, John T. *Unless the Threat of Death Is Behind Them: Hard-Boiled Fiction and Film Noir*. Johns Hopkins UP, 2006.

Johnston, Carol Ann. "Sex and the Southern Girl: Eudora Welty's Critical Legacy." *Mississippi Quarterly*, vol. 56, no. 2, 2003, pp. 269–87.

Kaplansky, Leslie A. "Cinematic Rhythms in the Short Fiction of Eudora Welty." *Studies in Short Fiction*, vol. 33, no. 4, 1996, pp. 579–89.

Kreyling, Michael. *Eudora Welty's Achievement of Order*, Louisiana State UP, 1980.

Kreyling, Michael. *Understanding Eudora Welty*. U of South Carolina P, 1999.

Mark, Rebecca. *The Dragon's Blood: Feminist Intertextuality in Eudora Welty's "The Golden Apples."* UP of Mississippi, 1994.

Marrs, Suzanne. *One Writer's Imagination: The Fiction of Eudora Welty*. Louisiana State UP, 2002.

Marrs, Suzanne, and Tom Nolan, editors. *Meanwhile There Are Letters: The Correspondence of Eudora Welty and Ross Macdonald*. Arcade Publishing, 2015.

McHaney, Thomas L. "Eudora Welty and the Multitudinous Golden Apples." *Mississippi Quarterly*, vol. 26, no. 4, 1973, pp. 589–624.

McMahand, Donnie, and Kevin Murphy. "'*Remember* right': Disenfranchised Grief and the Commemoration of Queer Bodies in Welty's Fiction and Life." *Eudora Welty Review*, vol. 6, 2014, pp. 69–82.

McWhirter, David. "Eudora Welty Goes to the Movies: Modernism, Regionalism, Global Media." *Modern Fiction Studies*, vol. 55, no. 1 2009, pp. 68–91.

Nissen, Axel. "Queer Welty, Camp Welty." *Mississippi Quarterly*, vol. 56, no. 2, 2003, pp. 209–29.

Pitavy-Souques, Danièle. "Technique as Myth: The Structure of *The Golden Apples*." *Eudora Welty: Thirteen Essays*, edited by Peggy W. Prenshaw, UP of Mississippi, 1983, pp. 146–56.

Plain, Gill. *Twentieth-Century Crime Fiction: Gender, Sexuality and the Body*. Fitzroy Dearborn Publishers, 2001.

Polk, Noel. "Water, Wanderers, and Weddings: Going to Naples and to No Place." *Faulkner and Welty and the Southern Literary Tradition*. UP of Mississippi, 2008, pp. 133–62.

Pollack, Harriet. *Eudora Welty's Fiction and Photography: The Body of the Other Woman*. U of Georgia P, 2016.

Pollack, Harriet. "Reading John Robinson." *Mississippi Quarterly*, vol. 56, no. 2, 2003, pp. 175–208.

Pollack, Harriet. "Story-making in *The Golden Apples*: Point of View, Gender and the Importance of Cassie Morrison." *Southern Quarterly*, vol. 34, no. 2, 1996, pp. 75–80.

Scott, Michael. "Easter as Sexual Pathfinder in Eudora Welty's *Moon Lake*." *CrossRoads*, vol. 1, no.1, 1992, pp. 35–38.

Smith, Dina. "Cinematic Modernism and Eudora Welty's *The Golden Apples*." *Mississippi Quarterly*, Special Issue: Eudora Welty Centennial, 2009, pp. 81–100.

Smith, Lillian. *Killers of the Dream*. 1949. Norton, 1994.

Stockton, Kathryn Bond. "Growing Sideways, or Versions of the Queer Child: The Ghost, the Homosexual, the Freudian, the Innocent, and the Interval of Animal." *Curiouser: On the Queerness of Children*, edited by Steven Bruhm and Natasha Hurley, U of Minnesota P, 2004, pp. 277–315.

Trefzer, Annette. "'Something Inarticulate': Sexual Desire in the Fiction of Eudora Welty and Hubert Creekmore." *Eudora Welty Review*, vol. 9, 2017, pp. 83–100.

Watson, Jay. "So Easy Even a Child Could Do It: William Faulkner's Southern Gothicizers." *Mississippi Quarterly*, vol. 72, no. 1, 2019, pp. 1–23.

Welty, Eudora. Afterword. *Morgana: Two Stories from "The Golden Apples,"* by Welty, UP of Mississippi, 1988, pp. 147–51.

Welty, Eudora. *Conversations with Eudora Welty*, edited by Peggy W. Prenshaw, UP of Mississippi, 1984.

Welty, Eudora. "In Yoknapatawpha." *Hudson Review*, vol. 1, no. 4, 1949, pp. 596–98.

Welty, Eudora. *The Golden Apples*. 1949. Harcourt Brace, 1977.

Welty, Eudora. *One Writer's Beginnings*. 1983. Warner Books, 1991.

Weston, Ruth D. *Gothic Traditions and Narrative Techniques in the Fiction of Eudora Welty*. Louisiana State UP, 1994.

Wolff, Sally. "'How Babies Could Come' and 'How They Could Die': Eudora Welty's Children of the Dark Cradle." *Mississippi Quarterly*, vol. 56, no. 2, 2003, pp. 251–67.

Yaeger, Patricia S. "Beyond the Hummingbird: Southern Women Writers and the Southern Gargantua." *Haunted Bodies: Gender and Southern Texts*, edited by Anne Goodwyn Jones and Susan V. Donaldson, UP of Virginia, 1997, pp. 287–318.

Yaeger, Patricia S. "The Case of the Dangling Signifier: Phallic Imagery in Eudora Welty's 'Moon Lake.'" *Twentieth Century Literature*, vol. 28, no. 4, 1982, pp. 431–52.

COURT'S OPENED

The Ponder Heart and Murderous Women

REBECCA MARK

... what was needed for the case was a motive, something
to show anger or sudden feeling.
—SUSAN GLASPELL "A JURY OF HER PEERS" (1917)

Although Eudora Welty's *The Ponder Heart* has not previously been read by critics as a detective story or a murder mystery, the narrative does indeed feature both a dead body and a murder trial, each of which present readers with serious questions concerning Bonnie Dee's untimely death. What happened to Bonnie Dee is under a reader's investigation. In considering ways to read this novella, I want to argue that the strange mystery at the center of *The Ponder Heart* may delineate a political crime of sorts, a crime of failed imagination that cannot be pinned on one person in the story, nor is committed by a single perpetrator, but is the product of an intersectional (and textual) web of enmeshed racism, class prejudice, and gender bias.[1] It is a comic story that presents why three women might seriously want to kill.

A reader of *The Ponder Heart* may understand that Uncle Daniel could have killed Bonnie Dee by suffocating her, literally and metaphorically, but the novella is not that straightforward. Uncle Daniel is not convicted by the story's end. Edna Earle, moreover—in her role as the book's focalizing unreliable narrator—floats strange scenarios as if to deliberately confuse, including the assertion that Bonnie Dee suffocated herself one night out of fear of lightning and thunder by holding Edna Earle's grandmother's pillow too close. Or alternately that a ball of lightning flew into the parlor and scared the girl to death. Or that she might have died laughing. Indeed, as Naoka Fuwa Thorton points out in her article, "A Hilarious Destruction:

93

'The Ponder Heart' as a Metanarrative," "signification is . . . a plurality of meanings produced in varying degrees independently by the speaker/writer, the listener/reader, and the context" (49). Edna Earle also reminds us that when Uncle Daniel is not giving away things, he is most likely eating or talking. When he talks, he takes possession: "Oh the stories! He made free with everybody's—he'd tell yours and his and the Man in the Moon's." Then pointedly, she adds: "Not mine: he wouldn't dream I had one, he loves me so—but everybody else's" (*TPH* 70).

Daniel tells everyone's stories and yet when it comes to the three female characters in the novella, Uncle Daniel has a complete collapse of resourcefulness. Uncle Daniel cannot conceive of Edna Earle having her own story, nor can he fathom where Bonnie Dee has gone when she leaves him, and he does not even consider that Narciss has a narrative to tell. These failures of imagination are important clues in this mystery. The three women stars of *The Ponder Heart*, I note, are fighting against limiting stereotypes of their time (the 1950s) as well as Uncle Daniel's misogyny. Edna Earle, for one, is cast as the poor spinster, Narciss as the put-upon Black servant, and Bonnie Dee as the suffocated and underage wife. The questions I ask are: Would any or all three of these women be willing to go after Uncle Daniel in retaliation? Could they be plotting his murder? Each of these women, to be sure, has a strong motive for it: Edna Earle, her rightful inheritance; Narciss, her power; and Bonnie Dee, money. And a motive that they all share is a desire to tell their own story, to control the narrative, and determine the parameters of the plot. Female desire to shut up blowhard men who take up all the air in the room is not the expected motive for murder, but it is certainly an understandable one.

And while many male noir and hard-boiled artists from this era would certainly acknowledge the possibility of women as murderers, the problem with their 1950s approach is that they rely on another stereotype: the femme fatale. The femme fatale character is the highly feminized seductress who leads men into temptation. Men who fall for her conniving plots and lies will commit horrible crimes for her and with her. The femme fatale character is both an inherently sexy/sexist trope *and* a potentially powerful indictment of patriarchy. We are taught, going back as far as ancient myths, to beware of the evil woman, fallen, who will devour and corrupt the innocent man. We are also, as in *Macbeth*, reminded that when a man has all the power, the woman must act as a femme fatale to entice the sovereign man to enact her wishes. Modern femme fatales, however, are complicated. They often act from disempowerment, poverty, from lack of control of their own lives, from being trapped in a system where they have no choice but to turn to men for help (thusly further exposing the horrific demands of patriarchy). They are punished for endeavoring to take control, to escape bad marriages, to cash in on insurance policies. By the twentieth century, then, femme fatales in film and literature become desperate, beautiful, women—certainly not the Circes, Medeas, Clytemnestras, or powerful queens of the past.

And yet, as critic Sarah Weinman has recently noted, in the very era when Welty was constructing *The Ponder Heart*, a host of female mystery writers were creatively responding to this problem by shaping a series of strong women characters.[2] This midcentury generation of American women crime writers," Weinman argues, "created a tradition that [she] calls 'domestic suspense.' . . . Novels of domestic suspense took the fantasy of suburban living and uncovered the bile and dreck subsisting underneath, a clever subversion that also doubled as a mirror to sublimated terror" (Weinman, "Introduction").[3] Whether or not Welty was reading these women crime novelists (and I believe she was), she engaged in clever subversion to expose the fantasy and yes horror of 1950s suburban and small town life.

Interestingly, one of the women's mysteries from this era, *The Case of the Weird Sisters* by Charlotte Armstrong (which became the film noir classic entitled *The Three Weird Sisters* in 1948) contains multiple surprising parallels to the plot of *The Ponder Heart*. Charlotte Armstrong's three sisters are old maids, and like Uncle Daniel, their brother Innis Whitlock is so selfish that he never thinks of their needs. The Whitlock family is a rich mining family and their house, once glamorous, sits out on the edge of town on the top of the hill and is increasingly neglected and isolated. The Ponders are a rich southern family who made their money from cotton and the economic legacy of enslavement. Their house sits on the edge of town suffering from neglect. Innis Whitlock, the rich heir to his parents' fortune, looks like and acts like Daniel. He has a pink pig nose, he is plump, scared of his sisters, and not at all sexually appealing. A storm, very like the one in *The Ponder Heart*, occurs in *The Case of the Weird Sisters* during one of the most egregious attempts to kill Innis. In both novels the electricity goes out at the worst moment. The marriage proposal of Innis to Alice is a sham as is the marriage of Bonnie Dee and Uncle Daniel. Both Bonnie Dee and Alice are in it for the money and never pretend otherwise. In *The Case of the Weird Sisters* Alice hides under the bed as Narciss does in *The Ponder Heart*.

But it's especially when the professor/detective character from Armstrong's novel, a man named Duff, who while contemplating the multiple possibilities behind who might have tried to kill Innis, suddenly says, "Yet why not all three?" that the various parallels between these two stories reveal a design to us. "Why *not* all three" women characters from *The Ponder Heart* very well may have been exactly what Welty wanted us to see in her story. There is a strong case to be made that the three women heroines of Welty's *The Ponder Heart* are each themselves potential murderers. In her extended ponderings, Welty even goes so far as to make the murdered body, death itself, less important than the story, the life force of human imagination. This is a story about how to stay alive, not how to die. And textual investigation of this mystery surprisingly resurrects one of the novella's most important and misunderstood characters—Bonnie Dee Peacock—from her seemingly ill-fated demise. Bonnie Dee is much more complicated than she might at first seem. She is, in fact, what we might call "undead."

Welty, I'll argue, is clearly fascinated with the notion of the undead in her fiction.[4] As Eric Anderson, Taylor Hagood, and Daniel Cross assert in their introduction to *Undead Souths: The Gothic and Beyond in Southern Litera-ture and Culture* (2015), "the dead contain cultural vibrancy in the present" and "if we let them in on the critical conversation, the still-living dead will speak volumes" (14). Indeed, we are quite familiar with undead characters in Welty's fiction, particularly undead women. In "Flowers for Marjorie" (1937), for example, its title character—arguably the most murdered of all Welty's women—is quite lively in death, suspended with her hand raised in a strange balance, and in her final fall, sticks her hand out the window as if to catch the wind (*CS* 115). When Little Harp kills and rapes an Indian girl in *The Robber Bridegroom* thinking it is Rosamond, and then chops off her wedding finger, "the finger jumped in the air and rolled across the floor into Rosamond's lap" (132). Ruby's imagination in "A Piece of News" is also quite alive when she reads in the newspaper of Ruby Fisher murdered (*CS* 34). Hazel, in "The Wide Net," authors the story of her own drowning to prepare her husband to follow her through her pregnancy. In "The Burning," undead Miss Theo writhes on the ground like a dead snake with eyes wide open (466). Drowned Clytie's legs are "like a pair of tongs" reaching for something from the deep well—her own face, her own life" (104). Gypsy in "Powerhouse" is both alive and dead simultaneously (142). We never know whether she has thrown herself out the window, but we do know the tale of her death drives Powerhouse to create and perform. Welty's older women characters in, say, *Losing Battles*, do not die easy; they create diva-like end-of-life scenarios, and when they die (if they die) they do not stay dead; their words and actions echo throughout the texts.

Undead women, then, are certainly plentiful in Welty's imagination. And yet, what we are still clearly less familiar with in Welty's fiction are female murder-ers. Although Miss Larkin in "A Curtain of Green" is certainly murderous, there are very few examples of women who ultimately kill. And yet, there is strong textual evidence that the three women heroines of *The Ponder Heart* are all potential murderers. We overlook their culpability because we cannot imagine these women as killers—cannot imagine them as fully three-dimensional figures who, too, may "have a story" to tell.

Welty, in *The Ponder Heart*, both invites and rejects the film noir femme fatale character. Her female characters, if they are potential murderers, are not beautiful or sexual. Instead of relying on their bodies, they use their brains to plot and plan ways to escape the traps that their circumscribed lives set for them. They use their power to secure the narrative thread. In *The Ponder Heart*, Welty evokes the film *The Postman Always Rings Twice* (1946) and its femme fatale character Cora to let us know she is well-versed in the type. Alerting us to the intertextual reference at play, Edna Earle referring to Bonnie Dee and Narciss's new phone out at the house, asks, "Do you think it's [the telephone] ever rung once?" (86) In *Postman*, a cat trips an electrical wire, creating a ball of fire (as in *The Ponder Heart*) and puts out the lights when Cora and Frank are trying to murder Cora's husband, Nick. The sign in front of the inn in *Postman* is blown down by the wind just like the hotel sign in *The Ponder Heart*. And as everyone in *Postman* says over and over, "That cat is deader than a door nail," Edna Earle repeats this same phrase referring to Bonnie Dee. But in *The Postman Always Rings Twice* Cora is dependent on Nick, cries like a femme when the lights go out, and makes Frank kill Nick with a bottle to the head rather than doing the deed herself. The rest of this article will lay out the case for Edna Earle, Bonnie Dee, and Narciss being, not femme but "butch" fatales who work on their own, and with each other, to overpower the men in their lives, stop their incessant talking and telling stories, trap them, take their money, and laugh at them. Femme fatale narratives are deadly serious tales of women's tragic culpability and eventual defeat. By contrast, my conception of "butch fatale narratives" allows the women to turn the tables on their male victims and win.

In *Fatal Women: Lesbian Sexuality and the Mark of Aggression*, Linda Hart argues that "the production of violent women in representation depends on a dis-articulated threat of desire between women" (x). My use of the butch fatale does not argue that Welty is creating lesbian characters in Narciss, Edna, or Bonnie Dee, but suggests that she opens the space of representation to the independent, queer woman in the shadow. As this butch fatale appears and disappears throughout the narrative, the possibility of performative space for women expands. This space includes women working with and for each other. When we take the butch fatale into consideration, we can understand that *The Ponder Heart*, unlike so many crime novels, is a comedy in the classic sense of the word, ending not just in female retribution but in female renewal, empowerment, and visibility.

Suzanne Marrs in *Eudora Welty: A Biography* points out that Welty was concerned about the murder scene in *The Ponder Heart*: "Eudora herself was not finished with *The Ponder Heart*. Late in May 1953 she began to worry that 'Uncle Daniel ought not to have finished Bonnie Dee off' but ultimately decided that there was no turning back on that. Still, she tinkered with the story, in June writing Diarmuid that she had 'fixed' it" (226–27). One must wonder: how did she fix it? One way that she might have "fixed it," I suggest, is by creating a multivalent text full of possibilities as to how Bonnie Dee might have died, who might have killed her, and whether in the world of fiction she is indeed dead.

Most readers have relegated *The Ponder Heart* to the category of comedy or spoof, and serious critics have virtually ignored this stand-alone Welty text, with one important exception. In "Judgements of *The Ponder Heart*: Welty's Trials of the 1950's" published in *Eudora Welty and Politics: Did the Writer Crusade* (2001), Sharon Baris historicizes *The Ponder Heart* by setting the text against the backdrop of troubling American trials of the years 1952 and 1953 when Welty was composing, first, the short story version called "Never Mind Uncle Daniel" (1952) and, then, the longer novella *The Ponder Heart* (1953). Baris asserts that the novella "speaks to the social and political tensions of its era—the period of the McCarthy hearings, the Rosenberg trials, and other tests of American loyalty that then prevailed" (180). Baris uses specific details, dates, and connections to *New York Times* articles about Ethel and Julius Rosenberg to argue her case. Her most remarkable bit of evidence is "that the Rosenberg funeral account, startlingly enough, appeared alongside the full description of a woman's freak electrocution—by a ball of lightning" (193). Building her case, Baris connects Eisenhower's unwillingness to offer Ethel Rosenberg clemency to Daniel's smothering of Bonnie Dee. This is not so far-fetched when we begin to see this moment from a feminist point of view. Eisenhower's reason for refusing Ethel Rosenberg clemency was that he needed to "protect American Women" from the threats of communism. As Welty knew all too well, this was the same deadly rationale that the KKK used to excuse lynching, extreme racism, and segregation in the South. The suffocating narrative of protecting white women became an excuse for the most reactionary political actions.

In fact, the other "test" of American loyalty being conducted at the time of the Rosenberg and McCarthy trials was on America women. American hegemony depended on white middle-class women going along with the 1950s story of a postwar "prosperous" America. Women, specifically American middle-class and upper-middle-class women were expected to stay in their place and abide by the racial and class dictates of the era. As Betty Friedan makes clear in her book about this period, *Feminine Mystique* (1963), passing this test meant that being married, having children, satisfying your husband's sexual desires, and becoming a master at the art of housework should be accepted as personally fulfilling. Of course, this formula for performing the role of the ideal feminine did not work for Black, LGBTQ, working-class, single, indigenous, or women of color who did not have the economic luxury or social capital to stay at home. The formula in truth worked for no one.

The 1950s feminine mystique only served to ensure that men would continue to dominate the work force and maintain economic control in the domestic sphere. During World War II women had taken jobs that men were not available to fill. As we know from the Rosie the Riveter image, women worked in factories and wartime production lines to build ships and planes. After World War II, in order to put women back in the domestic sphere "where they belonged" and make jobs available once again to men, every women's magazine, journal, television show, and advertisement in the *New York Times* perpetuated the image of the ideal white, middle-class housewife, mother and sex object, in her pretty clothes, buying china and sofa sets. The consumer feminine echoes throughout *The Ponder Heart* but is directly challenged and laughed at by Bonnie Dee and Narciss who order a washing machine but leave it on the porch, move the furniture—particularly the sofa—around willy-nilly, cook fudge instead of nutritious meals, and play house.

In 1952 when Eudora Welty was writing *The Ponder Heart*, instead of embracing this destructive misogynist mirage, she was shedding any desire of becoming "the perfect wife and mother." Welty's over-fourteen-year relationship (starting in 1937) with John Robinson, a gay man, would never become romantic marriage with children. By 1951 Welty recognized that John was in love with a young man named Enzo Rocchigiani. She took more time away from Jackson, Mississippi, moving instead for long periods to New York City. She travelled to Europe on a 1949 Guggenheim. She deepened her friendships with other intellectuals, writers, poets, literary agents, and artists who also traveled internationally. Welty (forty-three years old in 1952) was an award-winning, internationally recognized writer and more a member of the New York literati than the Jackson Garden club.

And if we follow the argument in Harriet Pollack's book *Eudora Welty's Fiction and Photography: The Body of The Other Woman* (2016), we will see that she never found the heterosexual plot of the married woman or the good mother particularly interesting, finding her muse instead in the body of the daring "other woman." Pollack writes, "With this pattern of attention to the body of the other woman, Welty's fiction enters southern literature's recurrent traumatic intersection between issues of class, gender construction, and race—all written on symbolic bodies. A prototypical Welty plot pairs a sheltered 'young lady' and an 'othered' body—usually underclass in Welty, but at times foreign or black" (1). Pollack finds that in these pairings of the protected observer and the daring other, Welty avoids and deconstructs the stereotypes and stifling expectations of 1950's white femininity that could so easily have destroyed her genius.

Participating in the feminine mystique, moreover, meant submitting to a commodity economy. It was the responsibility of middle-class women to become the ultimate consumers. Capitalism and patriarchy would win out over communism because the white middle- and upper-class woman would be able to stay at home with the children, let the father work, and consume the necessary goods to keep the economy moving. But this is not the whole story of women in the 1950s. Smoldering just beneath the surface were the beginnings of the second-wave feminist movement. In 1949 Simone de Beauvoir wrote *The Second Sex*. A poor translation was published in the United States in 1953 and there was a review of the book in the *New York Times* on February 22, 1953. This is exactly the moment when Welty was rewriting *The Ponder Heart*, deciding who kills who, and living in New York. We do not know whether Welty read *The Second Sex* or the book review, but the fact is, this brilliant critique of feminine roles was in print. Such a major moment in publishing would not have been overlooked by her circle of intellectual friends. In 1953, the civil rights movement was gaining momentum as well. During the fifties, Black women civil rights leaders including Ella Baker, Daisy Bates, Fannie Lou Hammer, Dorothy Height, Joann Robinson, Septima Poinsetta Clark, and a host of others were defining the course of resistance. By 1955, after the murder of the fourteen-year-old Black child Emmett Till, his mother Mamie shamed the world in front of his open casket: "I want the world to see what they did to my baby." And Rosa Parks's civil disobedience, the international outcry, and the resulting year-long Montgomery bus boycott revealed how poised for radical change the nation was.

In 1953, Welty's friendship with the Irish novelist Elizabeth Bowen was rocking her world as well. Bowen provided a role model who has not made housework, children, or sexual fidelity to a husband her primary life's work. As Dawn Trouard chronicles in her essay "The Promiscuous Joy of Eudora Welty: Missing Bowen in Mississippi," "everything conspired to make Bowen the jumping off point from which Welty could navigate to artistic freedom.

What Welty secured from Bowen was a glimpse at 'the other way to live.' Welty put it clearly: 'What writer now coming after her could fail to be nourished by her work, exhilarated by her example'" (260). Through her friendships with many professional women, Welty liberated herself from expectations that would have been stifling for a woman of such rare vision.

In 1952 and 1953 Welty was looking at the South from a distance and appalled by the highly conservative red-baiting nation and the horrifying racism of her home state. Adlai Stevenson, the one presidential candidate for whom she went out on a limb, had lost the election. She was fed up with southern town life and simultaneously beginning to enjoy her freedom. Trouard has chronicled that the other stories she was writing at this time, which become the collection *The Bride of the Innisfallen* (1955), tell a tale of an artist emerging into the full magnificence of her feminist voice. Each one exhibits an experimental and often extraordinary way of writing about women's imagination. The project of *The Ponder Heart* (1954) does not seem so different from the *Bride* stories when we notice that its main character and only narrator is a woman who runs her own business and manages everyone else's business—a woman with no children and no desire to have children, a woman who can only imagine marriage if her uncle is part of the picture— "in plenty of marriages there's three, three all your life" (28), a woman who could be passed over for an inheritance if her Uncle Ponder marries. When we get beyond criticism's obsession with Uncle Daniel, we can see that the plot of *The Ponder Heart* rests entirely on three women: Edna Earle, Bonnie Dee, and Narciss—their volition, their actions, their rules.

The timing of *The Ponder Heart* makes sense if we entertain the possibility that Welty writes the novella to present women characters who are deliberately outrageous, flamboyant architects of their own futures. Narciss, a Black woman, does what she wants when she wants. She drives Uncle Ponder's big Studebaker the moment she has an opportunity. Edna Earle, in full racist authority, bosses Narciss around but is not her boss. Narciss walks in and out of Edna Earle's plots creating her own much more radical and disruptive ones. Bonnie Dee is a colorful Peacock from the neighboring town of Polk who is more independent than her diminutive stature would imply, capable of "peacocking" her extensive wardrobe all over town. Bonnie Dee appears in the Five and Dime, wreaks havoc, and leaves. Even when she dies, she is reborn in her identical sister Johnny Ree, who wears her clothes, and in *all* her other sisters wearing her hand-me-downs. She is a quintessential undead character.

Likewise, other minor women characters are commanding attention and breaking stereotypes. Ms. Teacake Magee sings loudly at the Baptist Church and sends Uncle Daniel a black-and-white striped prison uniform cake when he is put on trial. Intrepid Elsie Fleming rides a motorcycle daredevil style around the wheel of death (defying death, she too is undead) revving her motor for the whole world to hear. These women act more like butches than femmes—fatale or otherwise. Edna Earle's grandmother was no shrinking violet. She owned the hotel by inheritance and according to Edna Earle, she told her son over and over that she was going to kill him. The plant that wins Edna Earle the blue ribbon at the county fair in the category "Best Other Than Named" is named Ouida Sampson. The real Ouida Sampson returns old as the hills to attend the funeral. Those from Laurel, Mississippi, however, will remember the name Ouida as Ouida Keeton, the daughter of a wealthy family accused of the gruesome murder of her mother in 1935.[5] Ouida Keeton cut off her mother's legs and left a horrible skin and bones trail that dogs picked up on; they found the missing parts from her mother's torso. Ouida Sampson's keen interest in the murder trial should not go unnoted nor should her putting out her "little skin and bones hand" (182) for what came her way. The women in this text are not frail southern ladies, nor are they sexy femme fatales. They are butch fatales revving their motors.

When the adapters of the New York production of *The Ponder House* in 1955 demoted Edna Earle from the narrator to a character in the play, Welty was outraged. In *Conversations with Eudora Welty*, many of the interviewers ask her about this production. Her answers are unwaveringly negative. Charles T. Bunting asks, "Were you pleased with the dramatization of *The Ponder Heart?*" and Welty responds:

> the book existed as a monologue by one of the characters, Edna Earle Ponder. We see everything through her; what we are interested in is how she looks at things. Well, naturally, on the stage she was made a character at whom we are looking from the outside, and made subordinate to Uncle Daniel, the one who is the subject of her story. So that to an author is rather wrenching. (56)

Furthering her objections in two other interviews, Welty explains: "Edna Earle was reduced to the background, sort of whimpering on the porch as Uncle Daniel goes through his antics. As I had written it, the whole story was seen through the eyes of Edna Earle. . . . There were times I thought I was in the wrong theater" (149). Welty insists on this point: "Edna Earle has captured an audience in *The Ponder Heart* and that's her character. I mean, she's got to tell you this story" (284). What infuriated Welty was that the producers, like Uncle Daniel, cannot imagine Edna Earle having a story, let alone being the narrator, the author of that story. By not making it her story to tell, they missed the whole point. In the play, Edna Earle is diminished and, as in a misreading of the novella, the subject is not Edna Earle, not the women, but Uncle Daniel, the Dandy, the uncle who moves too close, who plays creep-crawly, talks all the time, and eats everyone out of house and home.[6] His endless stories literally make Edna Earle "numb." But in my reading the person who does "not have a story" is Uncle Daniel himself.

When Edna Earle tries to get us interested in his story, she employs a string of clichés. Her favorite is to call Uncle Daniel "as good as gold"—which she does four times in the first third of the book. As we know from King Midas, being as good as gold is the kiss of death. One who is gold is not alive and not capable of human compassion. The repetition of this phrase is a not-so-subtle indictment of the upper class. Eva Sistrunk paints Coats of Arms (a symbol of the upper class) with gold paint to make a little extra money: "Eva can draw you a coat-of-arms—that's the one thing she can do, or otherwise have to teach school. That's ours, up over the clock. Ponder—with three deer. She says it's not her fault if the gold runs—it's the doorbell ringing or something. She never does anybody's over" (*TPH* 91). Coats of Arms are a symbol of the upper class, but Uncle Ponder's gold runs: he runs from marriage, from commitment, from responsibility. His mouth runs.

Uncle Daniel not only has no story of his own. He does not know how to read other people's stories. He gives people what they do not need: an incubator to the mailman, for example. He is an everyman and thus a nobody. He is both a capitalist, the richest man in town, and a communist, giving away his property, money, and material goods. He is a dandy, queer-looking man in a red bow tie, who does not seem to want to have sex with any of his wives. His Tom Thumb marriage at three is the same as his two marriages at fifty-three. He is a sexually creepy man who brings phallic banana ice cream to the chorus-line girls at the County Fair, who moves too close to anyone sitting with him on the couch, and is generally after every woman he meets but is totally uninterested once he has caught one—like a cat playing with a mouse (cat and mouse images abound throughout the text).

Fifty-three-year-old Uncle Daniel is a white-suited southern plantation owner with a big hat and a big head, as much a symbol of the old racist South, the nation in 1953, as anyone can be. At the trial he shouts out: "I'd rather be up there talking myself than hear you and every one of these other folks put together. Turn-a loose" (*TPH* 130) and says about Edna Earle, "'I'm going to beat her if she don't stop. And I'm going to fire him,' says Uncle Daniel.

'Deyancey, you're fired'" (*TPH* 130). Remember the words from the first pages of Edna Earle's story: "and then he's liable to give you a little hug and start trying to give you something. Don't do any good to be bashful. He won't let you refuse" (*TPH* 7) As we know all too well, white supremacists, creepy misogynists "rich as Croesus," are everywhere. What is surprising is that critics and most readers have not seen Uncle Daniel for the charlatan that he is.

The story then is not about Uncle Daniel, but about the three women's powerful responses to his attempts to belittle and trap them. Throughout *Ponder Heart* both Uncle Daniel and Edna Earle talk about Bonnie Dee in diminutive stereotypical terms: "She wasn't any bigger than a minute," "pretty as a doll" (*TPH* 44, 53, 79, 135). When Uncle Daniel and Edna Earle are not wearing out sexist clichés describing Bonnie Dee, Edna Earle begrudgingly admits that: "Bonnie Dee could make change and Bonnie Dee could cut hair" (*TPH* 73). The only time Uncle Daniel describes her in any unusual way is when he says: "She is a natural barber." In fact, he is so proud of her haircutting skills that he has "the hardware salesman bring her a whole line of scissors and sharp blades" (51). The first time Edna Earle sees Bonnie Dee back at the family home she is wielding a bone razor. Uncle Daniel calls out to her:

> "Edna Earle, Edna Earle, she's fixing to cut my throat!" . . . Here she came Miss Bonnie Dee sashaying around the table with her little bone razor wide open in her hand. So, Uncle Daniel climbed down, good as gold, and sat back in his chair and she got the doodads and commenced to lather his face, like it was any other day . . . "Miss Edna Earle," Bonnie Dee turns and remarks to me, "Court's opened." There she stood with that razor cocked in her little hand, sending me about my business. "Keep hands down," she pipes to Uncle Daniel. (*TPH* 61)

To fully comprehend the portent of this moment, Bonnie Dee with razor in hand, we must unpack two literary allusions: one is to Susan Glaspell's play, *Trifles* (1916), which was later adapted into a short story, "A Jury of Her Peers" (1917). I will focus only on the short story. The other intertextual allusion is to Herman Melville's antislavery story, *Benito Cereno* (1855). In these texts the entire plot depends on the fact that the characters cannot adequately interpret the murderous mystery that is unfolding before their eyes. In both stories this blindness is based on prejudice. The men in "A Jury of Her Peers" are bad readers of the crime scene because they cannot see the feminine and feminist domestic clues which reveal that Mrs. Wright has indeed killed her husband. In *Benito Cereno*, Captain Amasa Delano cannot imagine the slaves having successfully taken over the *San Dominick*. He cannot see what is unfolding right in front of his eyes because he cannot imagine enslaved people having the autonomy, humanity, and authority to rebel.

In Susan Glaspell's "A Jury of Her Peers," the county attorney Mr. Henderson, the sheriff Mr. Peters, and the neighbor Mr. Hale, accompanied by their wives, Mrs. Peters and Mrs. Hale, explore a crime scene at the Wrights' home. The day before, Mr. Hale had gone over to the Wright place to ask Mr. Wright to put in a telephone—to share a line with him. Mr. Wright had been unwilling to put in phone service because he liked peace and quiet, even though they lived "on a lonesome stretch of road" (2). Mr. Hale recounts finding Mrs. Wright sitting in a broken-down rocker "pleatin' at her apron" with her fingers (2). In fact, he repeats this phrase three times. When he asks her where her husband is, she laughs and then tells him that her husband is dead upstairs and that he died with a rope around his neck. The three men find, "Nothing that would point to any motive. Nothing here but kitchen things" (2), even though they find that it is so cold in the house that all Mrs. Wright's preserves have frozen and burst open. When the men leave to go looking in the barn, they tell the women to keep their eyes out for a clue adding, "But would a woman know a clue if they did come upon it?" (4).

After overhearing Mr. Henderson say, "that what was needed for the case was a motive, something to show anger or sudden feeling" (6), they remember that Mr. Wright would not buy Mrs. Wright any clothes and surmise that she did not go into town or socialize with the other women because she did not have anything nice to wear. The women left alone, however, while focusing on the one remaining jar of undamaged cherry preserves in the kitchen, do indeed know a clue when they see one—multiple clues at that. To their horror, the motive is gradually made clear to them: a neglected wife, given no money to buy a new stove, a telephone, or nice things, locked away from everyone in a cold, lonesome house.

At this point they find a quilting basket and a half-finished quilt. The two women become suspicious especially when they realize that one of Mrs. Wright's squares is unevenly sewn. They keep asking: "do you think she is going to quilt it or knot it?" (6) But when they look closely in the sewing basket and find a dead canary with a broken neck wrapped in silk, they know for certain what happened: that Mrs. Wright strangled her husband just like he had strangled her songbird. They know that she is the murderer, and they know her motive was rage. And yet they do not tell the sheriff or Mr. Hale. They protect Mrs. Wright from the law. Earlier Mrs. Peters remembers that Minnie Foster, Mrs. Wright's maiden name as a young woman, had sung beautifully in the church: "I wish you'd seen Minnie Foster when she wore a white dress with blue ribbons and stood up there in the choir and sang. . . . Oh, I wish I had come over here once in a while. That was a crime. Who's going to punish that?" (9, 10). While they are trying to decide what to do, Mrs. Peters remembers a boy who took a hatchet and killed her kitten when she was a young girl. She remembers that she almost took the hatchet and could have done the same to him. Women, too, can imagine being murderous.

The women in this novella cannot only *imagine* being murderers; unlike Mrs. Peters; they wield weapons. When Edna Earle finds Bonnie Dee with the razor and interprets this as a domestic quarrel, an important clue should be noted. Before Edna Earle leaves, she tells us that, "I just politely turned on my heel, leaving them both there with fourteen perfect quarts of peach preserves cooling on the back porch behind me" (62). Does Edna Earle, wishing that Bonnie Dee would kill Uncle Daniel for her, leave perfect peach preserves— a direct textual allusion to "A Jury of her Peers"—so no one will suspect Bonnie Dee? Edna Earle recalls that Bonnie Dee "just sat and picked at the Beulah food like a *canary bird*" (45; my emphasis). Narciss *pleats* Bonnie Dee's skirt. Uncle Daniel and his father never put a telephone line into the house. Bonnie Dee wears a white dress with a blue ribbon just like Minnie Foster. When Uncle Daniel and Bonnie Dee are in the last moments of Bonnie Dee's life, she pulls herself into a knot. Like Minnie Foster, Bonnie Dee laughs at death.

There is a biographical connection to "A Jury of her Peers" for Welty as well. In March of 1953, John Robinson sent Welty a story about a "19-year-old man . . . focused on an older artist named Tom" (Pollack 216). As Suzanne Marrs chronicles in *Eudora Welty: A Biography*, Welty writes a harsher than usual critique of his story: "She certainly resented the story's hostile view of women and its seemingly implicit criticism of her. To Tom, at one point in the text, 'a scolding female blue jay has come to seem' almost like another person—He and the bird were like two old maids who had lived too much alone, getting on each other's nerves, that sometimes he could have gladly wrung that bird's neck'" (Marrs 237). Marrs points to this moment as the breaking point in Eudora and John's relationship.

But neither Bonnie Dee (nor Eudora Welty) are Mrs. Wright. Bonnie Dee is not the dutiful housewife staying home and putting up preserves. She is not making dinner for Uncle Daniel. She is not doing anything but putting him on trial. Court's opened. She gets a telephone installed herself and buys herself and Narciss new clothes and a new stove. She is the antithesis of the antebellum southern woman. She is Bonnie Dee, the Bonnie Blue revenge spirit of the South's Scarlett, who ran successful businesses and used men for her own financial needs. As Edna recounts:

And to crown it all, she got a telephone. I passed by the place myself, going for a quick ride before dark with Mr. Springer when he was tired (so tired I drove) and Uncle Daniel sitting up behind. Bonnie Dee was out in the yard fully to be seen, in a hunter's green velveteen two-piece dress with a stand-up collar, and Narciss was right behind her in blue, all to watch the man put it in. They waved their hands like crazy at the car going by, and then again going back, blowing dust on all that regalia. Do you think it's ever rung once? (*TPH* 71)

Edna Earle can blow dust on them all she likes, but Narciss and Bonnie Dee write themselves into the story in full regalia. Bonnie Dee dresses herself in the fashion of her literary mother Scarlett, in the hunter-green curtain fabric from *Gone with the Wind*, rather than waiting for some Mr. Wright to do it for her. She goes against the plantation economic system and makes friends with Narciss across the color line. Bonnie Dee has kicked the richest man in town out of his own house. The last thing she does before she dies is order a large amount of ice to be delivered to the house. This order bodes poorly for Uncle Daniel. One cannot help but assume that she will be storing his body on this ice.

Throughout the text her ability to cut hair transforms Bonnie Dee from a diminutive victim to a murderer ready to slash loud-mouthed, pompous, gluttonous, plantation child Uncle Daniel down to size. She starts by loping off his "senator-like" hair, turning him into a fuzzy peach. Ouida Sampson, the plant's name, brings us directly to the textual universe of Sampson and Delilah. Delilah, who is furious at Sampson cries out to him, "You have mocked me and told me lies. Please tell me how you could be bound" (Judges 16.10). In a moment of weakness Sampson tells Delilah, "A razor has never come upon my head . . . if my head were shaved then my strength would leave me" (Judges 16.17). Bonnie Dee shaves Uncle Daniel and his strength leaves him. He passes out. Cutting is central to this text and Welty texts in general. Uncle Daniel buys Bonnie Dee scissors. In many Welty texts, particularly in *Losing Battles*, cutting, piercing, and trimming figure prominently. In *Losing Battles*, the Aunts cut Gloria's wedding dress down to size and Welty herself cut up her own typed drafts of her stories with scissors to edit them effectively and then "stitched" them back together with straight pins. Bonnie Dee has cut holes in all the pulp stories in the *True Love Story* and *Movie Mirror* magazines stacked all over the house, deconstructing these false narratives.[7] She fills up her own space and tells her own stories. She does indeed have a story to tell, but she is also a character in a vast intertextual tapestry of conspiratorial resistance which Welty stiches together throughout the text.

In Melville's *Benito Cereno*, Captain Delano of *The Bachelor's Delight* anchored off the coast of Chile, sees a strange ghost-like ship in the distance wandering off course. Captain Delano boards the slave ship *San Dominick*, thinking he is merely assisting a ship that has gotten into trouble after going through a bad storm. He cannot understand why the Spanish Captain Benito Cereno is so pale and languid, and he assumes the faithful Senegalese "slave" Babo is helping him through this ordeal. Captain Delano's misreading of the situation is its point. The enslaved Africans on the *San Dominick* have staged a revolt, killed Cereno's business partner, secured his skull to the masthead, murdered many of the crew, and are hiding the insurrection from the visiting Captain. Babo, the leader of the revolt, keeps Don Benito Cereno in line by pretending to be his loyal manservant. While Delano is watching, Babo shaves Don Cereno and nicks him with a razor to his throat, effectively keeping him quiet in front of their visitor. Cereno is often described as if he's on the verge of passing out. And when Edna Earle finds Uncle Daniel passed out, she expects to see a nick on his neck. Court's opened. And another mutiny's in motion.

In Melville's story, four older African men sit on the four corners of the deck of the *San Dominick*, separating threads of old rope or picking oakum and polishing hatchets. By echoing the weapons and threats of *Benito Cereno* in this narrative, Welty code switches and connects her feminist text to the inequity of the economy, the legacy of the slave trade, and the blindness of patriarchal white supremacy in the small town of Clay. The rich white family in it, including Grandpa, Uncle Daniel, Edna Earle, and Tip Clanahan, have similarly benefitted from and improved their status on the backs of enslaved Africans. Another name for "poor white trash" is "clay eaters." Now, the poor white trash and Black people are eating the town of Clay.

All three women—Narciss, Edna Earle, and Bonnie Dee—are not who they seem. Narciss is plotting and planning her freedom, economic and otherwise. Edna Earle is plotting how to get her rightful inheritance and enjoying the storytelling as she does so. Bonnie Dee wants the Ponder money and more. If she has a child with Uncle Ponder, she could change her status and her family's status in the town for years to come. But this is a trial marriage. As far as having sex and populating the town with Peacock and Ponder progeny, Uncle Daniel is no fertility god like King MacLain. He is a dismal failure. His idea of having sex is playing creepy-mousie. Teacake Magee leaves her marriage, and it is by all estimations because Uncle Daniel does not shut up or put up where it counts. These are not sweet and satisfied southern ladies.

These three women are simultaneously detectives and potential murderesses. They are looking out for number one at the same time they are working in cahoots. When Bonnie Dee and Narciss join forces, poor white and Black women coming together, they have the power to topple the southern racist structure that demands that they hate one another.

In case we are still dubious about the three women's intentions, note there are murder weapons everywhere in *The Ponder Heart*. Not only does Bonnie Dee have a razor to Uncle Daniel's throat, but Edna Earle carries a hatchet and shakes it at him when he comes to tell her Bonnie Dee has run him off. Narciss cuts up chickens with sharp blades. Teacake Magee has a gun under her pillow and does not scare easy. When De Yancey calls Edna Earle "Ma'am" (implying she is old), she says, "I could have killed him" (111). When Edna Earle asks if Bonnie Dee remembers it is Grandpa's house she is in, Narciss drives off "in a fit of giggles going zig zag" (70). When the three women are not wielding weapons, they are imagining other means of attack. Edna Earle says she is glad Uncle Daniel did not go after Elsie Fleming, as she might have bitten him. Edna Earle, Narciss, and Bonnie Dee are directly responsible for every heart attack and plot twist, every zig zag, and every sashay in this knotted-up story. They are the early predecessors of the heroines in *Thelma and Louise*, Jane, Lilly, and Dolly in *9 to 5*, and the women in *Big Little Lies*.

Edna Earle's motives are easy: she will get a huge inheritance if Uncle Daniel dies, and she will have the last word. Throughout the story she is literally reading a set of literary directions: the 1905 novel *The House of a Thousand Candles* by Meredith Nicholson is an intricate and murderous, often violent, story of a young man trying to get his inheritance. When "taking care of her grandfather," who has a heart condition, Edna gives him coffee and she feeds Uncle Daniel massive amounts of food—not so good for his ponderous heart in its precarious condition. As soon as her grandfather is in the grave (a fact which she repeats often), she removes all the lightning rods off the top of the Ponder house, an action potentially endangering Uncle Daniel.

Narciss has her own motives. If Uncle Daniel died, she would only have to listen to Bonnie Dee, and that would be an improvement. Bonnie Dee shares what she buys with Narciss. Narciss is so glad to see Bonnie Dee back at the house that she calls out "hallelujah prayers is answered" (62). It is in fact Narciss who aids and abets Uncle Daniel marrying the seventeen-year-old Bonnie Dee by driving him to Silver Lake. Seventeen was underage for Mississippi in 1945, and thus his action would make him guilty of statuary rape. Narciss may know this but does not stop the wedding that could have him sent off to jail. For Narciss, Bonnie Dee is not just company in that lonely old house, she is a foil able to help her rule over Uncle Daniel and a way to keep Edna Earle from gaining control of the inheritance. From the moment Bonnie Dee is on the scene, Narciss is in the driver's seat both metaphorically and literally; she wears fancy mail-order clothes; she finally gets electricity at the house saving her extra work; she has a washing machine delivered, even if it has not been hooked up yet, and she does not have to put up with, cook for, listen to, or obey either Uncle Ponder or Edna Earle. Narciss creates her own image, wears cool blues, dons Ella Baker-style sunglasses, treats her day in court as a performance, and is proud of her work. Edna Earle recalls that when she called for Narciss after Bonnie Dee dies—Narciss was nowhere to be found. Narciss "laughs from the back of the courtroom to hear how she did" (115). She is proud of her plot to foil Edna Earle and Uncle Daniel. Throughout the text, women laugh when they are outwitting men and Black women laugh when they are outwitting white rich people.[8]

Edna Earle and Uncle Daniel's courtroom version of what happened is proved false by the lawyers. Edna Earle tells us but not the court (or are we the court?), "that Uncle Daniel tickles Bonnie Dee with a tassel while playing a game of creep-mousie with her up her neck" and that "you cannot make a tickler stop unless you play dead" (142). While Uncle Daniel is torturing her, Edna Earle wants us to believe that Bonnie Dee suffocates herself with a pillow and dies laughing. Now this is possible. But I think the court is still open. Edna Earle tells the reader but not the jury, that she saw Bonnie Dee sitting on the couch with a turkey platter full of candy holding one piece with a knife. When Edna Earle and Uncle Daniel enter the house, it is dark, and they cannot turn the lights on. Thus, we must ask why, in this game of *Clue*, Miss Peacock is in the living room with a plate of grainy candy and a knife on a turkey platter? What makes the fudge grainy? Could it be poison? She knows Uncle Daniel loves sweets. A pan of grainy candy could trap a mouse. Why is Narciss hiding? Is Bonnie Dee in the middle of the living room with a knife because she's waiting to kill Uncle Daniel? She is hiding in the dark. Narciss pushes her into the perfect place for a trap as she rides the sofa. She can either knife him or poison him with the candy. Does he pass out when he sees what she's about to do, as he did when he was faced with the razor blade, giving Edna Earle enough time to kill Bonnie Dee with the pillow, or knife, or her hatchet? Or does he play "creep-mousie," once too often and drive her out of the text altogether. Court's opened.

When Uncle Ponder is playing creep-mousie up Bonnie Dee's arm, she makes her own body into a knot and slips away: "She pulled herself in a little knot at the other end of the sofa" (175). Bonnie Dee, trapped between Edna Earle, Uncle Ponder, and the ball of fire, simply removes herself from the story by making her body a knot that the others cannot disentangle. In *Benito*

Cereno when one of the Spaniards wants to give slow-witted Delano a clue to help him figure out what he is seeing on the slave ship, he throws him an intricate Gordian-like knot. Delano cannot interpret the knot and ultimately lets one of the Africans throw it overboard. In "A Jury of Her Peers," the male sheriff cannot interpret the quilted knots of Mrs. Wright's world. Bonnie Dee is the knot that Edna Earle can neither disentangle nor catch. Bonnie Dee is thrown metaphorically overboard, off the raft of a sofa on which she has been playing dead. Uncle Daniel even calls out to Edna Earle to catch her, but Edna Earle cannot. At this moment Edna Earle's failure of imagination dooms or saves Bonnie Dee depending on how we read her departure. Whichever way we read this moment Bonnie Dee leaves the text voluntarily. *She* pulls her body into a knot. *She* puts the pillow over her face. *She* dies laughing. All of these are volitional, autonomous, and clearly subjective ways of dealing with her situation. She cannot stand Uncle Daniel's creep-mousie anymore, and she cannot kill him because Edna is there and the punishment of poor white trash Bonnie Dee would be swift in the 1950s. She has the knife, the sticky candy, and the ice to put his dead body on, but now Edna Earle would be a witness. She has a sister that looks like her twin, so the Bonnie Dees of the world are in no danger of dying out. Simply slipping out of the story is a calculated strategy.

A female character volitionally disappearing from a text is not new to women's literature. The best example is Kate Chopin's Edna Pontellier in *The Awakening* (1899). Many critics see the ending of *The Awakening* as a moment when Edna, having lost her love, Robert, and unsatisfied with traditional marriage and motherhood, drowns herself in the sea. The problem with this reading is that it neglects the possibility of another ending. Edna has been learning to swim. She swims out to sea, and it is in the last two lines of the text that the most poignant and meaningful metaphors appear: "There was the hum of bees, and the musky odor of pinks filled the air" (303). At the very moment when Edna is supposed to have committed suicide by swimming out into the ocean, the text becomes alive and fertile. A "hum of bees" and "a musky odor of pinks" are symbols of regeneration and feminine-embodied renewal, not death. As a character and not a human being, Edna can simply swim out of a text that has trapped her. Bonnie Dee, also a character and not a human being, is trapped by terribly diminutive stereotypes. She is from a poor family but the metaphors and symbols surrounding Bonnie Dee's life are potent and fertile. The metaphors surrounding Uncle Ponder and Edna Earle are nonreproductive and dead-ended. Uncle Daniel seems to be a sexual predator and a failed fertility god simultaneously. As Bonnie Dee says, "you always do the wrong thing" (64). Laughing and sexual fulfillment are tied very closely in this novella. *Le petite mort*: Bonnie Dee only laughs when she dies. She fulfills herself when she "kills herself," thus escaping Uncle Daniel's tormenting. Free at last. She just "slips out of his hands" as the text reads, and never lets him have the satisfaction of killing her, possessing her, or tickling her to death.

There is a strange cat-and-mouse game going on throughout the text that reminds us that all the characters can be read as both hunter and hunted. In the shaving scene, Uncle Daniel jumps up on the table like a cat after drinking buttermilk and crackers and getting milk on his cheeks. Bonnie Dee yawns and spits like a cat. Her sisters are called mice. When they bring the tree in that was hit by lightning, it looks like something had skinned down it with its claws. The moment Bonnie Dee dies, the ball of lightning shoots through the room and hits the tree, and if she is a catlike ghost, her ghost could have clawed the tree. She never ages. She has nine lives. She cannot die. She is undead. When Gladney catches Edna Earle in a lie about the time of Bonnie Dee's death, he shouts out "Now the cat's out of the bag" (*TPH* 121).

We can find motives for all three of the women, but the question becomes: what are Welty's motives? And I would say the answer is plain and simple: rage. Her rage at the South, at the nation, at Eisenhower, at John Robinson, at the whole spinster stereotype. At the deadly depressing feminine mystique of the 1950s, at having to live in Jackson and wanting to flee Jackson. At tasting freedom but still being bound, at the old southern stories that relegated her to a regional writer's status. Need we go on? We rarely if ever think of Welty's rage. But I would go so far as to say that *The Ponder Heart* is her most angry novel. And once we add the ingredient of rage, we find that Welty has indeed killed off Scarlett's daughter, freed the enslaved Narciss, and muted the racist, opinionated Edna Earles of the world. If we have any doubt that Welty herself could be a murderer, we need only look at Welty's one and only Civil War story, "The Burning," where she has Miss Theo and Miss Myra hang themselves and has Delilah, their enslaved woman, readily help them complete the task. She wrote "The Burning" in 1951. And if Welty can be a murderer so can Edna.

Narciss appears as a domestic, Bonnie Dee as the underaged, diminutive, and dim-witted poor-white-trash Peacock, and Edna Earle as the doting spinster niece revolving around the planet Uncle Daniel. These are stereotypes that blind us to the characters' actual motives, desires, passions, and potentials. If we follow the *Benito Cereno* reference, then they have all staged a rebellion that they are trying to hide not just from the visiting Hotel Guest, who is listening to Edna Earle's story, but from the reader, from each other, from Uncle Daniel, and I am afraid to say, successfully from the critics. But

Edna Earle must tell this story. She wants us to know the truth. She wants us to know that she *has* a story. Narciss and Bonnie Dee, as African American and poor white trash, respectively, work together, playing jacks, figuring out the plan. The rich white people end up with no money, no property, a house that has gone to grass, and no audience to listen to their silly stories. *The Ponder Heart* is literally a set of directions on how to stage a textual heist, deflate male power, silence old southern myths, and shut down American white-supremacist hegemonic discourse. The African American characters, Narciss, and Big John, and the poor, white girl Bonnie Dee Peacock have made change and cut hair. Narciss gets the last word. She is no longer a good cook for white people. Her rice won't stand apart. Now she only cooks if she wants to–as Edna says, if she only would. Who killed Bonnie Dee? No one and everyone. She slips away unmurdered and undead.

Notes

1. Edgar Allan Poe's "Purloined Letter," and Agatha Christie's *A.B.C. Murders* create the idea of metatextual linguistic clues as part of the mystery. Truman Capote's *In Cold Blood* not only makes the notion of psychological culpability famous but explores the difference between the supposed truth of a murder and the ways that the fictional telling of the story with all its in-depth psychological exploration of character can in his words be the actual truth. Kafka's *The Trial* is an example of the ways in which literature can explore political crime.

2. Weinman is the editor of the much-acclaimed volume, *Troubled Daughters, Twisted Wives: Stories from the Trailblazers of Domestic Suspense* and an eight-volume series highlighting novels by women mystery writers.

3. The accompanying Library of America volumes for Weinman's introduction— *Women Crime Writers: Four Suspense Novels of the 1940s* and *Women Crime Writers: Four Suspense Novels of the 1950s*—came out in 2015.

4. The motif of the "undead" defined by Bram Stoker in *Dracula* and Edgar Allan Poe in many of his stories, and more recently in Zombie fiction, was already a widely known device in the nineteenth century.

5. Ouida was assisted by an equally wealthy businessman. This murder, known as the Legs Murder, was documented and analyzed in *The Legs Murder Scandal* by Hunter Cole, one of Welty's close friends. He came from Laurel and would undoubtedly have talked to Welty about Ouida Keeton.

6. Like Ozzie and Clare singing the song in Leonard Bernstein's *On the Town*, Edna Earle makes it clear in the very first paragraph that Uncle Daniel gets "carried away" (*Ponder Heart* 7).

7. Bonnie Dee looks like she sent away for a set of Balzac novels, but Edna Earle can't find it anywhere. Honoré de Balzac (1799–1850), one of the most prolific writers of the world, claimed to write the whole comedic history of all humans, striving to fill more

space in the literary universe than Welty or Edna Earle could ever want to fill. In this fashion, Balzac was another Uncle Daniel, pouring stories out into the world. The fact that Bonnie Dee either decided against reading Balzac or she never ordered the set, reveals that this is not the kind of woman who wants to listen to the world as portrayed by a man, even one of the greatest novelists of all time.

8. This is a direct reference to a scene in Mae West's *I'm No Angel* (1933). During the trial of West's character, her maid, Beulah Thordyke (Gertrude Howard), sits in the back and laughs out loud at the procession. Beulah also testifies to the court that West's character totally loved the man she is suing. It is a court case in which men are shown to be cheaters and sexual harassers.

Works Cited

Anderson, Eric Gary, Taylor Hagood, and Daniel Cross Turner. *Undead Souths: The Gothic and Beyond in Southern Literature and Culture*. Louisiana State UP, 2015.

Baris, Sharon. "Judgements of the Ponder Heart: Welty's Trials of the 1950's." *Eudora Welty and Politics: Did the Writer Crusade*, edited by Harriet Pollack and Suzanne Marrs, Louisiana State UP, 2001, pp. 179–202.

Beauvoir, Simone de. *The Second Sex*. Knopf Publishing, 1953.

Chopin, Kate. *The Awakening* (1899). Norton Critical, 1992.

Cole, Hunter. *The Legs Murder Scandal*. UP of Mississippi, 2012.

Friedan, Betty. *The Feminine Mystique*. W. W. Norton, 1963.

Glaspell, Susan. "A Jury of Her Peers." The Crowell Publishing Company, 1918.

Glaspell, Susan. *Trifles*. 1916. CreateSpace Independent Publishing, 2014.

Marrs, Suzanne. *Eudora Welty: A Biography*. Harcourt Books, 2005.

Melville, Herman. *Benito Cereno*. 1855. Harper Perennial Classics, 2014.

Nicholson, Meredith. *The House of a Thousand Candles*. 1905. CreateSpace Independent Publishing Platform, 2017.

Pollack, Harriet. *Eudora Welty's Fiction and Photography: The Body of The Other Woman*. U of Georgia P, 2016.

Trouard, Dawn, "The Promiscuous Joy of Eudora Welty: Missing Bowen in Mississippi." *Transatlantic Exchanges: The American South in Europe—Europe in the American South*, edited by Richard Gray and Waldemar Zacharasiewicz, Austrian Academy of Sciences and the British Academy, 2007, pp. 257–76.

Thornton, Naoka Fuwa. "A Hilarious Destruction: The Ponder Heart as a Metanarrative." *Southern Quarterly*, vol. 36, no. 1, 1997, pp. 43–50.

Weinman, Sarah. "Introduction to Women Crime Writers." *Women Crime Writers of the 1940s & 1950s*. http://womencrime.loa.org/.

Welty, Eudora. *The Collected Stories of Eudora Welty*. 1980. Harcourt, Brace, 2019.

Welty, Eudora. *Conversations with Eudora Welty*, edited by Peggy Prenshaw, UP of Mississippi, 1984.

Welty, Eudora. *The Ponder Heart*. Harcourt, Brace, 1982.

Welty, Eudora. *The Robber Bridegroom*. Harcourt, Brace, 1942.

THE SLEUTH OF PINEHURST STREET

TOM NOLAN

"Here's a mystery for you," the North Carolina writer Dennis Drabelle began a 2016 book review in the *Washington Post*. "What drew Eudora Welty, who wrote incisive short stories about the South, to the work of Kenneth Millar who wrote hard-boiled detective novels, set largely in the West, under the name Ross Macdonald?"

Drabelle's "mystery" had puzzled people for years, he wrote, ever since Welty told *New York Times* interviewer Walter Clemons in 1970 that she was an admirer of Macdonald. ("Oh yes! I've read all his books, I think. I once wrote Ross Macdonald a fan letter, but I never mailed it" [*Meanwhile* 12].) This news certainly startled Clemons's colleague John Leonard, then editor of the *New York Times Book Review*. "I was flabbergasted that she was a reader of Ross Macdonald's," Leonard said; he himself had been a Macdonald devotee since the 1960s (Nolan, *Biography* 302). Editor Leonard assigned author Welty to review Macdonald's 1971 novel, *The Underground Man*. Her front-page essay, a fourteen-hundred-word celebration, then flabbergasted a large part of the literary community, from Yaddo to Yale. "In our day," Welty wrote,

> it is for such a novel as *The Underground Man* that the detective form exists. I think it also matters that it is the detective form, with all its effects, demands and its corresponding charms, that makes such a novel possible. What gives me special satisfaction about it is that no one but a good writer—*this* good writer—could have possibly brought it off. *The Underground Man* . . . is not only exhilaratingly well done; it is also very moving. (Welty, "Stuff," reprinted in McHaney 161–62)

Welty scrutinized Macdonald's prose with her own remarkable writer's eye:

Ross Macdonald's style . . . is one of delicacy and tension, very tightly made, with a spring in it. It doesn't allow a static sentence or one without pertinence. And the spare, controlled narrative, built for action and speed, conveys as well the world through which the action moves and gives it meaning, brings scene and character, however swiftly, before the eyes without a blur. It is an almost unbroken succession of sparkling pictures.

The style that works so well to produce fluidity and grace also suggests a mind much given to contemplation and reflection on our world. Mr. Macdonald's writing is something like a stand of clean, cool, well-branched, well-tended trees in which bright birds can flash and perch. And not for show, but to sing. (162)

The Underground Man, Welty concluded, "comes to stunning achievement" (157).

"In our day" she wrote, in 1971: some 130 years after Edgar Allan Poe invented the detective story; eighty-four years after Sir Arthur Conan Doyle popularized it through his Sherlock Holmes tales; forty-four years after Dashiell Hammett pioneered the hardboiled American school of private-eye mysteries; thirty-two years after Raymond Chandler romanticized Hammett's innovative vision with his novels of private detective Philip Marlowe—and now at the peak of Ross Macdonald's own quietly revolutionary transformation of the private-eye novel from a black-and-white casebook of crooks and cops, to a sociologically and psychologically sophisticated chronicle of dysfunctional families and ecological abuse.

Welty's page-one *Book Review* piece helped propel *The Underground Man* onto the *Times*'s Top Ten bestseller list: "The first runaway mystery in many years," one industry source described Macdonald's novel (Barkham). Welty's review enhanced Ross Macdonald's literary reputation immeasurably, and she brought him (and the mystery genre at its best) to the attention of readers who would never before have dreamed of picking up a private-eye novel.

Future author Max Byrd was an assistant professor of English at Yale in 1972 when that school offered "an experimental course," *Literature X*, marking the start of a heightened recognition of crime fiction in the academy: "One of the books we read was [Macdonald's] *The Chill*," Byrd recalled,

which I think alternated with [Macdonald's] *The Galton Case* . . . along with Oedipus Rex, Dostoevsky . . . and various others, talking about how the mystery story was really connected at its basic plot level and thematic concerns with these other 'higher' literatures, and that there was a continuity. I don't think anyone had ever done that before in an

academic environment . . . and what went on at Yale had its reverbera-
tions throughout the whole business. . . . So when they introduced
Ross Macdonald . . . right after Sophocles, that was a pretty daring
thing to do, because of the strong distinction then between lowbrow
and highbrow . . . But . . . that was about the time when Eudora Welty
did her famous book review; and at Yale, anything that comes out of
the *New York Times* rather staggers them! They were busy rethinking
that. (Max Byrd to Nolan, 1990, qtd. in *Ross Macdonald* 6)

By 1971, Welty had been reading detective fiction for decades. She enjoyed
the "Golden Age" (1920s–1930s) mysteries of Margery Allingham, Elizabeth Donleavy, and Ngaio Marsh; reviewed William Faulkner's *Intruder in
the Dust* (1949) for the *Hudson Review*; and provided a jacket-blurb for
Helen Eustis's *The Horizontal Man* (1946). Of more modern thriller writers,
she especially liked the English jockey-turned-author Dick Francis. But the
detective-novelist she admired most of all, it seemed—and this had been true
for at least a decade before *The Underground Man*—was Ross Macdonald.
    In the front room of her home (where she had written most of her own
books and stories) in Jackson, Mississippi, one morning in 1990, seven years
after Ross Macdonald's death, Eudora Welty analyzed what it was she liked
so much about Macdonald's prose:

His style is so very much his own," she said, "and it's made to do
exactly what he wanted it to. . . . It's quite direct, but it's constructed
and organized—which I wish more people knew how to do. And the
way the action progressed, from paragraph to paragraph—and the
background was drawn into it in the same way, built up and revealing
things in the right order, to make for both honesty and suspense—and
all of that was something that he just knew how to do." (qtd. in Nolan,
"1990" 6)

Macdonald's ability to link movement with description and incident with
emotion in a seamless flow can be seen in this brief passage from *The Zebra-
Striped Hearse*:

It was clear late twilight when the jet dropped down over the Peninsula.
The light of its cities were scattered like a broken necklace along the
dark rim of the Bay. At its tip stood San Francisco, remote and brilliant
as a city of the mind, hawsered to reality by her two great bridges—if
Marin and Berkeley were reality.

I took a cab to Redwood City. The deputy on duty on the ground floor of the Hall of Justice was a young man with red chipmunk cheeks and eyes that were neither bright nor stupid. He looked me over non-committally, waiting to see if I was a citizen or one of the others. (36)

That compressed, infused technique was what Welty so enjoyed about Macdonald's books; she said: "That's why I enjoy reading them," and she went on, "why you enjoy reading them again . . . when you know how he was really manipulating things all the time, in order to bring about the revelation, about character and time and so on. All of this is functional, at the same time as it's—as he creates the suspense of the story and its atmosphere; it's all a unit" (8).

She would write that she found Macdonald a better and more serious writer than his hardboiled predecessors, Hammett and Chandler. Now she expanded on that:

I think he surpassed them. What he did had more—substance, reality and thought in it, and more penetration of that same world, I suppose, than they attempted or needed to do. They wrote what their stories needed, and he wrote what his needed. He had more to say. And he said it more sympathetically and more imaginatively, I think. . . . [and to show] more imagination and sympathy toward people than is usually accorded in a crime novel. (8)

Imagination and sympathy toward people were key, of course, to Welty's own character and art.

Reading was a serious matter to her, to say the least—as it had been to her mother, who once ran into a burning house to save a cherished set of Dickens novels. Welty's mother enjoyed detective novels, too, though her taste ran to the earlier authors: Agatha Christie, S. S. Van Dine, Mary Roberts Rinehart; the more hard-boiled authors set her teeth on edge. "I can remember, in the 30's I guess," Welty would write Macdonald in 1975, "my mother, a great mystery reader, saying, 'That old James M. Cain! I wouldn't give you 2 ¢ for all he's written!'" (*Meanwhile* 236). Welty herself didn't get around to reading Cain until 1975, but she was aware of Raymond Chandler's work in the 1940s, in part because of the enthusiasm it provoked in her lifelong literary agent Diarmuid Russell.

California writer Chandler's first book *The Big Sleep* was published in 1939, when Welty was thirty years old. His first-person mystery novels featuring Los Angeles private detective Philip Marlowe were soon hailed as the best thing to happen to the mystery genre since Dashiell Hammett. "Did I tell you," Welty wrote Russell in December of 1943, "FAREWELL MY LOVELY [Chandler's second Marlowe novel, 1940] appeared down this way in Pocket books and I was crazy about it—he has a new one out this winter, I saw somewhere, THE LADY IN THE LAKE [Chandler's fourth, 1943], but it's not here yet" (Eichelberger 110). Chandler's work won praise from W. H. Auden and Edmund Wilson as being not mere detective-stories but closer to (dare they say) "real novels." Russell (son of the noted Irish poet "A.E.") was considering writing something about Chandler for the *New York Times Book Review*; in early 1945, Welty queried: "When is your piece about Chandler coming out?—You told me you'd been asked to do it but first didn't think you would" (Eichelberger 155).

But he did: Russell's essay was printed in the *New York Times Book Review* of June 17, 1945, under the title "Raymond Chandler, and the Future of Whodunits." In it, the agent argued that superior authors of detective-fiction deserved to be marketed (and, by extension, critically considered) on a par with superior mainstream literature. "Chandler is undoubtedly one of the best of mystery story writers," he wrote, "and it is my belief that if he had not been subject to the blind pigeonholing which has affected all mystery stories, his novels might well have appeared on the best-seller list . . . Does it seem ridiculous? But has any publisher tried to see if it is ridiculous?" (7).

In a modest way, Russell had done for Chandler what Welty would do for Macdonald in much more spectacular fashion with her piece in the *New York Times Book Review* twenty-six years later.

Welty's opinion of Chandler's flamboyant style cooled over the years: "I think some of the time Chandler and so on got pretty self-indulgent, in what they did," she said in 1990 (Nolan, "1990" 8). Of Dashiell Hammett, though, she judged approvingly in 1969 that he "wrote with delicacy and in a fadeless kind of acid" (Welty, *Hanging by a Thread* xviii). And she never lost her appreciation for the older writers she learned early to love, including Agatha Christie ("endlessly diverting to me," *Meanwhile* 166) and Rex Stout ("I must have my Nero!" [Welty, from Nolan interview, 1990 Interview; unpublished section]).

A precocious Welty's first attempt at writing her own "tale of ratiocination" came at age 16, with a story set in Paris (like Poe's crime tales?) and beginning: "Monsieur Boule inserted a delicate dagger in Mademoiselle's left side and departed with a poised immediacy" (qtd. in Kuehl 85). "I like to think I didn't take myself seriously then," she said much later, directly after quoting that sentence on herself, "but I did" (85).

Some years after that aborted Parisian adventure, she attempted a more down-to-earth murder mystery. "It was meant to be a stage play," she said in 1990. "I had a good idea for one. . . . People used to go and spend the summer in the South in little country hotels with big wells. . . . [T]hey were little worlds in themselves, and people came from all around—you know, like a good cast for a murder. And wonderful ways to kill people: throwing them down the well or anything" (Welty qtd. in Nolan, "1990" 13). Her "closed community"-type mystery, so prevalent in 1930s detective fiction, became in time a 1945 short story, "A Sketching Trip," written then from a nostalgic perspective (those old hotels were already gone) in a manner no longer aping Christie's or Stout's—or S. J. Perelman's—but in Welty's now-well-developed own: a "marvelous style," to borrow Miss Welty's delineation of William Faulkner's *Intruder in the Dust*-era prose, "that can always search in new ways and also appeared to use from beginning to end the prerogatives of an impromptu piece of work" ("Stuff," qtd. in McHaney 89). Controlled, yet with a spontaneous feel.

She'd written another such tale a few years earlier, "Old Mr. Marblehall," concerning "a man who has multiplied his life by deception," leading a double life (96); and this sketch, in its long posterity, would multiply *its* own life by being reprinted in *Ellery Queen Mystery Magazine* (March 1985), and included, over the decades, in crime-story anthologies. "Literary" mystery fiction—that would be the tag given to Welty's story, the same qualifying tag given to similarly ambitious stories by Faulkner, Dickens, Wilkie Collins, Georges Simenon—all the way back to Poe.

That seminal creator was a great influence on Ross Macdonald—born Kenneth Millar in 1916 and raised mostly in Kitchener, Ontario, Canada. Other important influences on him were Dickens, Dostoevsky, D. H. Lawrence, Dashiell Hammett—and, inevitably, Sir Arthur Conan Doyle.

Kenneth Millar's own first attempted mystery story was a Sherlock Holmes parody, published in his high-school literary magazine.[1] While teaching at that same school a few years later, he assisted his wife Margaret Sturm Millar in the writing of her first few mystery novels featuring a psychiatrist-sleuth, Dr. Paul Prye. Then, while a graduate student at the University of Michigan, he wrote his own first novel in a month, a spy adventure, *The Dark Tunnel* (1944). While serving in the Navy during World War II, he wrote a second thriller, *Trouble Follows Me* (1946). In 1949, Alfred Knopf (publisher of both Hammett and Chandler) brought out *The Moving Target*, Millar's first book featuring Southern California private detective Lew Archer—and the first book to bear Millar's Macdonald pseudonym. By 1953, when he returned to Michigan from his Santa Barbara, California, home, to give a talk during a weeklong seminar on the popular arts, Millar had not only earned his Michigan PhD in English literature and criticism (with a dissertation on Samuel Coleridge), but Macdonald had established himself as a new leading light in the hard-boiled mystery field.

His was a reputation built on surprisingly lofty aesthetic and philosophical principles, according to Donald Pearce, a longtime friend of Millar's who knew him from his undergraduate days in Ontario, through graduate school in Michigan and his first two decades in Santa Barbara. Together they had taken W. H. Auden's legendary 1941 graduate seminar course, and then Cleanth Brooks's almost equally celebrated 1942 class in which Brooks worked out the literary principles later described in his classic work *The Well-Wrought Urn: Studies in the Structure of Poetry*—this, just three years after Brooks had published some of Eudora Welty's first short stories in his and Robert Penn Warren's *Southern Review*.

By 1953, Millar had adapted his own lofty principles to the writing of popular fiction. "Ken's vision of the artist," Pearce recalled when we talked in 1990,

> was that he was a shaman: a person who danced until he fell dead for the benefit of the tribe, danced away their sicknesses and illnesses so that they could be whole, healthy and well again. That's a well-known shamanistic rite, [as described in James Frazer's] *The Golden Bough*; Wyndham Lewis had a similar vision of what the artist is for, in civilization. . . . Ken thought the mystery writer particularly was a shaman who danced out in public print the nightmares and anxieties, the troubles and the evils of the time, in order that we can see them. His view was that what an artist must do is to get hold of the evil in his time and make it visible, so that it can be comprehended. . . . He had this noble vision of the artist's role—responsibility, rather—in civilization. He tried to pull the detective story in that serious direction; he thought and felt it should go to that ambitious place. (Pearce interview, conducted by Nolan, 1990)

In his lecture on the detective story at the University of Michigan in 1953, Millar, a recent recipient of the PhD, told a full-house Angel Hall audience that the mystery tale originated in the nineteenth century's freedom "to know evil as well as good," with the tales of Poe expressing the urge to evil, "which modern man accepted as part of the bargain when he took entire command of his own will" (Macdonald, "Scene" 18–19). Poe invented the detective story, Millar thought, "in order to grasp and objectify the nature of the evil and somehow to place the guilt. That is probably the function of all good detective stories: to confront us imaginatively with evil, to explain it in the course of a narrative which convinces us of its reality, if possible to purge the evil." Books that had worked such horrid wonders, he said, included William Faulkner's *Sanctuary*. (Faulkner's *Intruder in the Dust* he declared "probably our most ambitious American mystery novel" [Macdonald, "Scene" 17].)

Among other "first-rate and tormented geniuses" who'd put crime fiction to its most serious use, he judged, were Dostoyevsky and Dickens. And the line continued into the present, with many modern writers choosing to undergo "the sharpest pains and bitterest moral dilemmas of our society," voluntarily submitting themselves to "the involuntary anguish of the criminal, the insane, the dispossessed." Alas, Millar noted, the traditional detective story with its "brilliant" sleuth-hero (Sherlock Holmes or Nero Wolfe) did not lend itself well to such explorations. "It is the murderer rather than the detective who must be the center of attention," he thought, "if the mystery is to have a genuine tragic interest" (Macdonald, "Scene" 28).

When Millar began writing detective fiction in earnest—after a postwar move, with his wife and young daughter, to Santa Barbara, California, and after changing his pen name in 1949 to Ross Macdonald—he had focused his shamanistic eye on the moral and physical perils unique to his newly adopted region: a state whose cultural, moral, and political climate he often deplored but one whose progress and preoccupations seemed to predict those of the whole country.

Macdonald's earliest tales and plot notebooks were full of storylines involving fatal hit-and-run accidents—a natural enough concern in car-crazy postwar California. But in 1956, the author's fiction hit home: his and his wife Margaret Millar's sixteen-year-old child Linda drove a car which struck two youngsters, one of whom died. The shaman's vision had come true. Absolved, or exorcised, from this disturbing theme, writer Macdonald soon developed another recurring notebook fear: the adolescent who vanishes without warning from school. This one too came true for him: in 1959, when the just-published Macdonald novel *The Galton Case* included scenes of a distraught father seeking a daughter last seen in a Northern California city, nineteen-year-old Linda Millar disappeared from her Davis, California, campus after a Memorial Day weekend trip to a casino in Stateline. Once again, the shaman-author's vision had been made manifest in life. (Linda, to a great extent through her father's strenuous efforts over ten days in three cities, was found safe in Reno and returned to Santa Barbara.)

These events altered Millar's life forever, and they showed the way towards novelist Macdonald's mature themes. The hard-boiled heir to Hammett and

Chandler became a modern master in his own right. It's not known whether Welty was aware of Millar's personal trials and traumas throughout the 1950s (the two writers would not become acquainted until the 1970s), but surely she noticed the change in his books, which probed ever deeper into the psychopathological ills of "ordinary" lives.

After living through dreadful realities involving his troubled daughter, and having himself undergone psychoanalytic therapy to explore his own fear, sadness, and anger, this shamanistic author had "danced out in public print the nightmares and anxieties, the trouble and the evils" of his and his postwar-middle-class citizens' lives in a singular series of novels from *The Doomsters* (1956) through *The Galton Case* (1959) to *The Zebra-Striped Hearse* (1962). In 1963, he was at work on what he thought "my most horrible plot yet": a witch's brew of frustrated passions and malevolent manipulations which many would call his masterpiece and Welty would especially praise: *The Chill.*

While Macdonald handwrote this work in spiral-bound notebooks in his Santa Barbara writing room, sometimes wearing the type of green news-paperman's visor his father (a Canadian newspaperman at the turn of the twentieth century) had once worn, a midnight act of violence three thousand miles away, in Jackson, Mississippi, would shock Welty into writing her own shamanistic-trance of a short story which would fulfill in earnest Ken Millar's decade-old description of "the function of all good detective stories: to confront us imaginatively with evil, to explain it in the course of a narrative which convinces us of its reality" (19).

"A bullet from the back of a bush took Medgar Evers's blood," sang the first words of Bob Dylan's broadside "A Pawn in Their Game," the second quick work of indelible value born from the death of the NAACP Field Secretary murdered in Jackson in 1963. The first and near-instantaneous such work was Eudora Welty's "Where Is the Voice Coming From?," in which a cruel, jagged, tormented assassin's monologue spilled like ink upon a page in the early hours after a white man shot a Black man under a yellow moon.

"When that murder was committed," Welty told a *Paris Review* interviewer circa 1972, "it suddenly crossed my consciousness that I knew what was in that man's mind because I'd lived all my life where it happened. It was the strangest feeling of horror and compulsion all in one." The artist was possessed by her daemon. "At the time I wrote it—it was overnight—no one knew who the murderer was . . . I was like a real-life detective trying to discover who did it. I don't mean the name of the murderer but his *nature.* That's not really a short-story writer's prerogative, or is it?" It surely was a shaman's. "Anyway, as events went to prove, I think I came close to pinpointing the mind . . ." (Kuehl 83). One pictures Welty that fateful night, and the day after: upstairs, at home in her workroom, straight-pinning pieces of manuscript pages together to hang in a pattern on the wall—like a police investigator posting eight-by-ten pictures and drawing arrows on a homicide board: the sleuth of Pinehurst Street.

"Where Is the Voice Coming From?" (a listener's perplexed and urgent query, perhaps) was written in the first-person voice of its no-count narrator: a voice devoid of grace, as Joyce Carol Oates described it in a 2009 interview, "[the author']s most extreme, masculine, percussive, mean, vicious, *thug* voice" (Treisman and Oates). A voice that can't wait more than three sentences to spit out the n-word:

> I'd already brought up my rifle, I'd already taken my sights. And I'd already got him . . . Something darker than him, like the wings of a bird, spread on his back and pulled him down. He climbed up once, like a man under bad claws, and like just blood could weigh a ton he walked with it on his back to better light. Didn't get no further than his door. And fell to stay. . . . I says . . . [']Now I'm alive and you ain't. We ain't never now, never going to be equals and you know why? One of us is dead. . . . Well, you seen to it, didn't you?'" (*CS* 604)

Never had Welty inhabited such a coarse, wicked persona. And *inhabit* is the proper word. There was often something eerie about Welty and her art. To some it seemed to begin with the way she peered so intently at a person, with her enormous, all-seeing eyes—as if probing the chambered recesses of one's heart and soul. She could seem almost a sort of seer, a wizard of art. She made no secret of it. "What I do in the writing of any character," she said, "is to try to enter into the mind, heart, and skin of a human being who is not myself" (*CS* xi).

Indeed, when a suspect was arrested and charged in the Evers killing— after Miss Welty had sent her story to the *New Yorker*, but before it was printed there—the seized man in real life was enough like the fictionally summoned one, it seemed, to warrant altering the manuscript: "[T]he fiction's outward details had to be changed where by chance they had resembled too closely those of actuality," she recalled, "for the story must not be found prejudicial to the case of a person who might be on trial for his life" (*CS* 39). To quote from "Old Mr. Marblehall": "A moment of strange telepathies" (*CS* 96).

Welty, in writing this 1963 story, had fulfilled to the maximum the role of shaman- cultural priest that Ross Macdonald told his Michigan audience a decade earlier was key to the future of serious mystery fiction. "[M]any modern writers have felt the need to undergo and imaginatively express the sharpest pains and bitterest moral dilemmas of our society," the detective-novelist informed that auditorium filled with academics. "In a period of fear and loss, the artist deliberately assumes the experiences of the fearful and the lost—voluntarily submits himself to the involuntary anguish of the criminal, the insane, the dispossessed. . . . Devoid of easy hope as such work is . . . [it] casts light and compassion in the dark places where it is very badly needed" ("Scene" 20–21).

Macdonald as scholar could trace the shaman-figure in crime fiction all the way back to its use by the genre's inventor, Poe, in his story of extreme cruelty, "The Black Cat" (1843). That tale's narrator felt shame and remorse; Welty's assassin is merely vexed that his wife fails to praise him. But shaman-author Welty hints, at least, at eventual comeuppance for her villain, as the killer finds a hot evening now growing hotter—as hot, perhaps, as the hinges of the place to which he seems headed: "So I reach me down my old guitar off the nail in the wall. . . . and I start to play, and sing a-Down. And sing a-down, down, down, down." This dire four-note melodic descent, heard through the centuries in works as diverse as seventeenth-century English composer Henry Purcell's "Dido's Lament" and Ray Charles's 1962 single, "Hit the Road, Jack," here seems to insert itself into a murderer's ad lib country blues: "Sing a-down, down, down, down. Down" (*CS* 607).

That ending never failed to make the hair on the back of Welty's *New Yorker* editor (and fiction writer) William Maxwell's neck stand up (qtd. in Marrs, *What There Is* 384). The magazine thought it a good idea, now that a man had been arrested and charged with Evers's murder, to take out the actual people and places mentioned in this story and substitute made-up ones: names changed to protect the guilty, so to speak. Ken Millar might say that doing so validated "Where Is the Voice Coming From?" as fiction.

"What I was writing about really was that world of hate I felt I had grown up with," Welty said later, on television, to William F. Buckley, Jr., "and I felt I could speak as someone who knew it" (qtd. in Casey 55). Novelist Maud Casey, in her 2018 work *The Art of Mystery*, writes that Welty's story

offers us terrifying proximity to a character whose voice most of us would prefer not to imagine. The story imagines an event that should be unimaginable, that should be unbearable but is, unfortunately, neither of those things. If it was unimaginable, then the murder of Evers . . . wouldn't have happened; if the murder of black people were unbearable, we'd all be dead. . . . That Welty not only could imagine the mind of this man but that she did imagine it requires artistic

rigor . . . [T]he radical empathy of creating character . . . [requires] a
combination of hard-won knowledge and the mystery of all you will
never know." . . . "Welty's story may be born from rage and anguish,
but it doesn't end there. If it's to succeed it has to slip us into the *I* of
a man we don't want to be anywhere near . . . and then take us even
farther, even deeper, into the mystery and contradiction of the character's humanity. (54–59)

The narrator, Casey writes, is "so isolated he can't see how much sorrow he's
caused, or how isolated he is. . . . [The story] leaves one," Casey sums up,
"with a feeling that isn't pure anger or pure anguish but that includes both
and also a feeling that's difficult to articulate . . . something that requires our
desperate attention." Or, to repeat Macdonald's 1953 phrase, it "casts light and
compassion in the dark places where it is very badly needed" ("Scene" 20–21).

The story was recognized immediately as a unique literary achievement, a
masterpiece: this testament of obscene pride by the assassin of an Evers-like
figure, uttered in the quick aftermath of the wretched deed—and written,
Welty would say, in virtual synchronous time with whatever the real-life
murderer might be thinking, doing, and saying. It was also a significant contribution to crime fiction, akin to certain tales by Dostoevsky and Faulkner.
But few genre aficionados had the perspective of a Macdonald to appreciate
that aspect.

Welty wrote another story, "The Demonstrators," in 1966, whose plot
turned on murder and on how that murder's press coverage was used to
advance social agendas of a small town's establishment. Most of her creative
energy in the later 1960s, though, went into the completion of a long-in-
the-making novel, *Losing Battles*. It was in an interview in conjunction with
that work that Welty revealed her admiration for Macdonald's writing—
prompting a letter to her from him, her response, and all else that ensued:
the two authors met in New York in May of 1971, three months after her
Underground Man review was published; they became great friends and
constant correspondents.

In 1972, Macdonald returned the compliment of Welty's *New York Times*
tribute, as it were, by dedicating his follow-up novel, *Sleeping Beauty* (1973),
to her. In simple terms, the book recounts detective Lew Archer's search for
a missing young woman he fears may be dead, either from an overdose of
sleeping pills or from being killed by kidnappers. But the story is built on
the bones of the fairy-tale of the same name, the fable of the princess who
sleeps for years until awakened by the loving kiss of a savior-prince.

On October 15, 1972, Welty wrote Millar about the Macdonald novel, *Sleeping Beauty*, which she read in typescript. "You've made something unique," she told him,

> it seems to me . . . a continuation, in the natural logic of your writing, a pushing further. . . . This has been a wider fling of the net . . . it's extraordinary work . . . this time the connections will bring together and relate not only human beings, but those stronger, older giants— greed & fire & waste & hurt & killing—all kin. And your story, with its delicate sure threads, holds the whole thing together, holds idea and act & meaning in one—with mystery kept central, at the heart, where it belongs—the urgent meaning of a human life or a death, that needs to be found out "It's what it's all about, isn't it?" (*Meanwhile* 92–93)

Her long, loving appreciation, gratifyingly specific, continued for a thousand words. She pronounced the novel "a beautiful piece of work . . . and signifying a great deal. . . . I am so filled with joy & pride to have my name on that [dedication] page" (*Meanwhile* 94).

Reading and rereading her poetic, deeply felt appreciation of his book the day it arrived, with tears in his eyes, was, Macdonald responded, "one of the great moments of my life" (*Meanwhile* 95). There was another layer of meaning laid between the lines of his mystery story, he revealed: "I mean the use of the phrase [Sleeping Beauty] as a generalized abstract noun"—the world's own slumbering beauty, awaiting awakening, or the beauty of a single waiting soul. "Well," Macdonald wrote his most perceptive and admiring reader, after savoring her grand encomium, "the beauty is sleeping indeed but your sweet and penetrating thoughts, Eudora, awaken her continually, indeed become her" (96).

And there is another clue planted within the novel, indicating Welty's central place in its symbolism. The book's literal sleeping beauty, the missing girl, has a book of short stories, *Permanent Errors*, among her effects. A reader may realize, or easily discover, that the author of that real-life work is Reynolds Price (Welty's close friend) and that it too is dedicated to Eudora Welty.

Throughout 1973, Welty cheered her West Coast colleague through his selection of stories for inclusion in an anthology of suspense tales he was editing (*Ross Macdonald Selects Great Stories of Suspense*, 1974). Her comments and suggestions resulted from a pleasant immersion in the literature of apprehension, from Agatha Christie to Patricia Highsmith—and Margaret Millar.

Macdonald visited Welty in Jackson, Mississippi, for a public celebration of her life and art; she came to Santa Barbara several times to take part in its Writers Conference—but mostly to see Ken Millar. By early 1976, he had written what would be his final novel, *The Blue Hammer*, in which faint signs of his fading powers and faculties may be (at least in retrospect) discerned. Macdonald sent Welty an advance copy; and on February 23, 1976, she wrote him:

> I read it with admiration as I always read your work, but this time of a special kind, because I was watching how you were allowing yourself a little freer rein, more ease of the old strictness but still keeping the tension, & nobody knows better than you do how much that matters in plot and all its branchings—& more scope and more length. I applauded it all. . . . I've read the book twice & know the scene I think most powerful—it's when Gerard Johnson shouts in the street. It's marvelous. (*Meanwhile* 288)

Welty herself was working on a long mystery-laced story, she told him: "The Shadow Club," in which she'd used several of the same character-names and elements as he had in *Hammer*: "I too have a Mildred, also a Ralph, and a Gerard (as a last name), & I too have a greenhouse, in which the major critical event took place & in the past" (*Meanwhile* 96). Thus she returned the affectionate waves he had made to her in *Sleeping Beauty*: pulling tighter the knots that tied them together as writers, colleagues, and loving friends.

By 1981, Millar—eventually diagnosed with Alzheimer's disease—could no longer write letters. Welty though continued to write to him. In 1982, she traveled to Santa Barbara for a final visit. His mental acuity was for the most part gone, but that warm and welcoming nature was intact. Welty and Margaret Millar together went south ninety miles to Los Angeles, to the *Los Angeles Times* Book Prizes ceremony, where the absent Macdonald was presented the Robert Kirsch Award for career excellence. Welty then returned to Jackson, distraught but grateful for her one last meeting with this most kindred of spirits.

It had never been a case, with them, of artistic opposites attracting; rather, they were an example *par excellence* of elective affinities united by daring intellect, brilliant talent, and human sensitivity.

Kenneth Millar—Ross Macdonald—died in Santa Barbara, California, in 1983. Two years later, Welty attended the Mystery Writers of America's (MWA) annual Edgar Awards dinner in New York City, where the MWA presented

winners in several categories with small ceramic busts of that original sha-
manic mystery-writer, Edgar Allan Poe. Eudora Welty was that night awarded
a commemorative Raven—a bust of Poe's black bird—and named Mystery
Reader of the Year. She would display the Raven in a prominent place in her
Jackson home—as opposed to her Pulitzer Prize for fiction, which was stored
in a sitting-room closet. In a perfect world, the Raven would have nestled on
her mantel next to a bust of Poe himself, awarded Welty a decade earlier for
"Where Is the Voice Coming From?" as Best Mystery Short Story of 1963—
but of course that story was never given that award nor even nominated for it.

Note

1. Miller [sic], Kenneth. "The South Sea Soup Co.," *The Grumbler*, Kitchener Collegiate
Institute, 1931.

Works Cited

Barkham, John. "Where Writing Is No Mystery." *New York Post*, 21 Aug. 1971.

Casey, Maud. *The Art of Mystery: The Search for Questions*. Graywolf Press, 2018.

Clemons, Walter. "Meeting Miss Welty." *New York Times Book Review*, 12 April 1970.

Drabelle, Dennis. "A literary mystery: What drew Eudora Welty to detective writer Ross
Macdonald?" *The Washington Post*, 13 April 2016.

Dylan, Bob. "Only a Pawn in Their Game." *The Times They Are A-Changin'*, Columbia
Records,1964.

Eichelberger, Julia, editor. *Tell about Night Flowers: Eudora Welty's Gardening Letters,
1940–1949*. UP of Mississippi, 2013.

Eustis, Helen. *The Horizontal Man*. Harper Brothers, 1946.

Kuehl, Linda. "Eudora Welty." *Conversations with Eudora Welty*, edited by Peggy Whitman
Prenshaw, UP of Mississippi, 1984, pp. 74–91. Originally published in *Writers at Work
(The Paris Review Interviews, Fourth Series)*, edited by George Plimpton, The Viking
Press, 1976, pp. 271–92.

Macdonald, Ross. *The Blue Hammer*. Alfred A. Knopf, 1976.

Macdonald, Ross. *The Chill*. Alfred A. Knopf, 1963.

Macdonald, Ross. *The Doomsters*. Alfred A. Knopf, 1958.

Macdonald, Ross. *The Galton Case*. Alfred A. Knopf, 1959.

Macdonald, Ross. *The Moving Target*. Alfred A. Knopf, 1949.

Macdonald, Ross. "The Scene of the Crime: Social Meanings of the Detective Story."
Inward Journey, edited by Ralph B. Sipper, Cordelia Editions, 1984, pp. 11–36.

Macdonald, Ross. *Sleeping Beauty*. Alfred A. Knopf, 1973.

Macdonald, Ross. *The Underground Man*. Alfred A. Knopf, 1971.

Macdonald, Ross. *The Zebra-Striped Hearse*. Alfred A. Knopf, 1962.

Macdonald, Ross, editor. *Ross Macdonald Selects Great Stories of Suspense*. Alfred A.
Knopf, 1974.

Marrs, Suzanne, editor. *What There Is to Say Has Been Said: The Correspondence of Eudora Welty and William Maxwell*. Houghton Mifflin Harcourt, 2011.

Marrs, Suzanne, and Tom Nolan, editors. *Meanwhile There Are Letters: The Correspondence of Eudora Welty and Ross Macdonald*. Arcade, 2015.

Millar, Kenneth. *The Dark Tunnel*. Dodd, Mead, 1944.

Millar, Kenneth. *Trouble Follows Me*. Dodd, Mead, 1946

Nolan, Tom. *Ross Macdonald: A Biography*. Scribner, 1999.

Nolan, Tom. "1990: I Call on Eudora Welty." *Eudora Welty Review*, vol. 9, spring 2017, pp. 1–20.

Pearce, Donald. Personal Interview, 1990.

Price, Reynolds. *Permanent Errors*. Atheneum, 1970.

Russell, D. C. "Raymond Chandler, and the Future of Whodunits." *New York Times Book Review*, 17 June 1945.

Treisman, Deborah, and Joyce Carol Oates. "Joyce Carol Oates Reads Eudora Welty." *New Yorker*, 9 March 2009, https://www.wnyc.org/story/joyce-carol-oates-reads -eudora-welty/.

Welty, Eudora. "The Demonstrators." *The Collected Stories of Eudora Welty*. Harcourt Brace Jovanovich, 1980, pp. 608–22.

Welty, Eudora. Introduction. *Hanging by a Thread: A New Treasury of Suspense Fact and Fiction*, edited by Joan Kahn, Houghton Mifflin, 1969, pp. xv–xix.

Welty, Eudora. "In Yoknapatawpha." *Eudora Welty: A Writer's Eye: Collected Book Reviews*, edited by Pearl Amelia McHaney, UP of Mississippi, 2009, pp. 87–90. Originally published in *Hudson Review*, winter 1949, pp. 596–98.

Welty, Eudora. "Old Mr. Marblehall." *The Collected Stories of Eudora Welty*. Harcourt Brace Jovanovich, 1980, pp. 91–97.

Welty, Eudora. Personal Interview, 1990.

Welty, Eudora. "A Sketching Trip." *The Atlantic*, June 1945, pp. 62–70.

Welty, Eudora. "'The Southern Imagination': An Interview with Eudora Welty and Walker Percy." *Conversations with Eudora Welty*, edited by Peggy Whitman Prenshaw, UP of Mississippi, 1984, pp. 92–114.

Welty, Eudora. "The Stuff That Nightmares Are Made Of." *Eudora Welty: A Writer's Eye: Collected Book Reviews*, edited by Pearl Amelia McHaney, UP of Mississippi, 2009, pp. 157–62. Originally published in *New York Times Book Review*, 14 Feb. 1971.

Welty, Eudora. "Where Is the Voice Coming From?" *The Collected Stories of Eudora Welty*. Harcourt Brace Jovanovich, 1980, pp. 603–7.

DETECTING DR. STRICKLAND

The Author as "Mindhunter"

MICHAEL PICKARD

Eudora Welty enjoyed a good mystery novel. Visitors to the Eudora Welty House and Garden Museum (Welty House) in Jackson, Mississippi, can find hundreds of these books on her shelves. A glance at those shelves suggests Welty read widely across the genre. Her library includes Agatha Christie, John Dickson Carr, Dick Francis, Ross Macdonald, Ngaio Marsh, Ruth Rendell, Georges Simenon, many others. Indeed, Welty's love of whodunits was well enough known that the Mystery Writers of America (MWA) honored her with its 1985 Raven Award for Mystery Reader of the Year: a bust of Poe's beguiling bird. This honor so delighted Welty that she put it on display, even as she kept other awards—her Pulitzer Prize, for example—in a closet.

Today, the Raven Award presides over a spare bedroom just across the hall from Welty's own. On the Welty House tour, it signals the pleasure she found in this species of narrative art. But from another point of view it also draws a line. Welty may have read mystery novels, but she wrote literary fiction. After all, the Mystery Writers of America did not offer her its Grand Master Award, which Christie, Carr, Francis, Macdonald, Marsh, Rendell, and Simenon all received. But neither did Welty pine for this distinction, of course. In her mind the best fiction resisted all efforts at circumscription. In 1971, for example, she reviewed Macdonald's *The Underground Man*. Later, the two would grow close.[1] At the time, however, she only knew him on the page, from his books and a correspondence they had only just begun (Marrs, *Eudora Welty* 353–54). "What gives me satisfaction about" *The Underground Man*, she writes in the review, "is that no one but a good writer—*this* good writer—could have possibly brought it off" (*"The Underground Man*. By Ross Macdonald" 258). For Welty the novel has clear literary merit. It "suggests a mind much given to contemplation and reflection on our world" (*"The*

Underground Man. By Ross Macdonald" 259). She valued Macdonald as a writer, not merely as a writer of mystery fiction.

One could make the same case, but in reverse, about Welty: no one but a writer steeped in the mystery genre could have brought off many of her stories. More of them than one might suppose turn on crimes of various kinds. Welty's characters meditate or commit murder, theft, rape, assault, treason, arson, and bigamy, among other felonies. Many of her protagonists, in a sense, conduct amateur investigations. In "First Love," Joel Mayes must parse the mystery of Burr and Blennerhasset. In "The Wide Net," William Wallace must find out what happened to Hazel. In "The Winds," Josie searches for clues that can help her solve the puzzle of Cornella, the older girl who lives across the street. In "June Recital," Loch Morrison surveils the clandestine activities taking place in the abandoned house next door. One could go on. Still, few think of Welty as a writer of mystery fiction.

It is time to challenge that perception. From Welty's library we can see just how many occasions she had to study "the detective form, with all its difficult demands and corresponding charms" ("*The Underground Man.* By Ross Macdonald" 258). If she often used this form to explore what Ruth M. Vande Kieft called "mysteries of the inner life," however, Welty seldom observed its final rule (27). "*Revealing whodunit is the climax of the mystery novel,*" proclaims a popular guide to writing mysteries from 1986, in italics so we pay attention: "It is what the reader has been waiting for" (Norville 102). The author has titled this chapter, "The End Game." A traditional detective story, W. H. Auden once observed, ends in "innocence . . . restored" (264). The detective solves the crime, the officers make arrests, and everyone gets back to normal life, confident the evil has been expelled.

Welty plays a different endgame. She seldom restores innocence in her fictional worlds, even when she does give us a whodunit, as in "Where Is the Voice Coming From?" Readers waiting for resolution from her stories will have to keep waiting. So often these stories invoke the state of mind that Keats called "Negative Capability." They invite readers to dwell "in uncertainties, Mysteries, doubts, without any irritable reaching after fact & reason" (Keats 79). Fact and reason tell us we should abhor and convict the murderer of Medgar Evers, the African American civil rights worker shot dead on his own driveway in 1963. Welty, who abhors this man and wants his conviction just as much as we do, nonetheless takes us inside his mind, a hellish place.

Drawn to such explorations, critics have not often looked at Weltyan mystery through the lens of genre. Her late story "The Demonstrators" (1966) is an exception. In 2013, Rebecca Mark described "The Demonstrators" as a "murder mystery to be read by following the clues" (199). Mark's investigation leads to a surprising conclusion. The ostensible victims of the story's double murder, she claims, have in fact staged that crime as a performance "to educate the doctor and save their own people" (199). Harriet Pollack, in *Eudora Welty's Fiction and Photography: The Body of the Other Woman* (2016), argues that Welty recasts the traditional whodunit by implying that white medicine has "marginalized" Ruby Gaddy "to death, *as much as if* she had been murdered in a church bombing or burning" (218, her italics). Building on these readings, Jacob Agner proposes that Welty uses a "country noir" aesthetic to "pinpoint whiteness and its institutional support as the real darkness" in Holden, Mississippi (208–9).

In all three readings, the true villain of the story is institutionalized white supremacy, as represented by the story's ostensible protagonist, Dr. Richard Strickland, his town's newspaper, and the white officials it quotes. The Holden *Sentinel* claims to have solved the murder of Ruby Gaddy: Dove Collins did it. White people were not involved. Case closed. Innocence restored. But Welty invites us to suspect this kind of storytelling. More importantly, she calls our attention to a crime not so easily solved: a world organized on the principle that Black lives do not matter.

So much falls into place when one looks at "The Demonstrators" as crime fiction. But I think critics have not yet pursued this insight to its end. In the current consensus, Strickland is a dupe or, alternatively, a criminal operator. Seeing him in this way has the salutary effect, as Mark has observed, of decentering him within Welty's narrative (199). It also stands in stark contrast to some early interpretations, which cast the doctor as a good man caught up in a terrible situation.[2]

Strickland is not that good man, I will argue, but Welty also does not flatten him into caricature. "The Demonstrators" exposes medical racism and white supremacy, as the perceptive recent discussion of the story has made clear. But Welty goes beyond recognition of these forces to consider how they can reside within Strickland's educated mind and pass the muster of his human heart. How does a person who has devoted his life to healing others— who had suffered humanizing losses of his own and made personal sacrifices in order to pursue this profession—live with himself, when the system he lives within has turned him into an agent of discrimination and even murder? How, in short, is Richard Strickland possible? As racial violence continues to erupt around us, the unsolved mystery at the heart of "The Demonstrators" calls for renewed investigation.

In "The Demonstrators," Welty invokes—only to swerve from—what Auden called the "basic formula" of detective fiction: "a murder occurs; many are suspected; all but one suspect, who is the murderer, are eliminated; the murderer is arrested or dies" (262). When the story begins, someone has attacked Ruby Gaddy, a Black woman, with an ice pick. She later dies of the wounds sustained in this attack. Strickland is summoned to the scene and, as Agner puts it, "moonlights" as detective (201). The women at Ruby's bedside identify Dove Collins, Ruby's common-law husband, as the culprit. No other suspects come to light. Later, driving Holden's dark and empty streets, his mind on problems of his own, Strickland discovers Dove, who soon dies of wounds ostensibly caused by Ruby in self-defense. With this information in hand, the town marshal, Curtis "Cowboy" Stubblefield, arrives at his conclusion, double murder, and declares the case closed. The Holden *Sentinel*, as we have seen, dutifully reports this narrative and the official pronouncement that race had nothing to do with it. As the article's subhead proclaims, "No Racial Content Espied" (746).

But it's just not so. Determined readers not turned away by Welty's "sometimes-obstructing style," as Pollack puts it, know better ("Words Between Strangers" 77). Those readers become in effect the true detectives of "The Demonstrators." Drawing on the critical discussion, they can see that Holden's authorities have reached a false conviction and eliminate the official narrative. They realize that Welty may imply, but she never says outright, what happened to or between Ruby and Dove. As Rebecca Mark observes, "Welty, an avid reader of detective stories, never shows us the most important evidence in any good murder mystery: the dead body" (201). She presents us with reports from various officials, none of whom we can trust. Furthermore, detecting readers can see how the casual racism everywhere on display in the *Sentinel* belies its efforts to eject race from the discussion of this case. They can see that both Dove and Ruby are victims, and that the real murderer, white oppression, diffuse as a grass fire on the edge of town, eludes arrest.

So does its crony, Dr. Richard Strickland, who could have done more for Ruby and who has arrived at his own false conviction: that he cannot treat her wound. As a member of the town's white elite, moreover, Strickland also bears some indirect responsibility for the outcome of Dove's life. In Holden, Mississippi, Dove Collins never had a fair shake. From this point of view, the story presents a variation on one of the mystery genre's cherished conclusions: the doctor did it. But Welty veers from the expected endgame of detective fiction, refusing to restore innocence. Strickland suffers no appreciable loss of status for the part he plays in the deaths of Dove and Ruby, but he is not—in the end—the real focus of the story's investigation. As Pollack and Agner observe, Welty shifts the focus of the traditional whodunit to reveal the structural and medical racism that operates both above and below ground in her time and place and our own. This case, of course, remains unsolved.

Welty does even more than that, however. In writing "The Demonstrators" (as in writing "Where Is the Voice Coming From?") she takes on the role of a "mindhunter," in the broad sense. Her procedure could not be more different than that of John E. Douglas, the FBI agent and pioneer of criminal profiling whose bestselling book, *Mindhunter: Inside the FBI's Elite Serial Crimes Unit* (1995), popularized that kenning. Hers is the creative method. She makes no claims to science and offers us no types, schema, or classifications, only the conviction that we cannot change minds we do not understand; and that we cannot reach this understanding and the transformation to which it can lead, unless we establish some common ground, however treacherous, with people who operate on different value systems than our own. In "The Demonstrators," Welty profiles the mentality of a white, conservative Mississippian, complicit and complex. Both words come from the same root, which denotes something so plaited together with other things as to become almost inextricable from them. It is precisely this difficult work of unweaving that Welty attempts.

In this sense, her approach could not be more different than the one she gives to Philip, the young civil rights advocate whom Strickland invites to dinner at a tenuous moment in his marriage. An outsider pursuing a just cause, Philip has no qualms about "dramatizing" his experience of Mississippi to nonsoutherners: "they won't know the difference where the paper is read." In the parlance of our own time, he publishes fake news. His story about civil rights workers forced at gunpoint to pick cotton in the June heat ignores agricultural realities, but he doesn't care: racist Mississippians might have done (and we know they did) much worse ("The Demonstrators" 744). Welty might agree with his politics, but she does not use his means. She is not the kind of detective who will massage evidence, even to achieve needed social change. Moreover, she sees that Philip's tactics can only alienate someone like Strickland, who is open-minded enough to welcome the activist into his home.

In 1960s Mississippi, that kind of open-mindedness came with risks. Months after Welty published "The Demonstrators," Klan operatives Tommy Tarrants and Kathy Ainsworth set off a bomb in the author's own Belhaven neighborhood. Their target was Robert Kochtitzky, who did interracial work, chiefly in a religious context. He lived just blocks away from Welty, at the intersection of St. Mary Street and Poplar Boulevard. According to the

Clarion-Ledger, "Kochtizky, his wife and a house guest, a minister from Washington [DC], had left the living room only moments before the explosions tore the porch away from the house, blew a hole in the living room wall, and propelled debris across the room with enough force to penetrate the opposite wall." An AP wirephoto shows extensive damage to the facade. Its caption identifies Kochtitzky as a "civil rights sympathizer" even as it notes his own insistence that he "is not an activist in the civil rights movement" (Pearce 1A).

The accompanying article, "Bombing Here Puzzles Enforcement Men," evokes the parodic reporting in Welty's Holden *Sentinel*. Its author quotes an interview with Kochtitzky, who knows very well why he was targeted: "the attitude my wife and I have on race—our attitude toward Negroes as human beings is basically the issue" (Pearce 12A). The reporter, however, obfuscates. He cites "law enforcement officers" who claim that the attack on Kochtitzky "broke the pattern of past racial bombings" and fear "a siege of terror planned by an undisciplined band of extremists." "Investigators do not think" that the bombing stems from "organized Klan activities," he writes (Pearce 1A). Later investigations, of course, made clear that it did (Nelson 66–7).

No one will confuse Richard Strickland for Robert Kochtitzky. His wife Irene may sympathize with civil rights, but he remains aloof. He would never say the things Kochtitzky says in print. He invites Philip to dinner "for the sake of an old friend," not because he supports the cause. But his good deed does not go unpunished. "Later"—the story does not say when—someone comes to Strickland's house in the night and spreads broken glass across his driveway. He does not notice the vandalism until the next morning, when he has driven into it. He thinks the vandals have come for him "as a result of his entertainment" of Philip. Welty leaves the question open, but Strickland's conclusion, as Marrs notes, seems plausible (*One Writer's Imagination* 186). After all, Philip, like his historical counterparts, is almost certainly under surveillance. One can imagine proponents of white power wanting to send a message to the doctor, a prominent man in Holden: stay in line. Irene seems to have interpreted the incident this way, as well. "Standing in the door, [she] had suddenly broken into laughter," as though she appreciates the irony: on the very night Strickland objected to Philip "lying" about Klan "hostilities," he brought those hostilities to his own front door (744).

Following clues in "The Demonstrators," we can all too easily throw the book at Strickland for racism and culpable negligence besides. He does not recognize Ruby, who cleans his office, until one of the other observers at her bedside prompts him to do so. The one white man in the room, he deals with those observers, including the victim's family, with a manner by turns pompous and combative. If he commits no harm in his treatment of Ruby's stab wound, he omits measures available to him in theory, as Pollack has claimed, to attempt to save her life. His own wife calls him a hypocrite. He has resigned himself to seeing life through in the face of "bitterness, intractability, that divided everybody and everything" (744). In his acceptance of his helplessness, he helps prop up the system of white oppression. Strickland is, in short, a healer who cannot heal anything at all—Ruby, Dove, his daughter, his marriage, the town in which he lives, the inequities of his times.

But he also does not leave Holden for the easier life surely available to him elsewhere, even though he has the means to do so. He has made three other house calls by the time that he arrives at Ruby's bedside that Saturday evening. If he fails to consider driving her to Jackson or to the Taborian Hospital in Mound Bayou—he at least comes. Another white doctor might simply have dismissed Ruby's child sister when she summoned him or made excuses. In *The Most Southern Place on Earth: The Mississippi Delta and the Roots of Regional Identity*, historian James C. Cobb presents as commonplaces examples of white physicians who refuse to treat African Americans or demand payment up front (263). Ruby is worn out, dying. Like all patients then and now she has a right to be treated with respect. Although Strickland, unforgivably, is brusque, he is also exhausted, and the calls for help, we learn, keep coming well into the early hours of Sunday morning. He does not mention compensation.

Welty's scene recalls Hemingway's "Indian Camp" (1924), a story she admired ("Looking at Short Stories" 89). Hemingway also presents a physician "accustomed," to borrow Harrison's gloss on Strickland, "to wielding authority over bodies" (99). Of course, "Indian Camp" undercuts that authority with an irony absorbed by readers and, one suspects, by the doctor's son, young Nick Adams. Well-trained, Nick's father compartmentalizes the screams of the woman undergoing a difficult labor. They are "not important" to the procedure, which is everything. Having performed a successful operation under field conditions, he feels an understandable pride: "'That's one for the medical journal, George,' he said. Doing a Caesarian with a jackknife and sewing it up with nine-foot gut leaders" (18). However, the same clinical detachment that proves invaluable under duress also anaesthetizes him, in effect, to the emotional lives of the others in the room, who take in the woman's screaming without the doctor's self-assurance. He dismisses the extent to which the experience disturbs Nick, whom he has brought along as an "interne" (17) in order to teach him about childbirth. And he never imagines that the woman's husband, himself wounded and suffering on the top bunk just above her, would not as it were take his wife's screaming like a man. Unable to bear her pain, an afterthought to the doctor in the room, the husband slices his own throat. He performs with clinical precision, in other words, a terrible operation of his own. There to learn about birth, Nick learns a lesson about death, one that hangs over the rest of *In Our Time*.

At Ruby's bedside, Strickland, who leans as heavily as Nick's father on the social privilege that comes both with his profession and his whiteness, nevertheless seems more harried—or, as Marrs puts it, "befuddled"—than assured (*One Writer's Imagination* 191). He is a necessary evil in this house, a capitulation to oppression and the racial history of white medicine. He may not understand these things, or he may understand them only on some level, but his uneasiness suggests that he senses the combination of appreciation and resistance that his presence provokes. As many commentators have observed, Lucille, whom readers may infer is Ruby's mother, questions his competence: "'Let me see you do something,' she said with a fury. 'You ain't even tied her up! You sure ain't your daddy!'" (739). Strickland defends his diagnosis with an exasperation that belies his insecurity, but he does not challenge Lucille's judgment. Like Nick Adams, he is not the doctor his father was, and he knows it.

Moments before this exchange, Strickland has reproved Lucille for striking Roger, Ruby's baby, "a blow on the side of the head" (738). His tone is supercilious, but he also speaks as someone who understands how it feels to parent a child incapacitated. His own daughter Sylvia, now deceased, "had been injured at birth"—how, one wonders, and by whom? Have we here another of the doctor's culpabilities? Dead at thirteen, she "had never sat up or spoken" (743). Welty in 1965 knew very well what it meant to love and mourn family members trapped in a long debilitation. In the same month that she worked through line edits for "The Demonstrators" with William Maxwell, fiction editor at the *New Yorker*, she wrote to him about "a family crisis with two heads—my mother had a stroke and my brother [Edward], several weeks earlier, broke his neck and is in a hospital in Jackson" (186). With the possibility and then the fact of these losses in mind, she gave a family tragedy to the Stricklands. A willing patriarch, Richard has earned the family bread while his wife Irene has overseen Sylvia's care. Yet, when he reflects that he has "loved [Sylvia] and mourned her all her life," one feels that the story does not ironize his grief as it does, for example, his marriage or his politics (743). Compared with Lucille and her family, the Stricklands have, as the saying goes, first-world problems. Nevertheless, by making the doctor vulnerable, the story invites readers to place his complicities within a human context. His deep distress has to some extent humanized his soul.

At this point, most criticism on the story agrees that Strickland's reverie, which occurs while he waits for a long train to pass on his way back into town, culminates in a false epiphany. At Ruby's house, he has quenched his thirst from a teacup that, he thinks, could have belonged to his family or to Irene's. Lucille has reminded him that she used to do the family laundry, and on leaving the house he has seen dresses hung up to dry on the front porch. Spooked by these vertiginous, angelic garments, haunted by recollections of the paternalistic ties that bind Ruby's world with his own, the objects his family has handed down to hers, he somehow manages to find comfort for himself "in a house of murder" (743). With this comfort comes a fond recollection of "the way [things] used to seem," of intact marriages, private selves, and more efficient white paternalism (744). In this sense, the epiphany exposes a narcissistic element at the doctor's core. In Agner's words, he "uses [Ruby's] suffering to repair his own wounded masculine feelings, co-opting her tragedy as his own" (206).

That Strickland's personal life is in ruins, at least, is clear. Once a storybook union, his marriage has fallen apart, and he thinks he knows the reason why: Irene has replaced her single-minded devotion to Sylvia with a single-minded devotion to civil rights. Lost in thought, the doctor diagnoses his wife with the same self-certainty as he has diagnosed Ruby: "What do you do after giving all your devotion to something that cannot be helped, and that has been taken away? You give all your devotion to something else that cannot be helped. But you shun all the terrible reminders, and turn not to a human being but an idea" (743). On its face, Strickland's assessment of Irene appeals to what William Empson once called "permanent truths" (5). Some things—a child incapacitated by injury, an ice pick to the heart—can only be helped by degrees. The way forward out of bitter, intractable division surely involves facing up to terrible reminders, turning not to ideas but to human beings. If Strickland could set aside his own intransigent self-absorption, perhaps he could use these notions to begin healing his weary soul. Instead, he places them within a reductive, self-exculpatory narrative that enables him to free himself from blame for what he must feel as an excruciating personal failure.

"The Demonstrators" tells us very little about Irene and what has caused her desire for separation. She has left Holden, and her rejection of their marriage has hurt Strickland. He copes with this wound by adopting an ironic view of her behavior. This view helps him regain a measure of control at a moment of rending uncertainty. Striving to make sense of why the relationship has unraveled, however, he only exposes his own contradictions. On the one hand, he condescends to his wife. It serves Richard to see Irene as unable to process the grief she feels about Sylvia's life and death, and to see her as determined, in consequence, to throw herself at another lost cause.

On the other hand, he seems painfully aware of hearsay that she is, in fact, having a good time "back where she came from, where, he'd heard, they were all giving parties for her" (744).

In fact, this rumor says more about Strickland, who entertains it, than Irene, whose life away from Holden Welty does not disclose. She is (in her husband's view) at once naive, dedicated "to something . . . that cannot be helped," and compromised. She claims to believe in civil rights, but (again, in his view) she enjoys the entertainments of the very system she opposes. Commenting on this moment in *One Writer's Imagination*, Marrs writes that, through the lens of Strickland, Irene's "faith *seems* short lived" (191, my italics). Marrs is right: readers do not have enough evidence to know. That Strickland has framed Irene in a way that reflects his own divisions, however, we can know. He craves acceptance from both the Black and the white communities of Holden. He wants to have the courage of his convictions and, at the same time, the blandishments of privilege: nights at the club, membership in the town's respectable social elite. Put another way, the epiphany by the train tracks confirms Irene's judgment about Strickland's fundamental hypocrisy. In the argument with Philip, he appeals to honesty, but, as Irene observes, he does not scruple about "putting a false front on" when it comes to Herman Fairbrothers's terminal illness (744). He seems just as unable to square with himself. Moreover, the insights that he has acquired through his medical studies as well as through life experience have congealed into truths he does not question. Those truths drive the assumptions he brings to bear, among other places, by Ruby's bedside, where he can see no hope for survival.

At the same time, as I have said, Strickland perseveres in Holden, answering its calls, palliating if not healing its wounds. He will go on offering hospice to the white community pillars in their final illnesses, and he will go on—as he has "enough times" before—sewing up the Doves of the town on Sunday mornings after weekend scraps (737). He will go on conscientiously objecting to false journalistic representations of the hostilities of his state even as he puts his own "false front on things" (744). The Holden *Sentinel* reports that

> Collins was discovered on his own doorstep by Dr. Strickland who had been spending the evening at the Country Club. Collins is reported by Dr. Strickland to have expired shortly following his discovery, alleging his death to chest wounds.
>
> "He offered no statement," Dr. Strickland said in response to a query. (748)

Strickland withholds Dove's final words, and either he or the writer of the article omits the fact that he has gone out to Ruby's bedside to treat her. The article instead places him at the Country Club, a bastion of white power in Holden, all night long. Why? Moreover, even the lazy reporter for the *Sentinel*, who seems to have little interest in finding the facts, in theory would have determined the location of Dove's death. Although Welty places the interaction between Dove and Strickland downtown in an "arena of moonlight," she does not pinpoint the location (746). But it seems unlikely that it takes place "on . . . [the] doorstep" of his office, as the *Sentinel* reports—unless we take the phrase as shorthand for the surrounding blocks (748). Should we then infer that Strickland has moved Dove toward and perhaps into his office? Why would he have done so if not in an effort, at risk to himself, to honor Dove's request and perhaps also, as Marrs writes, to attempt treatment (190)? Why suppress Dove's plea for concealment from the paper unless he does not wish to lend his voice to the white narrative that has already criminalized the deaths of Dove and Ruby as an instance of Black-on-Black violence? Why make no mention of his trip to Ruby's bedside if not out of concern about how Holden's white community will receive this news? Drawing on contemporary accounts, Marrs writes of "the hysteria that had overcome white Mississippi" in the 1960s (*One Writer's Imagination* 186). Reactionary Holden has already strewn the doctor's driveway with broken glass in retaliation for his decision to welcome a civil rights worker into his home. How would white members of the community, who feel free to call up Strickland at all hours, have responded to the idea of the doctor going off their grid (literally) in order to care for Ruby Gaddy?

No demonstrator, to be sure, the doctor makes the authoritative pronouncements that white Holden expects him to make. In small ways, however, as he has done by inviting Philip to dinner, Strickland appears to resist his own instrumentalization within the racialized discourse of the town. That he may not want credulous newspaper readers to know that he has crossed those tracks "with a bad record" (742) to offer care on the other side of town, or that he has attempted to help Dove, does not ennoble the doctor, much less earn him an ethical pass. But it looks like a plausible response to pressure all too real for some white Mississippians in the 1960s. In that same decade, after all, Welty herself took the considerable risk of driving across Jackson's tracks for unpublicized meetings with students from Tougaloo College, then under surveillance by the Sovereignty Commission. According to the Reverend Edwin King as well as other sources, the license plates of white visitors to Tougaloo during this time "were recorded." Here, as with Sylvia,

Welty may be sharing a portion of her own experience with Strickland, an understanding of what one can and cannot place on the record. As the only doctor in dying Holden, he has an exceedingly complex balance to strike. Does he refuse to detail his actions on that Saturday night in order to protect himself, in order to preserve the conditions under which he can continue to provide what meager care he can on both sides of town?

Strickland remains, at story's end, privileged as ever. He fails to observe his own caste position and the labor that provides the amenities that he takes for granted (Harrison 107). *Hypocrite lecteur*, but also to some extent an obstructionist, he faces, in the *Sentinel*, his own complicities with the system that—as Mark and Pollack suggest—have failed Ruby Gaddy a long time before the ice pick ever found her heart. He faces but does not face up to them. Instead, he retreats into private suffering. He still grieves his daughter. He must see Herman Fairbrothers and Marcia Pope through their terminal illnesses. From one point of view, he is more respectable but no less self-justifying than the narrator of "Where is the Voice Coming From?"—the healer as broadly guilty as the murderer. In the same decade as Welty wrote the story, Hannah Arendt defined "the banality of evil" that Strickland's life, to some extent, manifests (252). From another point of view, he is a doctor of last resort, compromised by wounds of his own that he cannot heal, perseverant, an enemy in the house, better than no doctor at all.

Alongside its *exposé* of white medicine, white journalism, and the more diffuse structures of white power operative in 1960s Mississippi, "The Demonstrators" investigates but does not condescend to white mentalities shaped by these forces. Alongside agnosticism—as Mark puts it, "What can we actually know about one another?" (219)—the story calls for acknowledgment of complexity coterminous with complicity. Writing for readers of many times, many places, Welty probes a wounded world to "initiate" a "new experience" of it ("Must the Novelist Crusade?" 810). She refuses to anesthetize. She treats her physician *manqué* with dignity and searing probity. She both "indicts" and "understands" Strickland, as Ebony Lumumba writes (181). He lives in what he perceives (and the story presents) as a wasteland he feels powerless to revitalize, and so perpetuates. If the story asks us to empathize with him to some extent, then it also asks us to see the self-interest that underwrites his disillusioned appeal to what "cannot be helped." Here lies the force of Welty's demystification of the place she knew best of all. "The Demonstrators" explores both "the degree to which even private actions are politicized" (Harrison 107) and the pressure politicization places on "the human right to be a private, mysterious, dignified, and unrepeatable self" (Vande Kieft 43). Inexplicable tragedies occur. Between understandable grief and resignation

to the bitter divisions of social life, between a claim to privacy and acquiescence in an intractable system that does not burden everyone to the same
degree, stands a grade crossing with a bad record.

"No human being is out of bounds to [Anton] Chekhov," Welty once re-
marked: "His candor was exploratory and painstaking—he might have used
it as the doctor in him would know how, treating the need for truth between
human beings as an emergency" ("Chekhov" 69). In "The Demonstrators,"
a portrait of a doctor who does not know how, Welty shares Chekhov's
"exploratory and painstaking" candor. The story exemplifies her belief that
"the very greatest mystery lies in unsheathed reality itself" ("Chekhov" 81).
Chekhov himself once made a distinction that Welty would have appreci-
ated, between "solving a problem" and "stating a problem correctly." "Only the
second," he argued, "is obligatory for the artist" (Chekhov, "To A. S. Suvorin"
100). Writing to Mary Lou Aswell, Welty stated the problem of her story as
she conceived it: "I wanted to show however imperfectly the complexity of
what it's like today—the breakdown of the old relationships and the false
starts and the despairs and self-delusions of what it's like. . . . I called it 'The
Demonstrators' because that's what I feel everybody is reduced to being" (qtd.
in *One Writer's Imagination* 190). From her beloved home in the Belhaven
neighborhood—two miles from the infamous Jackson Woolworth's, where a
mob assaulted students and faculty from Tougaloo College engaged in a sit-in
at the store's "Whites Only" lunch counter; four miles from Medgar Evers's
blood-stained driveway—Welty witnessed the breakdowns, false starts, despairs, and self-delusions of her world. Writing at a time of emergency, she
refused to compromise her investigation of her fellow Mississippians, reduc-
ing them to mere ideological demonstrations.

In a new era of violence and ignominy, a Mississippi every bit as complex
as the one Welty knew again faces a crisis of candor, an emergent "need for
truth between human beings." In Belhaven, cracks spider up the walls of
respectable houses undermined by Yazoo clay. Burst pipes pierce asphalt,
shooting geysers thirty feet into the air. Gunshots punctuate the night.
Legally free to deny service on the ground of "sincerely held religious beliefs
or moral conviction" to same-sex couples, couples living out of wedlock, and
individuals who live outside gender binaries, Mississippians go on electing
governors that, one feels sure, Welty would have abhorred (HB 1523). Outside
of bars, and at the one health clinic in the state that provides abortions, furious
demonstrators cry shame on patrons, patients, and passing cars alike, hand-
ing down sentences no one asks for. Why they bother is a mystery we need
some latter-day "mindhunter" to help us understand. Twenty-first-century

Stricklands anesthetize themselves with fatalisms like stopped clocks. They do not care what critics think. This is the world that we who would continue Welty's work must understand and reach.

Notes

1. See the introduction to Marrs and Nolan.

2. For a discussion of these early interpretations, see *Eudora Welty's Fiction and Photography*, p. 208.

Works Cited

Agner, Jacob. "Welty's Moonlighting Detective: Whiteness and Welty's Subversion of the American Noir Tradition in 'The Demonstrators.'" *New Essays on Eudora Welty, Class, and Race*, edited by Harriet Pollack, UP of Mississippi, 2020, pp. 189–213.

Arendt, Hannah. *Eichmann in Jerusalem*. 1963. Penguin, 2006.

Auden, W. H. "The Guilty Vicarage: Notes on the Detective Story, by an Addict." *The Complete Works of W. H. Auden: Prose, Vol. 2, 1939–1948*, edited by Edward Mendelson, Princeton University Press, 2002, pp. 261–70.

Chekhov, Anton. "To A. S. Suvorin." 27 Oct. 1888. *Letters of Anton Chekhov*, translated by Constance Garnett, Macmillan, 1920, pp. 99–103, *Archive*, archive.org.

Cobb, James C. *The Most Southern Place on Earth*. Oxford UP, 1994.

Empson, William. *Some Versions of Pastoral*. New Directions, 1974.

Eudora Welty House and Garden Museum. "Tour of the Eudora Welty House," 2012.

Harrison, Suzan. "'Racial Content Espied': Modernist Politics, Textuality, and Race in Eudora Welty's 'The Demonstrators,'" *Eudora Welty and Politics: Did the Writer Crusade?*, edited by Harriet Pollack and Suzanne Marrs, Louisiana State UP, 2001, pp. 89–108.

Hemingway, Ernest. *In Our Time*. 1925. Scribner, 1996.

Keats, John. "To George and Tom Keats." 21, 27? Dec. 1817. *Selected Letters*, edited by John Barnard, Penguin, 2014, pp. 77–80, Kindle.

King, Edwin. Email message to author, 11 Dec. 2019.

Lumumba, Ebony. "Demonstration of Life: Signifying for Social Justice in Eudora Welty's 'The Demonstrators.'" *New Essays on Eudora Welty, Class, and Race*, edited by Harriet Pollack, UP of Mississippi, 2020, pp. 171–88.

Mark, Rebecca. "Ice Picks, Guinea Pigs, and Dead Birds: Dramatic Weltyan Possibilities in 'The Demonstrators.'" *Eudora Welty, Whiteness, and Race*, edited by Harriet Pollack, U of Georgia P, 2013, pp. 199–223.

Marrs, Suzanne. *One Writer's Imagination: The Fiction of Eudora Welty*. Louisiana State UP, 2002.

Marrs, Suzanne. *Eudora Welty: A Biography*. Harcourt, 2005.

Marrs, Suzanne. Email message to author, 4 Jan. 2021.

Marrs, Suzanne, and Tom Nolan, editors. *Meanwhile There Are Letters: The Correspondence of Eudora Welty and Ross Macdonald*. Arcade, 2015.

Mississippi, Legislature, House, House Bill 1523, Protecting Freedom of Conscience from Government Discrimination. http://billstatus.ls.state.ms.us/2016/pdf/history/HB/HB1523.xml.

Nelson, Jack. *Terror in the Night: the Klan's Campaign against the Jews.* Simon & Schuster, 1993.

Pearce, John. "Bombing Here Puzzle to Enforcement Men." *Clarion-Ledger,* 20 Nov. 1967, p. 1A. *Newspapers.com.*

Pollack, Harriet. *Eudora Welty's Fiction and Photography: The Body of the Other Woman.* U of Georgia P, 2016.

Pollack, Harriet. "Words Between Strangers: On Welty, Her Style, and Her Audience." *Welty: A Life in Literature,* edited by Albert J. Devlin, UP of Mississippi, 1987, pp. 54–81.

Vande Kieft, Ruth M. *Eudora Welty.* Twayne Publishers, 1962.

Welty, Eudora. "The Demonstrators." *Stories, Essays, & Memoir,* edited by Richard Ford and Michael Kreyling, Library of America, 1998, pp.733–50.

Welty, Eudora. "Looking at Short Stories." *The Eye of the Story: Selected Essays and Reviews,* Random House, 1977, pp. 85–106.

Welty, Eudora. "Must the Novelist Crusade?" *Stories, Essays, & Memoir,* edited by Richard Ford and Michael Kreyling, Library of America, 1998, pp. 803–14.

Welty, Eudora. "Preface to 'Collected Stories.'" *Stories, Essays, & Memoir,* edited by Richard Ford and Michael Kreyling, Library of America, 1998, pp. 827–29.

Welty, Eudora. "Reality in Chekhov's Stories." *The Eye of the Story: Selected Essays and Reviews,* Random House, 1977, pp. 61–81.

Welty, Eudora. "*The Underground Man.* By Ross Macdonald." *The Eye of the Story: Selected Essays and Reviews,* Random House, 1977, pp. 251–60.

Welty, Eudora, and William Maxwell. *What There Is to Say We Have Said: The Correspondence of Eudora Welty and William Maxwell,* edited by Suzanne Marrs, Mariner Books, 2012.

WHEN A MYSTERY LEADS TO MURDER

Genre Bending, Hommes Fatals, Thickening Mystery, and the Covert Investigation of Whiteness in Eudora Welty's *Losing Battles*

HARRIET POLLACK

As a modernist writer in the 1940s and 1950s, Eudora Welty created what I have elsewhere called signature puzzle-texts.[1] Strategies of secrets, surprises, and thickening mystery frequently invite her readers to play detective and search for clues in stories that defy readers' expectations. Her trademark story-puzzles typically delight by first calling up and then refusing to conform to familiar literary conventions. In signature works such as "A Memory," "Powerhouse," "The Wide Net," "The Burning," and too many others to name, discovery happens not only in plot, but also when readers are delighted by the writer's nonfulfillment of the expectations her texts initially conjured— that is, by her clever and complicating uses of point of view, allusion, genre, and other traditional devices.

Now the essays of *Eudora Welty and Mystery* underscore what research-ers also know from encounters with her correspondence and her house: Welty was fond of the genre. And as this volume shows, Welty often fooled with, alluded to, and innovated on the various mystery forms that she, as a reader, enjoyed. Her bookshelves show she collected whodunits by writ-ers such as Agatha Christie, Margery Allingham, and Ngaio Marsh. These writers in particular were bestselling practitioners of a popular crime story subset: the country house mystery. In this formula, a murder disrupts the pastoral life of a British country estate, and those gathered there become a closed circle of informants and suspects to be investigated. These novels typically culminate with a reveal that wins the day, divides good from evil, and restores comforting order.

Bringing this critical background to *Losing Battles* (1970), her longest work, I'll argue that—while neither spare nor whittled as her earlier short stories are—the novel is another puzzle-text, one that monkeys with country house mystery conventions, not to conform to the genre but to adapt, alter, and even question it. If the mystery genre traditionally seeks to create order, Welty's modernist/postmodernist adaptation, as its title suggests, discomfortingly confronts disorder.

THE MYSTERY AND THE MURDER

In *Losing Battles*, mystery unexpectedly leads to murder.

The novel's mystery elements emerge only gradually, embedded as they are in a general profusion of other raucous plotlines. In the book's first sections, comic subplots are numerous. At the annual Renfro-Beecham family reunion, on the birthday of ninety-year-old matriarch Elvira Jordan Vaughn, grandson Jack Renfro returns from 1930s Parchman Farm Prison to his expectant family. He comes home as well to the bride whom he was snatched from on his wedding night and to the infant daughter born in his absence. On the road home he begins Good Samaritan efforts—clumsy, comical, and episodic—to help a stranded couple—without at first recognizing that he is unwittingly helping the Judge who sentenced him. This misadventure reopens the identical high jinks that sent Jack to Parchman in the first place: competitive male shenanigans with his longtime rival Curly Stovall. And in the meanwhile, the larger community arranges to bury a storied schoolteacher while local candidates stump for the office of Justice of the Peace. Yet, in spite of the wild whirl of this large book, it is the family gathering as stage for haphazard tale-telling and abundant story-making that is principal and central. And amid this familial tale-telling, their conversations swerve towards a mystery. Oddly nestled within the sprawling book's middle sections, its "whodunit" investigates an out-of-wedlock birth and produces a murder confession. Then the tone of the novel becomes ambiguous and changeable, moving—as Welty so often does—to skate the boundaries of literary conventions, to merge genres, and to surprise readers.[2] Comedy unpredictably flares into scenes of violence, cruelty, and will collide even with the history of white supremacy.

In its unceasing clamor, the garrulous Renfro-Beecham clan undertakes to construct a crime story of illegitimate birth to solve the puzzle of Gloria Short—a county orphan now married into the family—by purporting to identify Jack's bride's possible birth parents. In droll modification of familiar conventions, Welty flips the country house mystery's traditionally English upper-class setting on its head by locating this case in an entirely other sort of country house—the porch and yard life of a mountain Mississippi "shotgun" tin-roofed homestead. There, no celebrated detective is working the puzzle. Instead, those who have gathered come to deem themselves a sort of kith and kin investigative team.

In their two days of storytelling, they generate a closed circle of parental suspects for standoffish Gloria, a strategic inquiry with which they attempt to dominate her, intending to forcibly bring her into their own closed circle of family by defeating her resented postures of superiority, individuality, and above all, independent self-creation. They fully intend to diminish her to a mystery which they have solved. Their opening gambit is to disclose her as her husband's cousin, and thus give her no option to resist family membership.

And while there is no super detective in this gathered party, in its midst—unpredictably come in from the road—there is that hard-boiled and prosecuting judge—brought by a car wreck. In consequence, while the reunion group formulates Gloria's out-of-wedlock birth as a cold-case mystery and attempts to decide on a reveal, the interpretative question of what constitutes evidence is explicitly deliberated, along with definitions of hearsay and law but, I'll argue, not of justice. Given the opportunity to opine on their examination, Judge Moody flatly asserts, "I don't think much of your proof. . . . In fact, there's not a particle of it I'd accept as evidence. Fishing back in old memories. Postcard from the dead. Wise sayings." The dubious relationship between family storytelling and truth has earlier been suggested and corroborated by a girl of seven years, when young Elvie responds to Uncle Curtis Beecham's narrative of Granny's birth. Elvie sensibly objects to the story of her grandmother "born squalling . . . by the licking fire" as they are currently assembled to celebrate Granny's birthdate: "In August?" Elvie cried. "On the first Sunday in August?" (180).

Meanwhile, the reader herself must become the suspicious detective who evaluates the clan's hearsay, and moreover, spot and assess small details in the text that ultimately show their relevance. Think now of Welty's habit in her short stories and her photographs of telling-all through a detail or punctum. Recall, for example, the moment in "Powerhouse" when, in the jazzman's telling of Gypsy's suicide, we meet this small but altering detail: "'I got a telegram my wife is dead,' says Powerhouse, *with wandering fingers*" (CS 133, my emphasis). Those few words efficiently signal that Welty's story is not about a relationship between Powerhouse and his possible wife, but about the relationships between the pianist's two performances, one musical and one narrative, that convey and transform his artistic Black-and-blues. That same sort of epiphanic clue is at work in this sprawling novel, in which some quietly dropped remarks can eventually be meaningfully unpacked if they have been noticed. With these pointers in mind, I'll suggest the reader may, over the course of the novel's development, identify and consider a ring of suspect parental pairings, following more clues than the reunion members think—or previous critics have thought—to use.

What is more, while Welty takes care to thicken rather than resolve the novel's mysteries, she stunningly has these several versions of the past all lead to the same unexpectedly revealed vigilante murder and acceded-to racial lynching. For, although no detective investigates a murder, a murderer confesses. And shockingly and bewilderingly he confesses closer to the middle than to the end of the novel and quite without consequences.

There, Uncle Nathan Beecham suddenly and startlingly responds to the clan's musings on the relationships between Julia Mortimer, Rachel Sojourner, Sam Dale Beecham, Herman Dearman, and himself, announcing: "I killed Mr. Dearman with a stone to his head and let 'em hang a sawmill n----r for it" (344).[3]

As Rebecca Mark made clear in her 2001 essay, "Cross-mark Ploughed into the Center: Civil Rights and Eudora Welty's *Losing Battles*," Welty worked on this book throughout the long unfolding civil rights era. In 1955—the year when young Emmett Till's racist murder led to the infamous Mississippi trial that acquitted his killers, disturbing media events that would spur the Movement for racial equality and justice—Welty drafted the novel's first rudiments as a short story. In 1970, after piece-working her novel's narrative for a decade and a half, she finished and published the book in a climate animated by the enactment of 1960s civil rights legislation. These fifteen years marked a period of great upheaval in the Jim Crow South, and of national challenge to (as well as considerable maintenance of) the American racial status quo. It is in that time and place that Welty constructs her ambiguously comic novel about the white folk of Tishomingo County, one that orbits a white Christian community casually acceding both to law taken into individual hands and to Black lives not mattering.

Having explained this much about my topic, here are my essay's further intentions. To identify Welty's adaptations and subversions of the mystery genre and its resolutions: her playful adaptation of the country house formula, but also her anticipation of contemporary conventions both of "femme noir" written today by women regendering the notoriously problematic hard-boiled detective genre, and of "civil rights noir." Also, to notice a recurrent pattern of spirited homage to William Faulkner's mystery-loving novels and dark house repetitions. To litigate the detective-readers' real-time discovery and inspection of Gloria's case in order to ultimately propose a suspect parent-set not yet probed in criticism. To investigate all suspects by assembling crime-boards of textual evidence (informant verbatims in the form of quoted dialog) in order to reach a new reading of Gloria's enigma, one connecting the mystery of her birth to the novel's buried murder mystery. And at last, to further explore the novel's preparation for and quiet anatomy of murder and lynching.

WELTY, GENDERED GENRE BENDING, AND HOMMES FATALS

Welty, in earlier fictions and now here, is in some ways a clear predecessor to today's contemporary women writers of crime fictions and "domestic noirs," writers such as Megan Abbott, Gillian Flynn, Lucie Whitehouse, and Natalie Young.[4] In contemporary women's revision of the genre ("Chick Noir"), interest is shifted from reveal to backstory. And female crimes—the sort ranging from hiding out-of-wedlock pregnancy in *Losing Battles* to the murder of an abusive husband in Welty's unpublished drafts of "Alterations"—are rendered as following understandable motives; women do what they need to do to work, to end being bullied, and to resist having their desires and needs subordinated (Kennedy 33).

More curiously perhaps for understanding the arc of her career, Welty—like today's women writers—sketches hommes fatals. Femmes fatales are the more or less misogynist convention honed in her time period by the American crime fiction writers Raymond Chandler and Dashiell Hammett as they transformed the genial detectives of the English country house into "hard-boiled dicks" and gave the form gendered and sexist leanings. If their femme fatales are attractive and sexually dangerous, ultimately villainized, signaling cultural anxieties about the aggressive "New Woman," Welty's hommes fatals are attractive, sexually exciting, customarily idolized, but ultimately incomplete, faulty, and thus, dangerous, reflecting an era interrogating white male mythologies of heroic masculinity. Across Welty's canon there is a progression of hommes fatals. Jamie Lockhart in *The Robber Bridegroom* is one when, bandit of the woods, he robs Rosamond "of that which he had left her the day before," her clothing and her virginity, and on marrying her, installs her in a "house of marble and cypress wood on the shores of Lake Pontchartrain" (183). Billy Floyd in his relationship with Jenny Lockhart in "At the Landing" is one when "he violate[s] her . . . without care" (*CS* 251) and leaves her, deserted and damaged, to attempt self-repair while compulsively cleaning house. *Delta Wedding*'s George Fairchild, although a family hero, is another. While his sister-in-law Ellen is busy preparing her house for her oldest daughter's wedding, he casually and bafflingly reports inexplicably having had sex in a shed with the young and vulnerable runaway girl whom Ellen had herself met in the woods and correctly worried over, for the at-risk and abused girl is soon dead. King MacLain in *The Golden Apples* is the quintessential homme fatal when he abandons his wife to wander for adventure but returns to invite her to "meet me in the woods." Katie Rainey, reporting the incident, tells us Snowdie MacLain did not ask "what for?" but wryly follows with: "Then, twins," sons that Snowdie will without recourse single-parent as King's extended absence promptly resumes (*CS* 264), Overall, these ambiguously attractive hommes fatals figuratively and literally roam the woods, while their female partners—like those in the contemporary genre of femme noir—are routinely left to discover (and this is key) the perils of home confinement and, only when very lucky, independence there as well.[5]

In *Losing Battles*, as I'll show, Herman Dearman and Nathan Beecham are each candidates for the title "homme fatal"—but the convention's connotations perhaps ultimately touch even charming Jack, who is incapable of listening very well to his wife Gloria's plans and goals to build a life apart from his family. Gloria's frustration replays, in a different tonal register, *Delta Wedding* Robbie Reid's resentment of her husband George Fairchild's attachments to his family and to their addictive mythologizing of him. Like George, Jack hopes and perhaps expects his wife will soon subordinate her needs and desires to his family's. Note that femme noirs are typically set in relationships that women have been taught to expect fulfillment in—romance, marriage, or motherhood—relationships that seemed wonderful but then are not (Kennedy 34). For Gloria and Jack, sex is good, and Jack is kind and adoring, but at the same time he isn't at all troubled by Gloria's desires being diametrically opposed to his own.

DETECTING GLORIA SHORT AS MYSTERY

The mystery of Gloria's birth emerges from the stories occasioned by Miss Julia Mortimer's death. The passing of the novel's absent pivotal figure, like the demise of Addie Bundren in Faulkner's *As I Lay Dying*, sets in motion the journeys of the novel's second half and in particular the inquiry into Gloria's parentage. Comparison to the puzzle-loving Faulkner novel that Welty had read and admired is not an aside[6]—rather, it is impressive to recognize the number of playful plot parallels Welty incorporates into this counterpart comedy about Mississippi hill folk. For example, Willie Trimble's careful construction and presentation of a tribute coffin echoes Cash Bundren's crafting Addie's "on the bevel" (*AILD* 78). Doc Carruthers, like Doc Peabody, is called to precariously scale the family's mountain in a storm. Julia Mortimer, when she occasionally expresses the "token of her meaning"—her willful imposition on her students—with "her fresh-cut peach-tree switch" (*LB* 274), recalls the more severe schoolteacher Addie asserting to her students "with each blow of the switch: Now you are aware of me" (*AILD* 162). Vaughn Renfro's lyric interlude echoes Darl's distinctive sections in Faulkner's novel: the "different" brother's stream-of-consciousness. And of course, the Banner-Alliance community's fraught internment parade itself parallels the Bundren burial journey and drives one of *Losing Battles*'s most pivotal plot strands. All this is characteristic Weltian fun with literary transformation.

And yet of course Welty's novel is quite distinct in both the puzzles it builds and how it constructs them.

At Jack's family celebration of his Granny's 90th birthday, a marker of his matriach's near-death that gradually merges into Miss Julia's already underway funeral preparation, the detective-reader discovers Mortimer's life as paradoxical enigma: revered-and-yet-despised, tyrannical-while-heroic teacher of all the family and all the region. Whatever else, Mortimer's lifetime commitment to education had been total. She had battled with the likes of the Renfro-Beecham's pleasure in their unmodified selves. "She had designs on everybody. She wanted a doctor and a lawyer and all else we might have to holler for some day, to come right out of Banner. So she'd get behind some barefooted boy and push" (235). Altogether she intended to be an agent of change in Mississippi or as Uncle Percy comically rephrases it, "she wanted us to learn something if it was to kill us" (235).

While teacher to all, Julia Mortimer has been a particular mentor to Gloria Short. Aunt Cleo Beecham—the ficelle character newly married into the family who drives the day's storytelling forward with her inquisitive not-yet knowing—asks how the school system did "ever get ahold of [Gloria]?" She's told of a State spelling match won when the girl was only twelve years old. Mortimer had pitched schoolchildren against the members of the Legislature in the New Capitol's Hall of Representatives. There

> an orphan spelled down grown men. It gratified Miss Julia's soul, . . . [then] she coached that child so she could go to Alliance High School and keep up with ordinary children, till she got a diploma like they did, and she boarded her in her own home while she did it. She put

her on the bus after that and sent her to Normal, headed to be a teacher. (242)

Gloria confirms that Mortimer's "dearest wish was to pass on the torch.... What she taught me, I'd teach you, and on it would go" (244).

But a crisis in the relationship has occurred when Gloria informs her sponsor of what she acknowledges will bring Mortimer pain: "I may not ever be the wonderful teacher and lasting influence you are.... [T]here's a boy pretty well keeping after me," whom Gloria has announced intending to "pull ... through" and marry. Julia's spontaneous response is flat and quick: "Oh, you can't do that.... It's a thoroughly unteacherlike thing to do." Living in a time and place when a married woman is not permitted to teach, Mortimer, in settled protest, itemizes her objections. And she emphasizes two above simple youth and ignorance, advising her student both to "give a little mind to the family you're getting tangled up with" and also to ask a strategic question: "just who are you? You don't know.... Use your head.... Find out who you are. And don't get married first.... Get to work on yourself" (251–2). As Gloria tells it: "Miss Julia told me there was a dark thread ... running through my story somewhere.... Or my mother wouldn't have made a mystery out of me" (252).

RACHEL SOJOURNER

Hearing this story recounted as Gloria struggles with what she feels towards and owes to the now dead Mortimer, the family members who have bristled at Gloria's superior attitudes and aloofness presume to solve the secret of the newlywed orphan's parentage in spite of her adamant insistence that she "didn't mind being a mystery" and that if she'd been "born a mystery, [she]'d be married a mystery" (251). Granny's tiny voice speaks with clan authority to assert: "'Sojourner.... Prick up your ears. Once is all I'm going to tell it.... That's your mother....' She flicked her fan at Gloria. 'Fox-headed Rachel.'" One and all note the evidence of Gloria's flaming red hair.

Reconstructing Rachel Sojourner to take Gloria down, the Renfro-Beecham clan locate the orphan's postulated mother's Banner family "clear [at] the bottom of the hill.... Lower than Aycock...." They assert that Julia Mortimer taught her mother sewing because "Rachel couldn't learn to do mental arithmetic, so while the rest of us was firing off to beat the band, she sat ... putting in a seam." Moreover, Mortimer "[s]aw she's starving" and they called her into Granny's house to "help ... with this brood, mending their stockings," saying "At least you'll get fed." In conclusion, Granny asserts: "Well, that's who you are. You're Rachel's" (253–54).

Respecting Granny's proclamation, others embellish, adding details and telling stories they cannot reliably tell. Aunt Cleo—who has only just arrived in Banner for the first time with her new husband—informs Gloria, "You was tiny." "She was red as a pomegranate, and mad," adds Aunt Nanny (254). And Gloria's mother-in-law, Miss Beulah, turns Granny's reasonably open-to-doubt speculation that Rachel had ever had a baby into a forgone conclusion by insisting: "But Rachel's baby has to be somewhere. . . . And I think with Granny that somewhere is right here" (256).

While Granny's declaration takes on life, Gloria repeatedly resists it: "I'm not hers. I'm not Rachel's. I'm not one bit of hers" (254). "How do you know I'm Rachel's secret? . . . The more you tell it, the less I believe it" (256). "Granny can't prove I'm Rachel's. . . . Nobody can." (262).

It's Aunt Birdie who bids to disarm Gloria's protest with another stripe of argument: "I can show you the proof right now. . . . Like mother, like daughter!" (262). Birdie is censuring Gloria for having herself "jumped the gun" of marriage, evident from her having a daughter who is fourteen months old when she and Jack married eighteen months before—that is, Gloria was likely about five months pregnant when she married. Detective-readers, however, might resist Birdie's adage as in other respects a glaring misfit: Gloria excelled at learning while Rachel was so unsuited for the classroom that Mortimer provided for her a trade education in sewing, a skill that Gloria's rough homemade wedding dress suggests is not the young bride's forte.

It is at this point that the family switches its focus to "picking out" Gloria's father.

SAM DALE BEECHAM

Again, it is Granny who declares: "'Sam Dale Beecham. Sam Dale Beecham was going to marry fox-headed Rachel.' There was uproar at the table. Gloria's shriek came out and ran through the middle of it" (265).

Granny, we notice, is and will repeatedly be the source of most theories of and speculative solutions to Gloria's mystery. Granny, we know, is not our trusted detective because she is not in the least interested in discovering what she may not already know. But there is a Miss Marple-like resonance in her role as the aged sleuth who slowly announces her discoveries to a captive audience whom she leads—while the professional police officers in Christie's stories routinely dismiss Marple as too old and too female to be taken seriously. Christie's police, like the judge here, want documentable evidence while Miss Marple makes deductions based on intuitions of human nature; Granny's method, by and large, is also deduction. But now, Granny does offer something more.

As in the case of Bon's letter in Faulkner's modernist mystery novel *Absalom, Absalom!* that is a single tangible artifact of evidence appearing in a sea of subjective storytelling, Granny produces a picture postcard extracted from the family Bible. Here Welty plays on the mystery genre's traditional forms of substantiating clues—the family Bible, the found letter, the tell-tale photograph. Granny's Bible, an expected location for discovering an illuminating record of births and deaths, is instead studded with a trove of mementos whose meanings are imprecise: a lock of Ellen's hair, the ribbon that held Ellen's now lost ring, and Grandpa's spectacles, which Granny pokes free and places over her own as if to amplify her sleuthing vision. Then "she turned one more page and drew out what looked like a brownish postcard. . . . 'Let 'em hear that and see how they like it,' she told Uncle Nathan" (266).

What Miss Beulah then handles is "real-picture postcard" displaying Sam Dale Beecham in his soldier suit.[7] On its backside, there is a message that she haltingly reads, her voice having "suddenly lost all its authority": "'Dear Rachel. . . . Here is a—present for our—baby save it for when he gets here. Bought it with today's—pay and'—something—'trust it keeps good time. I miss one and all and wish I was in Banner.' Something—'Sincerely your husband Sam Dale Beecham'" (266–67).

The detective-reader may now, for a while, be comfortably cajoled into believing that red-haired Rachel and Sam Dale Beecham are Gloria's parents. But Welty will undermine the mystery genre's uncomplicated conventions of evidence. "Postcards from the dead" are not, as the Judge later declares, "proof." Textual evidence is open to interpretation in more than one way. Even when pulled from The Text.

As if already aware of the flaws in their testimony as it meets Gloria's steadfast resistance, the reunion women aggressively act to force feed this narrative to Gloria, along with dripping chunks of red seeded melon. The rancorous watermelon fight that ensues is frequently analyzed as a gang rape:

"Come on, sisters! . . . Let's cram it down her little red lane! Let's make her say Beecham! *We* did!" . . .

"Say who's a Beecham!" Then swallow it!" . . .

"Wash it down her crook!" . . .

A melony hand forced warm, seed-filled hunks into Gloria's sagging mouth. "Why, you're just in the bosom of your own family," somebody's

voice cried softly as if in condolence. Melon and fingers together went
into her mouth. (269–70)

In a novel that contains murder, this food fight may weirdly rate as its most
brutal scene; it is a fierce, ferocious episode of violation that quite over-
whelms the novel's alternate vision of family as comfort and refuge. The
episode assists our growing understanding of Gloria's insistent preference
to remain a waif of unknown origin; she dreads definition by family, and
like another central Welty orphan—Easter in "Moon Lake"—her identity is
rooted in a possibility of self-creation that abrogates lineage, belonging, or
family assignment. After the assault, limp with the cruelty inflicted, "Gloria
lay flat," stunned and molested, "an arm across her face now, its unfreckled
side exposed and as pale as the underpelt of a rabbit." Nevertheless she
stands her ground as "one to myself, and nobody's kin, and my own boss,
and nobody knows the one I am or where I came from" (315).

But of course, that is not quite true. As her intimate backstory with Julia
Mortimer suggests, we do know that Gloria has had, at minimum, a surrogate mother in her past.

JULIA MORTIMER

Gloria's initial account of her relationship to her sponsor described a dedicated bond. An underpaid school teacher who perhaps only once received as
much as seventeen silver dollars for her month's work, Mortimer nonetheless
boarded the orphan girl and sent her to high school while simultaneously,
in hard times, keeping Banner School running ("she'd do that if she had to
walk over the backs of forty supervisors" 242) from her own pocket. Aunt
Beck's opinion—which perhaps expresses faint praise for Gloria—is, "if she
sent you to high school and coached you in the meanwhiles, and was fighting
your way to a diploma from Normal for you, she must have come mighty
near to thinking you was worth it, Gloria. . . . A heap of times, people sac-
rifice to the limit they can for nothing. But now and then there'll be a good
excuse behind it." (245)

Thinking on this remark, a Welty reader familiar with "June Recital" may
be reminded of Miss Eckhart's love for her student Virgie Rainey's talent, as
well as Cassie's thought that the teacher's "love never did anyone any good"
(*CS* 306). But then again, as a detective-reader mulls the mystery of Gloria's
parentage and the possible "good excuse behind" Mortimer's support, Julia

herself rises as a parent-suspect. While other students at the Normal read aloud letters from their mothers, it's Julia's letters that Gloria reads.

There are additional inklings and supporting intimations to contemplate, hints that may be mused while the detective-reader learns of Julia's harassment, humiliation, and virtual imprisonment by Lexie Renfro, the "settled, white, Christian lady with no home ties" who has answered the call to nurse the now elderly teacher. Lexie Renfro's "care" for Julia is perhaps the second-most-violent assault in the novel, second only because we receive it secondhand. Perversely Lexie now shares the specifics of her callous brutality, telling the extended family how mercilessly she isolated the woman who devoted her life to the community, tied her to her bed, and flatly showed her the harsh truth that, without *family*, no one was coming to her with aid or concern. The detective-reader notes that Lexie reports Julia repeatedly enquiring "where's Gloria Short," as if she were her missing family (277). Pitilessly, Lexie tells Gloria that, in spite of being "straight along" asked for, "[y]ou were right in style when you didn't come" (279, 277). Abandoned, without support, Julia attempts to reach former students whom she might expect to help her; she writes letters, laboriously and desperately, tongue splayed out as if "words, just words was getting to be good enough to eat" (282). When Lexie takes even her pencil from her, Mortimer writes with her finger and "a little licking" on the bedsheet. Again in this "comic" novel, cruelty and savagery overwhelm, and skate comedy's boundaries.

Moreover, guilt is a stinging theme.[8] Hearing the details of this end-of-life assault, Gloria moans aloud in grief. And so does another member of Lexie's audience: Judge Oscar Moody who had, after all, randomly blundered into this year's Renfro-Beecham reunion while attempting, wholly too late, to come to Mortimer's aid. And now to make his own reveal, he pulls from his pocket and reads Julia's last letter to him.

In it, Julia pens lines that make a detective-reader linger in questioning conjecture.

Written on what may be the gold-edged flyleaf torn out of her own Bible (again textual evidence pulled from "The Text"), Julia's self-account and deathbed request to Moody is both penetrating and mysterious. She's ferociously clear as she writes of the losing battle of her life's cause: "All my life I've fought a hard war with ignorance. . . . Year in and year out, my children at Banner School took up the cause of the other side and held the fort against me." Reading the letter aloud, the Judge, himself one of Julia's receptive and grateful students, provides the reunion with "one more lesson" in Mortimer's confidence to change their futures. Refusing to admit defeat even as she writes from illness and imprisonment, she asserts herself "alive as ever," though "on the brink of oblivion" (298).

And then, mysteriously, she acknowledges, "I caught myself once on the verge of disgrace" (299). "Disgrace" is a word used in Julia's time and place for rebellious women, for women exposed as inappropriately sexual, for teachers caught in scandal, for fallen ladies, for out-of-wedlock mothers. Amplifying, she frames this sort of life-crisis as "put in your path to teach you," and "a warning," in what at first seems a delirious non-sequitur:

> There's been one thing I never did take into account. . . . Most likely neither did you. Watch out for innocence. Could you be tempted by it, Oscar—to your own mortification—and conspire with the ignorant and the lawless and the foolish and even the wicked, *to hold your tongue*? . . . Oscar Moody, I want to see you here in Alliance at your earliest convenience. Bring your Mississippi law with you, but you'll have to hear the story. It leads to a child. If I'm finally to reach my undoing, I won't be surprised to meet it in a child. You better get here fast. (300)

The detective-reader might now ask, whatever innocence is Julia referring to? Perhaps it could simply be Gloria's innocence, as she chooses Jack. Or, more tantalizingly, does Mortimer refer to her own inexperience as a young woman, who having in innocence made a mistake, found herself on the "verge of disgrace?" Who, both informed and naive about future consequences, decided to "hold her tongue" and hide a pregnancy and confinement in fear of losing her career and mission? Might she have once conspired "with the ignorant and the lawless and the foolish and even the wicked," by hiding her motherhood while her daughter grew? Is she calling on the Judge to hear her deathbed confession and then to help her legally recognize the child that she has both kept close and lost?

Gloria admits to having at one time thought Julia Mortimer was her mother, stunning the reunion with her "unbridled imagination." She acknowledges, "That would have explained everything. If once *she'd* made a mistake—and had me" (315). Beulah responds by uncharacteristically defending Mortimer: "if she had, Julia would have stuck to her guns . . . and brought you up for the world to see and brag on. She wouldn't make a mystery out of you. Had no use for mystery" (316). But what if Julia—the woman who "saved [Gloria] from the orphanage"—*had* made a mystery of her daughter, and then tragically lived to regret her choice? Her letter to the Judge certainly suggests remorse and a story withheld, a secret "disgrace" she on her death-bed is ready to expose. She asks him to "bring . . . Mississippi law" to "hear a story" that "leads to a child." And she fears her "undoing" is that child. A detective-reader certainly may add Julia Mortimer to the parent suspect list.

Julia's letter and the Judge's recitation display a depth of connection between Moody and his mentor as well as a profundity of pain as he acknowl-edges what it "cost that beleaguered woman" to reach him, only to have him fail to respond to her in time (301). His wife, a little jealous on discovering her husband's history of correspondence with this other woman, further upbraids him: "But here you are. . . . [And] you said 'anything for Miss Julia.'" Her comment boosts Moody's grieving disappointment in himself.

Strategically, Welty has the reunion—which, as in country house mystery formulas, typically identifies heroes and villains depending on whether or not they are family—at this moment comically and of course erroneously decide that the Judge must be "kin to that woman, . . . that's got to be it," as if all kinship, and now his to her, must be explained biologically (301).

That is, just as the detective-reader considers the possibility that the bond between Julia and Gloria is perhaps one of biological motherhood, Welty straight away redirects the reader to acknowledge the power of another sort of connection—one that results from seeing promise in, encouraging, and mentoring another's talents. As the Judge testifies, "If I was the first of Miss Julia's protégés, this girl [Gloria] was her last" (325). Welty critic Rebecca Mark, who forcefully argues that Julia *is* Gloria Short's mother, nevertheless concedes what I'll argue here, that "Welty makes sure we don't know" (145).

THE CRIME OF COUSIN MARRIAGE

While all the family still believes Sam Dale is her father, Gloria now fears that Judge Moody could prosecute Jack [Sam Dale's sister's son] for illegal cousin marriage, and might pronounce their wedding "null and void," leaving her baby without a name and returning Jack to Parchman Farm prison, where he has spent eighteen months for egregious tomfoolery with his habitual rival, Curly Stovall. Gloria fears she now understands other evidence from Julia's letters, letters that at least temporarily complicate the detective-reader's con-sideration of Julia's possible maternity:

> "It's still in words of fire on my brain. It said if I was going to marry who I threatened to marry, to stop right there. And come to see

her—there were still things I needed to know. . . . She said she'd been delving into her own mind and was still delving." (314)

. . . .

"Then Miss Julia let fly at me a second letter! She wrote and told me the wedding would be crossed off the books and Jack would have to go to the pen." (316)

. . . .

"The letter said a baby, if one was to get here, might be deaf and dumb . . . and go without a name. . . . [A]ll I could think of were the two words I'm scaredest of, null and void." (317)

As Aunt Birdie wonders aloud what Julia had "against these two sweethearts?" Moody judiciously replies, "She thought of the child" (316), voicing concern for possible reproductive risks. Jack's insular family on the other hand can only recommend the complete naturalness of marrying one's cousin, "the only safe thing in the world" (314). The Judge corrects them: "Not safe if that's what has happened and supposing the State has any way to prove it" (315). As Stephanie Rountree, discussing "Private Bodies and Public Policy" in the novel has recently explained, Mississippi had in 1922 "passed legislation criminalizing marriage between first cousins, making it the thirtieth . . . state to pass such a law" (4).

Fearful now of prosecution, Gloria begs the Judge to exonerate them, while the Judge is relatively unconcerned, doubting the reunion's evidence of Sam Dale fathering Rachel's baby Gloria. "The fact is," he concludes, "you could be almost anybody and have sprung up from almost anywhere" (315). "I saw there was a postcard. . . . But a postcard isn't the same evidence as a license to marry, or a marriage certificate, and even that. . ." (322). Rather, the Judge's trepidation is that he himself "will end up doing" what he has most hated and deplored: "Here I am, taking the law into my own hands," a remark Welty has him casually direct to Nathan Beecham. That is, he speaks the words "to Uncle Nathan, the one who was looking at him now with fixed eyes, over Granny's bowed head" (325), words that we will eventually understand, in retrospect, as pertinent to Nathan and secretly felt by him.

Then Beulah, unable to hold her tongue a moment longer, all at once blurts out a story that destabilizes the "proven" narrative of Sam Dale as Gloria's father. She's covertly suffered from a guilty memory of the time when—on her watch—a random hot coal burst into her younger brother's lap. Beulah has feared and supposed that Sam Dale, maimed, could not have fathered a child. And although the Judge dismisses this narrative too as "hearsay," he now attempts to close the matter, firmly announcing that "there was no prior knowledge [of kinship] between the partners and [therefore] no crime" (324–5).

The detective-reader assessing these conversations might indeed construe that since, according to Gloria, Julia Mortimer's letters proposed her concern for the consequences of cousin marriage, she could not be Gloria's mother after all. Should we then understand that Julia herself believed Gloria's parents were Rachel and Sam Dale?

Unless there might be another possible route to cousin marriage that concerns her.

What if Julia herself had been involved with a Beecham—that is, with Nathan Beecham, who had been "her shining light" when he was among her first students, as Jack had been among Gloria's (235)?

Hold that thought as we consider further evidence and learn of Herman Dearman and young Nathan Beecham—hommes fatals.

EVIDENCE: READING THE WEDDING PHOTO

To frame a "prettier view" of the family, Beulah now brings out her conspicuously large wedding photo—"nearly two feet long, seven or eight inches high"—taken, for a silver dollar, by a man on a mule passing through, and delivered by mail a month later. It is the clan's only picture of their whole family: "three deep . . . on the porch and steps of this house where they themselves now were" (327).

Like Sam Dale's "real-photo-postcard" and Julia's letter, this third artifact from the past is tangible and potentially informing testimony. Viewing it evokes new questions from Cleo (and the detective-reader) about family history. As always, both the meaning of the images and the stories they evoke are open to interpretation. As if to make clear both the credibility of this evidence and simultaneously, its questionable authority, Welty has now-vanished Sam Dale clearly and prominently pictured in it, but as false twins: "Evidently by racing the crank of the camera and running behind [the family's] backs, [he] had got in on both ends of the panorama, putting his face smack and smack again into the face of oblivion. Though too young and smooth to print itself dark enough not to fade, his face could not be mistaken; the hair stood straight up on his forehead, luxurious as a spring crop of oats" (328). Yet again, Welty has taken care to demonstrate that even photographic evidence can be manipulated and misleading.

And for the detective-reader, this thought-provoking photograph both reveals and withholds. Groom Ralph Renfro is seated by his standing bride, his leg "set out . . . like a loaf on a table," then only recently injured when blasting stumps of trees that Herman Dearman had clear-cut, though now Ralph is forever crippled as a result. Elsewhere in the photo, there is a "blur where someone moved." Aunt Beck interprets this haze for Gloria as "your mother" Rachel Sojourner, where Beulah had "never noticed her before." Gloria strains but "can't see what this girl looked like" (329). Just as Gloria does not want her mystery to be solved by the family, and like the woman in Natasha Trethewey's "Gesture of a Woman-In-Process" who "won't be still" and proves it with the "the white blur of her apron/still in motion" (3), the mysterious moving figure that might be Rachel escapes confinement both by this photograph and by the family's desire to contain her story.

Curious about another figure, a young man in a jaunty straw hat and "flowing tie," flaunting "a walking cane," Aunt Cleo asks, "What kind of dandy is this?" In a surprising revelation, a family chorus "full of glee" cries "That's Nathan!" Dumbfounded, Cleo challenges, "Well, he's got both hands." The image—worth pondering now—is startlingly and utterly different from the ascetic man whom we and Cleo have recently met, who, "surrendered to the lord," currently wanders the world fasting, posting signs that carry spiritual warnings, and bearing the infirmity of one "play hand," "a line-less and smooth" prosthesis gifted by his brothers (329, 220). By contrast, the photo's image of Nathan is very much a young man courting worldly attention to his physical self. Who was that young man, and what caused his change?

Further inspecting the wedding lineup, Cleo gives the "prize" for "pretty" to a woman who, by looking off into the horizon similarly seems to escape the photo's boundaries (quite like the figure that might be Rachel) and the limiting stories told from it. "[S]tanding the last one on the back row," as Welty noticeably dwells on this figure,

> her head turned away from the crowd and ignoring the camera, look-ing off from this porch here as from her own promontory to sur-vey the world. The full throat, firm long cheek, long-focused eye, the tall sweep of black hair laid with a rosebud that looked like a small diploma tied up in its ribbon, the very way the head was held, all said that the prospect was serious. (330)

It's Judge Moody who finally identifies this figure: "Miss Julia Percival Mortimer," a young stone-cold fox.

HERMAN DEARMAN

Now night and moonlight noir come to the reunion. Looking back, it does indeed appear that Welty, over the course of the novel, has gradually turned from evocations of Christie's country house formula to Chandleresque shades of darkness and disorder. The world of *Losing Battles* is "dosed with moonlight" "the thickness of china"—this is the look of noir echoing the technique of the spotlight moon that Welty had used so effectively to color her 1966 story "The Demonstrators" (363, 362; see Agner, "Moonlighting" 204–10).[9]

And suddenly Granny recalls that "on moonlight nights like tonight . . . they'd mount 'em the same steed and ride 'em up and down the road, and then hitch the bridle to the tree." Shocked voices ask: "'are you telling us about Miss Julia Mortimer and a sweetheart?' . . . 'Call him Dearman. That's his moniker'" (340). Her-man Dear-man is itself a name that makes a resounding ironic announcement of fatal attraction.

Although all laugh in dismay at this possibility, Beulah acknowledges, "A rascal like him's just the kind that some over-smart old maid would take a shine to" (340). Hence, the story of Herman Dearman's pillage of the family, the region, and the virgin land is told—in a narrative that calls up the sort of land-changing, avaricious, hubristic misdoings familiar from Faulkner's Yoknapatawpha, Mississippi novels: *Go Down, Moses, Absalom, Absalom!*, and the Snopes trilogy. The deeds of Herman Dearman echo those of Major DeSpain, Thomas Sutpen, and Flem Snopes, and notes of literary homage ring throughout this brief Mississippi history.

Initially Cleo incorrectly surmises that Dearman had been able to steal the general store that Ralph Renfro inherited from his father because Renfro came home injured from "German-hunting" in the war, but she is corrected; as Ralph himself explains, he never went to war:

> "I was right here in Banner, and watching him, and lost it to him." . . .
>
> "Dearman is who showed up full-grown around here, took over some of the country, brought [Black labor] in here, cut down every tree within forty miles, and run it shrieking through a sawmill. . . ."
>
> "Went through our hills and stripped 'em naked, that's all." (341)

Having literally followed the railroad's progress to Banner, Dearman "lived
with men in boxcars, . . . drank liquor," and put up a sawmill.[10] Ostensibly
partnering, Renfro blew stumps, cleaning up after Dearman. But "all at once
he had my business" (341).

Herman Dearman shared Julia Mortimer's capacity for unrelenting drive,
but his Snopesian goals were for himself, not for the community. As Percy
Beecham tells, in words that echo the family's descriptions of Julia herself—
but with a different inflection on the word "make"—"It was a tearing ambi-
tion he had to make all he could out of us":

> "What he left us was a nation of stumps," said Mr. Renfro.
>   Granny put out both hands in an amazingly swift predatory gesture.
>   "That's him!" said Miss Beulah. "Just a great big grabber, that's what
> Dearman was."
>   "Then after the store he took my house away from me," Mr. Renfro
> went on. "I had a little bad luck just at the perfect time to suit his needs,
> and he put me out and moved himself in. Thinking he was going to
> dwell in it forever, I reckon, and lord it over Banner forever and aye.
> He didn't get to do that." (341–42)

Looking for the denouement, Cleo asks: "What happened to Dearman?" and
Granny's riposte swaggers: "I sent him home" (342).

But as if in involuntary response to Cleo's question, Nathan Beecham
now precipitously and suddenly suffers some species of nervous attack,
ostensibly induced from panic, stress, or triggered epilepsy. His arm jerking,
his face darkening, he tumbles to his sister Beulah's breast, head back and
mouth open, recovering in stages of "gray-faced" coughing. Cleo, relentlessly
inquisitive, probes the meaning of his reaction: "what's he got to hide?" Then
it's Jack who drives the question home: "One day . . . I wish you'd tell it. . . .
Whatever caused you to go off among strangers, and never stay still" (343).

And that is the invitation that elicits Nathan's unexpected murder confession: "Son, there's not but one bad thing either you or I or anybody else
can do. And I already done it. That's kill a man. I killed Mr. Dearman with
a stone to his head and let 'em hang a sawmill n----r for it. After that, Jesus
had to hold my hand" (344).

Before probing the meaning of this startling and racist admission for the
novel as a whole, first consider its relevance to Gloria's mystery.

Granny's sudden response to Nathan's revelation, for example, is, "Never
said Sam Dale was the father. . . . Going to marry the girl, I said. Think Sam

Dale was pulling her out of a pickle" (345). Notably, Granny has now revised her story to present Rachel Sojourner and Herman Dearman as Gloria's parents. She pictures Dearman—the homme fatal who Percy bemoans had made "some of our girls . . . sweet on him" (344)—leaving Rachel pregnant. The detective-reader now pictures Sam Dale fondly intending to marry this girl whom he possibly loved or at least meant to chivalrously aid. In Granny's latest crime report, Nathan "did it for Sam Dale" (345). That is, to avenge his brother or to clear the path for him, while permanently sentencing a culprit who had been devastating the family and the region.

But, on the other hand, Granny had also begun the night with a tale of Dearman's nightly moonlight rides, not with Rachel, but with Julia Mortimer. The detective-reader may remember now that Ralph Renfro has earlier let fall a connection between Julia and Dearman in the story of the teacher's finances:

> "The first month . . . they paid her with seventeen silver dollars. But afterwards, they wasn't ever able to come up to that brave start," said Miss Beulah. . . .
>
> "Teachers just got a warrant," said Mr. Renfro. "And there come up Mr. Dearman. . . . Well, he was going around the country buying up teachers' warrants at a discount. . . . That's telling the least of him, Mother." (274)

Julia's situation recalls the caption Welty scrawled on an early print of her photo now known as "Window Shopping," but first titled "Teachers Don't Get Paid." That is, instead of receiving salary earned, women were routinely given promissory notes—"warrants"—until there might be tax money enough to eventually pay them. And needing cash to live on, schoolteachers frequently sold those vouchers at a discount to those who would have them or would trade on them. Economic complications, often mainstays of conventional mystery plots, are thus palpable here too. Could Julia, in backstory to an attraction, have been grateful for, or indebted and vulnerable to Dearman, as a result of financial transactions?

Readers then may well consider that Gloria could be the child of a relationship between Mortimer and Dearman, rather than Rachel and Dearman. Then again, those possibilities are undercut by Julia's seemingly insistent warning that Gloria is related to Jack.

But suppose it was Nathan Beecham that Julia was involved with *before* entering a relationship with Herman Dearman?

WHAT ABOUT NATHAN BEECHAM?

Just as those few earlier lines about warrants suggest past history between Dearman and Mortimer, prior details have intimated a now noteworthy youthful attraction between Julia and Nathan. Noah Webster remarks that, as a new teacher in Banner, Julia "about cut her teeth on Nathan. He was her shining light" (235). Recall too that Nathan—in keeping with his current self-chastising asceticism—had hardly spoken a word during the reunion celebration before he strangely but strikingly "broke his long silence to say, 'Many a little schoolhouse I pass on the mountainside today is a sister to Banner, and I pass it wondering if I was to knock on the door wouldn't she come running out all unchanged'" (294). Does that out-of-the-blue nostalgic longing, let fall by a short story writer with a habit of telling much in a detail or two, suggest this other possible solution to Gloria's mystery? When counseling Gloria to pass on Jack, Julia had knowingly "said teachers falling in love with their first pupils was old at the Flood" (250). And consider too, when Julia advises Gloria to think not only of Jack, but to "give a little mind to the family you're getting tangled up with," could the older woman be revisiting her own decision to abandon a lover with a vexing family?

Now thinking across a possible repetition, Nathan to Jack, there could indeed be a case for Birdie's accusing adage, "like mother, like daughter."

Recall too Mortimer's counsel to "watch out for innocence." Was Julia recalling the naiveté of having once been attracted to and enamored of the young Nathan? In innocence, might an adolescent Nathan have once imagined Julia, who like Rachel boarded with the Beechams, would choose him and his family, and in consequence end her career for the sake of head-in-the-clouds love? Could his youthful, guiltless, and now evermore and eternally lost innocence have vanished in anger and fraught revenge when the family adversary and homme fatal Dearman perhaps became her next man standing? And notice that Nathan goes to none other than Julia to report his act of murder, and she—quite out of character—does not sternly deliver him to the law but rather unpredictably conspires for him to "start again . . . from there, to go on [his] way and be good," to wander the woods and world, as do so many other of Welty's hommes fatals.

"Like mother, like daughter" would in this case be a phrase suggesting an intergenerational repetition of a mistake—a haunting inheritance as in Faulkner's *Absalom, Absalom!* Could Julia have carried Nathan Beecham's child and refused to choose his family, only to have her daughter bear Jack Renfro's child and erroneously believe she *could both* choose him and cast off his family? And the tragedy would be that, in bequeathing Gloria the advice to "give a little mind to the family you're getting tangled up with," Julia loses her own family when Gloria retreats from unwanted counsel. Like Thomas Sutpen when *his* "trouble was innocence," was Julia doomed to watch her offspring reenact her fate, in this case attraction to a young man and not to his family?

"Like mother, like daughter" is also an axiom further complicated by Gloria's trusting that she can avoid Julia's unhappiness—as we see it in the dying woman's final isolation—by choosing Jack over teaching. This sort of attempted reversal is characteristic in the contemporary femme noir genre that Welty anticipated: women trying "to distance selves from mothers and previous generations of women [only to] discover to their horror that they are not so far removed from the struggles faced by women in previous decades" (Kennedy 35). Readers need wonder how Gloria, if indeed attempting a difference from her mother-surrogate who chose career over family—will now manage the tension between the future apart that she envisions for herself, her daughter Lady May, and her husband Jack, and the future serving the family that Jack seems headed for and that his kinfolk count on.

I argue this possibility, which has not to my knowledge been noted before, not to solve Gloria's mystery, but to remind readers that Welty does not. Rather, my point is that the expectation of solving mystery is one of the novel's losing battles. Gloria's is not the only mystery unsolved: the reunion's tellings of how their Beecham parents died on the Bywy Bridge, for example, thickens into the puzzle of what they were doing there in the first place—were they "running away from" their children, as Noah Webster believes (217)? Welty's habit in consistently thickening mystery rejects the assumptions of the country house form's conventional endings and their tidy, uncomplicated solutions to knowing. And Welty underscores the provisional and speculative aspects of all her novel's various "solutions" by having Beulah ask, "Granny, which would you rather? Keep Sam Dale perfect, or let him be a father after all?" as if to acknowledge that the various resolutions offered are all "stories." Certainly Mrs. Moody is accurate when she reassures Gloria, "You could be anybody's." Withholding solution, Welty's comic fiction refuses the mystery novel's "aha moment" that too perfectly separates the innocent from the guilty. Rather her comedic country house mystery turns out to be a noir novel in disguise, toying with the genre while showing—as she writes in *The Golden Apples*—"all the opposites on earth were close together," country houses and dark houses, "unrecognizable one from the other sometimes, making moments double upon themselves, and in the doubling double again, amending but never taking back" (*CS* 452–53).

Resisting solution, Welty is subverting a mystery genre mainstay that is also its foible. The traditional mystery genre undeniably has been notoriously critiqued for its escapist appeal and satisfactions: in British country house mysteries of the Golden Age, the horrors of World War I were obscured by and displaced in stories that in every respect resolve, that easily divide good from evil, and that comfortingly steer clear of the complex realities of actual world disorder. In contrast, I'll suggest that Welty, some fifty years later, by extending Nathan's crime beyond the killing of Herman Dearman to the execution of a Black man in his stead, pointedly incorporates and acknowledges the great disorder of her own time and place, 1960s Mississippi.

FROM MYSTERY TO MURDER: WHITENESS, RACE, AND THE CONVENTION OF EVOLVING SECRETS

Elsewhere I have connected a narrative lesson that Welty learned and described in *One Writer's Beginnings* to the mystery blueprint in which the investigation of a secret reveals another, worse, which is of course exactly what happens in *Losing Battles*.[11] In her memoir, Welty recounts asking her mother about the secret of sex and unexpectedly provoking the reveal of a lost sibling, "not how babies could come but how they could die. . . . The future story writer in the child must have taken unconscious note and stored it away: one secret is liable to be revealed in the place of another harder to tell and the substitute secret when nakedly exposed is often the more appalling" (17).

In *Losing Battles*, Welty makes use of this mystery formula of the substitute secret. That is, the various versions of love-crime enigma emerging from hearsay in this comic country house investigation expose a worse crime: a double murder of sorts in which a Black workman at Dearman's lumber mill is hung for Nathan's felony. This conviction of a Black surrogate, possibly by law but more likely by lynching, raises the subject of race in a novel that has not side-stepped it and has, on second glance, prepared throughout for this topic.

Rebecca Mark in her groundbreaking 2001 essay writes that Nathan's confession "takes up no more than two or three lines . . . [but is] a key to reading the whole novel" (123). I quite agree, though here I substitute and use a crime-novel key to enter the same white room through a different door. And in a mystery that has otherwise undercut all available evidence, the sudden confession further opens, rather than tidies, the book's borders.

In this context, the detective-reader might reconsider the mixed tone of this book to recognize and appreciate Welty amalgamating comedy, mystery, and social commentary. We've noted scenes in this comic novel where brutality fully overtakes humor. To my mind, its complex tones are similar to Coen brothers films in our day (think *Fargo* or *Raising Arizona*)—tonally ambiguous noir comedies that show occasional affection for the more wholesome merits of a region but also, at any moment, expose and inspect appallingly vicious behaviors—as well as the cultural patterns and presumptions that led to those acts. Like noir narratives and the Coen brothers' films, the novel discloses moral offenses "just beneath the innocent surface of everyday . . . life" (Rzepka 230), and among them, racism.

This novel's particular attention to issues of racism have not always been recognized. In 1972 Charles Bunting accused Welty of having dodged the topic in this civil rights era novel, pointing out its "rather conspicuous absence of Negroes." Welty denied the description and flummoxed her interviewer by responding: "There is . . . a very telling and essential incident in *Losing Battles* . . . that involves a Negro as such. Perhaps you remember" (*Conversations* 48). Bunting did not remember. Creating a conspicuous absence of his own, he did not respond and changed the topic.

Today, nearly fifty years after that interview, in a world that better understands whiteness as a racial concept, it is considerably easier to see that a novel set in Mississippi's predominately white Tishomingo County exposes whiteness and concerns race. A reader responding today to Bunting's inquiry will more readily see these subjects emerge as we learn Nathan sentenced Dearman with vigilante justice and then silently benefited from community assumptions that culprits are Black. The detective-reader may also appreciate that Nathan's suddenly divulged racial crime has quietly been prepared for throughout this novel.

To spot that readying groundwork, first consider the uses and meanings of the n-word throughout.[12] It is uttered first in relationship to Parchman Farm Prison. A well-versed reader of Mississippi fiction today may be conscious of the extreme difference between white Jack Renfro's comic experience of and even escape from Parchman in *Losing Battles* and Jesmyn Ward's Black character Richie's killing and haunting experience there in *Sing, Unburied, Sing* (2017). Life at this now-infamous penitentiary in the Mississippi Delta, viewed by the Beecham-Renfros in their infertile Mississippi hills, is to them, in their ignorance, a relative paradise:

> "Jack's in the Delta . . . Clear out of the hills and into the good land."
> They smiled. "That Jack!"
> "Where it's running with riches and swarming with n----s everywhere you look," said Uncle Curtis. (70)

In these lines the speakers grieve their own adversity on a Banner farm that "wouldn't hardly give a weed comfort and sustenance" while they picture free Black labor as profitably "swarming" at Parchman. Swarming to produce wealth but swarming like vermin.

Then later, Miss Beulah and Aunt Nanny describe Dearman who "brought n----s in here, cut down every tree within forty miles, and run it shrieking through a sawmill. . . . Went through our hills and stripped 'em naked, that's all" (341). There Beulah spits out her white resentment of the Black body used as a tool for the invasion and destruction of what their unfortunate family had of value.

The third use is of course by Nathan himself in his confession: "I killed Mr. Dearman with a stone to his head and let 'em hang a sawmill n----r for it. After that, Jesus had to hold my hand." Sister Beulah's reply to Nathan's desolate and wretched confession to what he ultimately has realized he has done and permitted is: "Now what did you want to tell that for? . . . We could've gotten through one more reunion without that, couldn't we? Without you punishing yourself?" Beulah is disturbed for Nathan's health and future, as well as for the mood of the reunion, but she is clearly not troubled that Black lives matter.

In this context of the everyday moral offense of racism, is it also relevant that every chapter header of the novel's first edition carries a recurring illustration (fig. 8.1), an image that was also embossed on the book's cover (fig. 8.2) and embedded in its dust-jacket art (fig. 8.3), and later represented in most subsequent editions as well (fig. 8.4)?[13] The recurring drawing likely represents the Bois d'Arc tree introduced in Jack and Curly's competition to save Judge Moody's car from running off Banner top—which is to say, the tree that figures in the distracting comedy of their "man-foolishness" (379). But is it also not the duplication of a haunting hanging tree? Early on, Jack's pal Aycock Comfort shares a bit of the tree's history when Welty has him say: "Old timers hung a rascal from this tree, my grandmaw used to tell" (131). Welty carefully made room for that detail, irrelevant in the scene where it occurs, but perhaps ultimately terribly pertinent in the novel as a whole, in which an innocent Black man swings for a white man's crime.

Trees of course signify variously in Welty's imaginary. In *One Writer's Beginnings*, she associates them especially with her mother's Andrews Family Tree, "drawn as a living tree, spreading from a rooted trunk, every branch, twig, and leaf in clear outline." Darkening, Welty recalls its "most riveting feature was the thick branch . . . broken off short to a jagged end, branchless and leafless, and labeled 'Joseph, Killed by lightning'" (66). Also memorably, in *Some Notes on River Country*, Welty describes the trees of the Natchez

Fig. 8.1. These tree images recur throughout *Losing Battles* (Random House, 1970) at the start of each of its six sections. It also appears on the title page, on the hardcover, and its dustjacket.

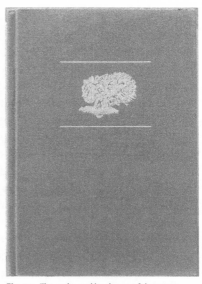

Fig. 8.2. The embossed hardcover of that same edition.

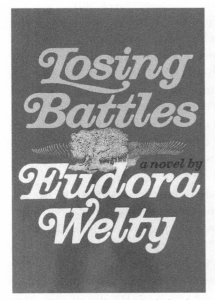

Fig. 8.3. The dust jacket for *Losing Battles* (Random House, 1970) and its version of the image.

Fig. 8.4. Here again is the tree, now realistic and eerie, on the dust jacket for the 2002 Book Club of America edition of *Losing Battles* (Random House, 1970).

Trace region as witnesses to history, an encumbered past haunted by Native Americans as well as Aaron Burr, by merchants and outlaws both. Traveling the same troubled Trace, Phoenix Jackson in Welty's "A Worn Path" reads the southern woodland's "big dead trees" as "like black men with one arm," depicting a landscape haunted by racial violence (144). Donnie McMahand and Kevin Murphy in an essay subtitled "Trees, Trespass, and Political Intelligence," illuminate those trees as "signposts of the lynched black male body, the branches rearticulating the suppressed history of southern atrocity." Reading the trees as complex, multi-vocal signifiers, they additionally interpret them as "potent life forces," and as counterposing "death and destruction" with survival and regeneration (42–43). Similarly, I read the recurring Bois d'Arc of *Losing Battles*—hidden in plain sight—as both family tree and lynching scaffold.

Another puzzle for the detective-reader is the question of why Judge Moody, who has at considerable length been precisely weighing the nuances of whether or not Jack can be prosecuted for marrying his cousin, now has absolutely nothing to say—at all—about Nathan's murder confession?

The Judge of course is not the arm of the law that arrests. That would be a local officer: marshal, justice of the peace, or sheriff. Curly Stovall is the region's marshal. Early in the novel, in connection with Jack's having comically "smothered, tied, and robbed" Curly, Cleo wonders "why . . . Stovall couldn't do his own arresting. . . . A marshal's got every right in the world and a justice of the peace is very little better than he is" (42). The justice of the peace who is apparently better charged with taking lawbreakers into custody is Homer Champion, who begrudgingly "arrested Jack, his own nephew, and then electioneered for a fresh term . . . on how bad he hated to do it." Not really a champion, Homer is an ambitious family-favoring man who nevertheless believes if it weren't for his kin pulling him down, he'd be "no telling how high up now. Maybe even sheriff" (83). These are lawmen suggestively in cahoots with Old Red (whose diabolic name could have come out of a Flannery O'Connor story), who "owns Foxtown" and "can deliver its votes" (415). They are white-town officials whose actions we would be hard pressed to identify as driven by anything but reelection calculations. Their arms of government are shown to be motivated not to serve impartial justice but more simply and entirely to "win." They judge every action by its effect on election (and I note the opposing pun on "election" in this novel so filled with religious reference). The elaborate white-male shenanigans that drive broad comedy throughout extend to government and law and are more than comic horseplay. Their concern is not for social good, not for unprejudiced administration, certainly not for Black lives, but for the clan and county votes of their very white constituencies. Note that in the final scenes of the novel, at Mortimer's funeral, Stovall and Champion suggestively gravitate toward Dearman's memorial "shaft," suggesting affiliation with his destructive force: "As though magnetized to the tallest monument in the cemetery, both Curly Stovall and Uncle Homer Champion stood at Dearman's grave, both glaring straight in front of them, both with their candidate's hats laid over their hearts. A little taller than they were, Dearman's shaft rose behind them" (428). This is surely Welty's pointed satire of Mississippi governments— written in well-timed distinction from the then-recent Civil Rights Acts of 1964, 1965, and 1968, all resisted by local Mississippi rule, but legislated as Welty wrote her book.

On the issues of whiteness, we as readers want to find Julia and the Judge better than what Moody describes as the Renfro-Beecham "pocket of igno- rance" to which he believes Julia has "maneuvered him," to show him "the root of it all, like the roots of a bad tooth" (303). Recall—as Rebecca Mark does—that in "Where Is the Voice Coming From?" (1963), Welty had a white- supremacist murderer reproach "meddlesome" institutional leaders: "Aint it about time . . . to starts to telling the teachers and the preachers and the judges of our so-called courts how far they can go?" (*CS* 607). That remark is one that we have all but heard, yet can well imagine, in the mouths of some members of the Renfro-Beecham clan. But in the murky-toned Coenesque comedy of *Losing Battles*, the teachers and the preachers and the judges are not so clearly exempt from complicity with the injustice of a Black man being convicted for a white man's crime. To that point, we should review the Judge's complete silence on hearing Nathan's confessions and assess Julia's astounding advice to Nathan to "start again, and go on your way, and be good" as possible indicators of their acceptance of atrocity and resignation to predominate white silence. This is culpable acquiescence in a country struggling mightily with the term "all" in its theoretical national principal of "liberty and justice for all."

Thinking still of the good, the bad, and the ugly, recall the surprisingly bigoted speech made by Willie Trimble, who is otherwise one of the novel's most likable characters. Irritated by the rejection of his tribute coffin, Welty has him say:

> I got it made to a T, a nice coffin, got all the way over there with it, and the crowd in the yard run me off. . . . She's already fitted, they says. Don't need any present. I thought they'd be having a fit over it and

welcome me with open arms. Seems like they opened up and got her
one in Gilfoy. It's a Jew. They don't believe in Jesus—I reckon Sunday's
just like any other day to him. (231)

The choice to heap a Jew with prejudice when expected entitlement fails is
Welty's topic here.

White acceptance of racism is thus detectible even in the novel's most
open-minded characters. Sensitive and intelligent young Vaughn, often her-
alded as the hopeful promise of a changing family future, whose stream-of-
consciousness is a lyric interlude in the novel, thinks about Nathan: "Among
all who slept here slept one who had killed a man" (365). Is it unfortunately
utterly predictable that a child in this family, even an aware and growing
one, feels his uncle has killed only one man, and not two?

When it comes to Black lives mattering then, the novel's retrogressive and
progressive characters—along with government and law at large—have been
and continue to be complicit with white prerogative. When Nathan confesses,
he shows his remorse by revealing his stump (another of those appearing
in Dearman's wake), the moral disfigurement that Nathan penitently made
visible through self-mutilation for crimes he, in a religious context at least,
recognizes as sinful: "There was good moonlight to see it by, white and clean
with its puckered stitching like a flour sack's" (344). This is noir whiteness
that Welty shines her spotlight on—the wrong so quickly passed over in
the novel. And its final judgement is left to God and the detective-reader.

I note concurrently that Nathan does not linger at the reunion this year,
but takes his departure early, saying

"Sister, I must needs not stop to take comfort."
  "You won't even stop in Banner to help bury Miss Julia Mortimer?"
  He shook his wet locks. "If the Lord has left me to outlast her, He
must want me to go my road further than I ever gone it before," he told
her, and hoisted his pack (375).

Nathan's final lines emphasize his history with Julia as well as his readiness
to flee before Judge Moody has any additional thoughts about him. Homme
fatal like the femme fatale of hard-boiled crime fiction, he has not obtained
what he desired, and yet the white male offender is ultimately left free to
wander the world. As is characteristic of Welty's puzzle-texts that repurpose
and transpose conventions, the thickening mysteries of *Losing Battles* flout
crime fiction's underlying desire for order, its closures, and even its murders

are passed by long before the novel concludes. And it is exactly that passing-over along with its racist implications that *is* the murder's reveal.

Notes

1. In "Evolving Secrets: The Patterns of Eudora Welty's Mysteries" and in "How She Wrote and How We Read: Teaching the Pleasure and Play of Welty's Modernist Techniques."

2. This is my topic in several works including the two in the above note, but foundationally in "On Welty's Use of Allusion: Expectations and Their Revision in 'The Wide Net,' *The Robber Bridegroom*, and 'At the Landing.'"

3. Throughout this essay, I have avoided revoicing the n-word, and replaced its middle letters with representative dashes.

4. For discussion of contemporary women's mysteries, see Victoria Kennedy, "'Chick Noir': Shopaholic Meets *Double Indemnity*" and Terrence Rafferty, "Women Are Writing the Best Crime Novels."

5. See Joyce and Sutton, *Domestic Noir*, on women in the noir house (viii).

6. Welty writes of her great excitement on reading *As I Lay Dying* in her December 31, 1946, correspondence to Diarmuid Russell, "All the evening we had been talking about Faulkner, Foff had lent me 'As I Lay Dying'—'My mother is a fish' is out of a Faulkner mouth, have you ever read it? I think I'll send it to you—Mod. Library seems to have got out 'As I Lay' & 'The Sound & the Fury' in one volume—It is a magnificent story—well, both are" (qtd. in Marrs 150).

7. Throughout the early twentieth century, consumers had photos turned into postcards though a process Kodak introduced in 1907. In the process, the company printed any photo on standard 3.5x 5.5 postcard backs.

8. The guilt that recurs throughout is Gloria's, Oscar Moody's, Nathan's, and the reunion's. It is also difficult to read Lexie's report of her appalling "caretaking" without picturing Welty's trepidation concerning future choices for her own ailing mother's circumstances, even as she read bits from this newly drafted work aloud to her as evening entertainment. To recall that Chestina Welty had herself once, like Mortimer, been a schoolhouse teacher in the hills of West Virginia is to sense both a daughter's tribute and her worry for time ahead, glancing through these scenes.

9. Jacob Agner in "Welty's Moonlighting Detective: Whiteness and Welty's Subversion of the American Noir Tradition in 'The Demonstrators'" has shown Welty using this moonlight noir to throw whiteness into relief.

10. Dearman's history also recalls Homer Barron's in Faulkner's "A Rose for Emily," coming to town with the construction company, building streets, courting the well-placed spinster, and getting killed.

11. See Pollack, *Eudora Welty's Fiction and Photography* and "Evolving Secrets: The Patterns of Eudora Welty's Mysteries."

12. I wish to thank Joyce Pully for this insight, who, in one of the Welty House's May through July 2020 "Welty-at-Home Book Club" discussions of the novel, modeled the

reading strategy of focusing on the novel's recurring use of this racial slur. Thanks too to all the other members of this project who, by reading together during a historic year of necessary quarantining and staying put, helped me think my way through this essay. Especially grateful for Sarah Ford and Suzanne Marrs who in postdiscussion phone calls so helpfully continued the dialog and then read this essay in early draft.

13. Credit as well as thanks to Adrienne Akins Warfield who first brought the recurring image and its possible meaning to my attention.

Works Cited

Agner, Jacob. "Welty's Moonlighting Detective: Whiteness and Welty's Subversion of the American Noir Tradition in 'The Demonstrators.'" *New Essays on Eudora Welty, Class, and Race*, edited by Harriet Pollack, UP of Mississippi, 2020, pp. 189–213.

Bunting, Charles T. "'An Interior World': An interview with Eudora Welty." *Conversations with Eudora Welty*, edited by Peggy Prenshaw, UP of Mississippi, 1984, pp. 40–63.

Faulkner, William. *Absalom, Absalom*. 1936. Modern Library, 1964.

Faulkner, William. *As I Lay Dying*. 1930. Vintage, 1957.

Ford, Sarah. "Rewriting Violence in Eudora Welty's *Losing Battles*." *Mississippi Quarterly*, vol. 54, no. 1, winter 2000–01, pp. 23–36.

Joyce, Laura, and Henry Sutton, editors. *Domestic Noir: The New Face of 21st Century Crime Fiction*. Palgrave Macmillan, 2018.

Kennedy, Victoria. "'Chick Noir': Shopaholic Meets *Double Indemnity*." *American, British, Canadian Studies*, vol. 28, 2017, pp. 19–38.

Mark, Rebecca. "Cross-mark Ploughed into the Center: Civil Rights and Eudora Welty's *Losing Battles*." *Eudora Welty and Politics: Did the Writer Crusade?*, edited by Harriet Pollack and Suzanne Marrs, Louisiana State UP, 2001, pp. 123–54.

Marrs, Suzanne. *Eudora Welty: A Biography*. Harcourt, 2005.

McMahand, Donnie, and Kevin Murphy. "The Lynched Earth: Trees, Trespass, and Political Intelligence in Welty's 'A Worn Path' and Morrison's *Home*." *New Essays on Eudora Welty, Class and Race*, edited by Harriet Pollack, UP of Mississippi, 2020, pp. 35–36.

Peters, Fiona. "The Literary Antecedents of Domestic Noir." *Domestic Noir: The New Face of 21st Century Crime*, edited by Laura Joyce and Henry Sutton, Palgrave, 2018, pp. 11–25.

Pollack, Harriet. *Eudora Welty's Fiction and Photography: The Body of the Other Woman*, U of Georgia P, 2016.

Pollack, Harriet. "Evolving Secrets: The Patterns of Eudora Welty's Mysteries." *Detecting the South in Fiction, Film, and Television*, edited by Deborah Barker and Theresa Stuckey, UP of Mississippi, 2019, pp. 142–59.

Pollack, Harriet. "How She Wrote and How We Read: Teaching the Pleasure and Play of Welty's Modernist Techniques." *Teaching the Works of Eudora Welty: 21st-Century Approaches*, edited by Julia Eichelberger & Mae Miller Claxton, UP Mississippi, 2018, pp. 24–31.

Pollack, Harriet. "On Welty's Use of Allusion: Expectations and Their Revision in 'The Wide Net,' *The Robber Bridegroom*, and 'At the Landing.'" *The Southern Quarterly*, Fall 1990, 5–33/*Eudora Welty (Bloom's BioCritique Series)*, edited by Harold Bloom, Chelsea

House Publications, 2004, 113–40/ *The Past Is Not Dead: Essays from the Southern Quarterly*, UP of Mississippi, 2012, pp. 183–207.

Rafferty, Terrence. "Women Are Writing the Best Crime Novels." *The Atlantic*, July–Aug. 2016, www.theatlantic.com/magazine/archive/2016/07/women-are-writing-the-best-crime-novels/485576/.

Rountree, Stephanie. "'Visible, Unfamiliar, Remarkable': Private Bodies and Public Policy in Eudora Welty's *Losing Battles*." *south: a scholarly journal*, vol. 48, no. 2, spring 2016, pp. 225–45.

Rzepka, Charles J. *Detective Fiction*. Polity Press, 2005.

Smith, Murray. "Film Noir, The Female Gothic, and *Deception*." *Wide Angle*, vol. 10, no. 1, 1988, pp. 62–75.

Trethewey, Natasha. *Domestic Work*. Graywolf Press, 2000.

Welty, Eudora. *The Collected Stories of Eudora Welty*. Harcourt Brace, 1980.

Welty, Eudora. *Losing Battles*. Random House, 1970.

Welty, Eudora. *One Writer's Beginnings*. Harvard UP, 1984.

Welty, Eudora. *The Robber Bridegroom*. 1942. Atheneum, 1978.

UNSOLVED MYSTERIES

Reading Eudora Welty's *The Optimist's Daughter* with Agatha Christie's *The Body in the Library*

SARAH GILBREATH FORD

In Eudora Welty's 1972 novel, *The Optimist's Daughter*, a dead body lies in the library. A group of mourners trade stories and gossip until the wife of the deceased man enters the company and puts on a grand performance of grief. When she is later congratulated, however, for the wealth she has now inherited, she responds, "I think things have gone off real well" (940). The daughter of the deceased man heard that same woman (her stepmother) physically attack her ailing father in the hospital before his death and wonders if she has enough evidence to get a verdict. Add to this plot a group of gossiping women who speculate about the deceased man's scandalous marriage to this much younger woman, a next-door neighbor who may have been in love with him, and a gathering of characters from different social classes in a confined space, and you have all the ingredients of a classic country house murder mystery novel.

The recipe for this familiar genre was concocted by Agatha Christie, a writer Welty remarks was "endlessly diverting to me" (*Meanwhile* 166). The proof that Welty was indeed an avid reader of her work can be found in Welty's house, which contains no less than nineteen books by Christie.[1] Christie's diverting books were products of the "Golden Age" of the detective story between World War I and II. Although the detective story was "invented" in the early nineteenth century by Edgar Allan Poe and was further developed into its generic form in the late-nineteenth century by Sir Arthur Conan Doyle, the genre became truly popular in the aftermath of World War I. Edmund Wilson in his 1944 essay "Why Do People Read Detective Stories?" explains that the world "was ridden by an all-pervasive feeling of guilt and a fear of impending disaster which it seemed hopeless to try to avert because it never seemed conclusively possible to pin down the responsibility." While a tale of murder might seem an odd mechanism for relieving fear, the murder mystery's offers of a solution to a crime and a clear villain to blame fit the needs of the time period perfectly. Paul Grimstad explains that even the high modernist T. S. Eliot found in detective fiction a "pleasing orderliness"; Eliot valued that "ghastly disruptions [were] restored to equilibrium with the soothing predictability of ritual."

Key to the generic trappings of a Golden Age detective story is the device of the closed society, which functions, as W. H. Auden explains, "so that the possibility of an outside murderer (and hence of the society being totally innocent) is excluded." Instead, the stories depict "a closely related society so that all its members are potentially suspect" (407). In many of her books, Christie relies on the confines of a country house to assemble her group of suspects. To explore how Welty borrows the framework of a country house murder mystery, I will be referencing Christie's 1942 novel *The Body in the Library*, a book Michael Cook describes as "one of the quintessential texts of the Golden Age, so redolent of its genre that it has acquired a metonymical relationship with the classic detective story" (43). In Christie's foreword, she admits that the plot device of "the body in the library" was already a recognized cliché when she wrote the book. In the first pages of her narrative, in fact, the wealthy library owners, the Bantrys, are incredulous that an event that supposedly "only happened in books" has now happened to them. The plot device works because the library setting heightens the shock value of a murdered corpse within the seemingly incongruous space of a sedate, book-filled room in a supposedly quiet country house.

The impact of the library setting yields an even greater jolt, as Christie explains, if the body is "wildly improbable and highly sensational" (vii). Cook points out that the library signals the "social privilege" of the country house's occupants, so the appearance of a lower-class character's body adds tension. In Christie's novel the body is that of a "cheap, tawdry, flamboyant figure," a thin, fair-haired girl in a backless "spangled" evening dress, heavy makeup, and fingernails "enameled in a deep blood-red" (11). Rather than showing concern for the death of the poor girl, Mrs. Bantry initially proclaims it all "rather thrilling" because if "one has got to have a murder actually happening in one's house, one might as well enjoy it" (8). The neighborhood gossips, though, are soon wondering with obvious innuendo about Mr. Bantry's connection to the victim. Mrs. Bantry protests that her husband "isn't like that" (44). He only gets a "little silly about pretty girls," and, after all, she has her own interests: "I've got the garden" (45). Judge McKelva and Fay's relationship in *The Optimist's Daughter* echoes this eyebrow-lifting pattern

of older man/younger woman, and Christie's description of the "tawdry" figure perfectly fits Fay. Although the positions are reversed in Welty's text,
with the older patriarch dead and the younger woman the object of suspicion, the narrative positions his dead body conspicuously in the library. I
will argue that in *The Optimist's Daughter* Welty borrows the dynamics of
the classic murder mystery formula with its heightened attention to social
tensions in a confined environment to explore the problematic connections
of marriage, property, and class.

With the encircling library signaling metafictional space, Welty then conducts a genre-bending exercise. After evoking a murder mystery plot that
promises a simple solution, the text veers from this narrative line. The mystery of the judge's death remains unsolved as his daughter Laurel ultimately
decides to employ a different genre to think about her father's death. While
Laurel initially plays detective by searching for clues in both of her parents'
desks, the all-important texts she finds are not, in the detective tradition of
Edgar Allan Poe, purloined objects that only need to be located for a narrative to be complete. Instead, I argue that the texts are read, bringing Laurel's
parents back to life. Eschewing the easy clarity and finality of a classic detective story, the novel's genre bending reveals a valuing of complexity and the
abiding mysteries of character.

LET'S PLAY CLUE: HOW TO LOCATE A SUSPECT

To posit that a body is murdered, a narrative must have a murderer, a nefari-
ous individual clever enough to contrive a plot and immoral enough to see it
through. In the case of *The Optimist's Daughter*, the obvious suspect should
be Fay because she is the dubious outsider who has married into an upper-
class family. Yet Fay appears too superficial and silly to be a criminal master-
mind. Cleanth Brooks calls her a "shallow, little vulgarian," while Thomas H.
Landess labels her "both vulgar and selfish" (227, 550).[2] The narrator describes
her as a kind of innocent: "perhaps" forty but with hair of a "childish tow"
and "round, country-blue eyes" (897). Major Bullock declares her to be "the
helpless kind," and Missouri describes her as Judge McKelva's "somebody
to spoil" (914, 917). Even Laurel, when thinking about Fay's violence at one
point, portrays her as childishly ignorant: "Fay didn't know what she was
doing" (963). The text seems to portray Fay as effectively inconsequential
and lacking the intelligence to plot a murder.

Other critics argue that although her character appears shallow, Fay's
otherness impacts Laurel positively. Robert H. Brinkmeyer, Jr. finds that in

opposition to Laurel's "rigid refusal to embrace a joyful openness to experience embodied in the carnival spirit," Fay has "carnivalesque power" (432,
437).[3] Rebecca Mark argues that Welty writes Fay as a "regenerative character," who causes Laurel to look "deeply" at her parents' lives (334). Dawn
Trouard finds Fay's reactions to be both "funny and true" and is confident
that Fay will "arrange to be happy beyond Mt. Salus" (240). These critics'
readings of her as a positive, rebellious spirit make Fay appear even less
suspicious. If a murderer must be both clever and bad, Fay seems neither.
However, paying attention to what Fay does instead of what the community
says about her might result in yet a different Fay—one who is, as Welty
herself pronounced, "evil" (*Conversations* 227).

Consider: What Fay does is marry a lonely widower of means, allowing
her to quit her day job as a typist and to sleep late every morning in a bed
swathed in peach satin until the servant brings her breakfast. The other
characters are so concerned with why Judge McKelva would marry the lowly
Fay that they do not bother to talk about why she married him. Miss Tennyson proclaims, "we all knew exactly what the sort of thing *was* that Fay'd
be good for" (949). Judge McKelva marries Fay because he is, in Miss Adele's
estimation, "a lonely old man" (953). Fay provides him company and sex, but
Laurel's friends do not explicitly name what Fay receives in return: money.
Apparently Fay's low-class status makes pondering this question unneces-
sary, but the characters in Christie's novel are more blunt about class issues.
When Christie's detectives shift from investigating the Bantrys to suspecting
the Jeffersons, a family whose members knew the dead girl, they discover
that the elderly Mr. Jefferson had changed his will to leave £50,000 to the
now-murdered girl. In exchange for being a companion to Mr. Jefferson in
his old age, the girl could drastically improve her life circumstances. The
other characters do not, however, look on this relationship favorably, and
three times various characters declare that the girl was a "common or garden
gold-digger" (104).

Marrying a man thirty years her senior suggests Fay may be one as well.
She certainly shows no emotion for her husband. When Judge McKelva explains that the onset of his vision problems came while he was pruning roses,
Fay interjects with a laugh "as derisive as a jay's" (884). Dr. Courtland's comment, "Yes, that's disturbing," could be in response to the judge's eye problem
or to Fay's inappropriate reaction. Told that her husband needs surgery, Fay
exclaims, "I don't see why this had to happen to *me*," and during his hospital
stay seems most concerned that she is missing Mardi Gras: "What a way to
keep his promise. When he told me he'd bring me to New Orleans some
day, it was to see the Carnival" (886, 889). She even sees the judge's death

in selfish terms, complaining that the doctor "picked my birthday" to let the judge die (907).[4] Fay's callousness towards Judge McKelva is clear, and she is indeed reborn on the day of his death because she has succeeded in becoming a new person: a widow of means.

To be a convincing suspect, however, Fay must have the opportunity to commit the crime. Marrying Judge McKelva and then ridding herself of him requires her to operate without supervision. Laurel remembers that when she came home for their wedding, Fay greeted her with marked animosity: "It wasn't any use in you bothering to come so far" (898). She repeats this sentiment daily at the hospital (898). After the doctor tells Laurel and Fay that they need to take alternating shifts watching the patient to make sure he remains still, Fay tells Laurel again, "No point in you staying just because the doctor said so" (891). With Laurel hovering, Fay is not free to do as she pleases.

When it seems clear that Fay is saddled with an invalid who cannot provide her with the good life, though, she dares to make her move. Because Laurel has a premonition and comes to the hospital during Fay's shift, Laurel unexpectedly witnesses Fay's actions. Earlier the nurse had warned Fay: "Don't go near that eye, hon! Don't nobody touch him or monkey with that eye of his, and don't even touch the bed he's on, till Dr. Courtland says touch, or somebody'll be mighty sorry" (891). On this night, however, as Laurel approaches her father's room, she hears Fay's declaration: "I tell you enough is enough!" and then sees the nurse struggling to pull Fay off of Judge McKelva. The nurse's accusation of Fay's assault is clear: "She laid hands on him! She said if he didn't snap out of it, she'd—. . . . She taken ahold of him. She was abusing him" (901).[5] The doctor rushes into the room only to declare the man dead. If Fay's attack is merely a childish, unpremeditated tantrum, it is odd that she times it for exactly when Laurel should not be there to protect her father. Is Fay's timing coincidence or calculation? That she is capable of violence is confirmed at the funeral when she "struck out with her hands, hitting at Major Bullock and Mr. Pitts and Sis, fighting her mother, too, for a moment. She showed her claws at Laurel" (934–5). Her sister tries to warn everyone: "she bites" (935).[6]

Everyone ignores the warning, continuing to posit Fay as lacking in class but essentially harmless. Her tackiness, though, hides her threat, as the other characters assume that members of their class, including the esteemed judge, could not be harmed by someone of such little consequence as Fay. In her characterization, the novel echoes a sister genre to the detective story, film noir, as Fay plays the role of femme fatale.[7] Helen Hanson and Catherine O'Rawe explain that although the femme fatale is best known from films (Phyllis Dietrichson in *Double Indemnity* and Cora Smith in *The Postman*

Always Rings Twice), the character's place in Western literature is indeed much older and broader (2). The classic femme fatale's beauty hides her menace. Mary Ann Doane explains that her "most striking characteristic, perhaps, is the fact that she never really is what she seems to be. She harbors a threat which is not entirely legible, predictable, or manageable" (1). The young, petite, blond Fay displays this requisite mixing of beauty and peril, and her opaque quality renders her unreadable to the other characters, thus masking her danger. Her tendency to strike out and bite indicates her willingness to do what she has to do to get what she wants when she has the opportunity.

What she wants, i.e., her motive, is yet a different question. Joan Acocella asserts that the most common motive in Christie's sixty-six mystery novels is money, and indeed the two classic motives in murder mysteries are money and love (85). The novel explores both, in scenes that occur in the McKelva home. In constructing these scenes, Welty borrows from the mystery genre the closed circle: an isolated setting that gathers all the main characters in one place and then turns up the heat.[8] For Christie's works, the closed circle uncovers tensions over class differences, marriage, and property.[9] In *The Body in the Library*, in addition to the concerns over Mr. Jefferson's will, another plot thread involves a young movie executive who lives near the Bantrys, playing the nouveau riche to their established upper class. Since the characters declare their town "such an unlikely place" for a murder, they imagine that this outsider, Basil Blake, could be "the only possible explanation," so they discuss his wild parties with "the most *terrible* noise" and women "with practically *nothing on!*" (16). The angst about Jefferson's choice to leave money to Ruby in addition to Basil Blake's disturbing parties reveals one frequent engine driving mystery novels, the fear over who is crossing class lines. In fact, the classic aha moment of "the butler did it" indicates not just plausible opportunity as butlers hover in the background, but the radical violating of class lines when a servant would dare to kill an employer.

In Welty's novel, if Fay evidences no emotion for Judge McKelva and only marries him to share his money, then it is plausible she kills him so she can have it to herself. After his death, she appears especially attuned to her inheritance.[10] When Fay and Laurel arrive at the McKelva house after the judge's death to find several townspeople there, Fay asks, "What are all these people doing in my house?" immediately declaring her new ownership of property (913). She reiterates her claim when complaining about Laurel's friends: "And who's making themselves at home in my parlor?" (914). Major Bullock, in imagining Fay as a "poor little girl," assures her, "I reckon you know you *get* the house and everything in it you want" (94). Fay, however, is already well aware: "I sure do know whose house this is" (940).

Fay's desire to claim sole ownership of this property explains her odd behavior to her own family. When Fay's family arrives from Texas, their lower-class manners immediately distinguish them from the McKelvas' friends. After they barge into the house, Mama Chisom is uncouth enough to comment aloud on the costliness of the coffin: "A grand coffin my little girl's afforded" (922). Moreover, only a minute into her conversation with Laurel, Mama Chisom has the temerity to remark that Laurel "ain't got father, mother, brother, sister, husband, chick nor child" (923). The Chisom family's coarse manners provide a stark contrast to the genteel denizens of Mount Salus, and the closed circle heightens the class tensions.[11] Fay, however, is notably bothered by her family's presence. She had earlier told Laurel at the hospital that she had no family: "None of 'em living" (898). When she sees them, she cries, "Get back!—Who told *them* to come?" (934). Her distress stems from their threat to ruin her plan to be the sole proprietor of the judge's property. When Bubba Chisom remarks, "Wanda Fay, you got enough stuff in sight to last one lone woman forever," Fay agrees that "I think things have gone off real well," clearly indicating her motives but also her intention to remain "lone" (940). Later, the family becomes more direct, with her mother asking, "who're you ever going to get to put in this house besides you?" and announcing, "there's room for the whole nation of *us* here" (941). To head them off, Fay announces that she wants to ride back to Texas with them for a visit.

Even if Fay's acquisition of property is not her primary motive but just a "happy" consequence of her husband's death, an alternative motive might be the problems evident in her marriage. Although the town describes a relationship where the elder man "doted" on his young wife by, for example, taking her out to eat on Sundays when the cook had the day off, other clues suggest that he might have been controlling or even demanding (947). When Judge McKelva tells the doctor about first noticing his eye malady, he was standing "at the end of my front porch there, with an eye on the street—Fay had slipped out somewhere" (884). He is watching as if she has escaped the house when she was not supposed to leave. As he says this, the narrator notes that Judge McKelva "bent on her his benign smile that looked so much like a scowl" (884).[12] When Fay later shows off her green stilettos, she remarks, "But just let me try slipping *out* in 'em, would he ever let me hear about it!" (28). The money gained by associating with a wealthy man seems to have a corresponding cost in the loss of autonomy. In *A Body in the Library*, Mr. Jefferson likewise tries to control his proposed ward, forbidding her to associate with young men and requiring her to obtain "education and polishing" (69). While Fay could be just teasing Judge McKelva about his controlling behavior, when she claims in response to hearing his "grinding and gnashing his teeth," "That's only the way he wakes up . . . I get it every morning" (890), and later when she responds to Laurel waking her up with, "Oh no, no, not any more!" (910), these clues suggest a darker element of their marriage: Judge McKelva's demands for her sexual attention and Fay's desire to be rid of them.

The closed circle gathering intensifies the spotlight on their marital problems. When Fay comes downstairs and sees his body in the coffin, she screams, "Why was he so *bad*? Why did he do me so *bad*?" (935) She then twice asserts that he was "unfair" to her, though these comments are couched by "Oh, Judge, how could you go off and leave me this way?" (934), suggesting it was unfair of him to die and leave her grieving. However, she then exclaims, "You cheated on me!" (934). While she may be indicating that he cheated by dying, "cheated" could also mean that he was somehow unfaithful to her. Instead of a complaint about his dying, it might be a revelation of their marital problems and her motive for killing him. The question is, with whom did he "cheat?"

One possibility hinted at in the text is the next-door neighbor Adele, who is ever-present, offering to help Judge McKelva prune his first wife's rose bushes and taking the agency to wash and put away the dishes "in their right places" because she is that familiar with the house (915). When Laurel looks out a window and sees Adele at her clothesline, she realizes her father could have watched Adele. Although Adele's automatic "wave toward the window" was "beckoning," Laurel, perhaps wanting to think the best of people, imagines that her father "looked out at her without ever seeing her" (956). The community certainly would have preferred this relationship to Judge McKelva's marriage to Fay. Miss Tennyson claims that if she had known he "was casting around for somebody to take Becky's place, I could've found him one a whole lot better than Fay," seemingly indicating Adele's feelings for him (953). Adele then deflects this attention, but whether she is embarrassed that she was not his choice or guilty because she was is not clear. When Laurel protests at the funeral that her father would never stand for lies being told about him, Adele counters with "Yes he would. If the truth might hurt the wrong person" (933). Although hints about their relationship remain only innuendo, Welty herself comments that "the unspoken attachment Miss Adele Courtland has long cherished for the Judge makes itself as strongly felt in the room as Fay's throwing herself upon his coffined body" (*Occasions* 310).

A different possibility for the infidelity Fay alludes to might be that Judge McKelva was *not* looking to replace Becky, and his continued feelings for his first wife provide Fay's complaint that he "cheated." That Judge McKelva's eye problems began when he was taking care of Becky's roses suggests that his feelings for her are likewise alive. Fay dismisses the connection: "One of those briars might have given you a scratch, hon, but it didn't leave a thorn" (884). She then complains, "Why did he have to go back there anyway and get mixed up in those brambles?" (884–85). The persistence of the "old roses" that Fay wants to "go on and die" indicates that she sees Becky as a continuing threat. Laurel recalls that Fay had "once at least called Becky 'my rival'" (976). Judge McKelva even forgets that Becky is dead when he wakes up from surgery, asking Laurel, "What's your mother have to say about me?" (890).[13] Laurel obviously has a biased view of her father's feelings, but her assessment that "He loved my mother" in response to Fay's complaining that Judge McKelva was "so *bad*" to her appears to be true (936, 935).

Between the potential problems in her marriage and her desire for property, Fay therefore has the two clichéd motives of love and money to kill the judge. To make sure that Laurel does not suspect her, however, she has to cover up the crime. She first deflects her actions by focusing on the doctor as the source of blame. When Dr. Courtland announces that Judge McKelva is dead, he adds, "and his eye was healing," suggesting that it was not the eye surgery or by extension the surgeon who caused his death. Fay, however, answers, "Are you trying to tell me you let my husband die?" (906). She asserts that her husband's eye did not even need surgery, that "he just took a scratch from an old rose briar," subtly blaming the doctor and Becky together (907). Fay then performs grief in that closed circle context to make it appear that she cared. She waits until everyone is in attendance and then "burst from the hall into the parlor" running towards the coffin. She shouts at the dead body about unfairness and cheating and has to be "dragged back" from the coffin. That she is simply performing is obvious; Miss Adele says that Fay acts "the most broken-hearted, most distraught behavior she could manage on the part of the widow" (949). When Fay's mother comments on the money that Fay spends on the funeral and the casket, Fay confesses, "It was no bargain, and I think that showed" (95). The show is what is crucial to counteract any suspicion.

LET'S PLAY DETECTIVE: HOW TO ASSESS THE CLUES

With a dead body in the library and a widow more interested in her inheritance than her grief, Laurel's suspects foul play. To complete Welty's mimicking of the murder mystery, Laurel takes on the role of detective, looking for clues that would lead to a legal consequence for her father's death. In doing so, Laurel follows in the footsteps of detectives from Poe's C. Auguste Dupin to Doyle's Sherlock Holmes, but the detective she most closely resembles is Christie's Miss Marple. While Laurel is not exactly a spinster sleuth, she sees herself as isolated in pursuing clues to the truth, as Miss Marple often proves to be when the official police follow other and ultimately false leads. In *A Body in the Library* Miss Marple, for example, quickly rules out the young, wealthy Basil Blake. Beatrix M. Brockman explains that Miss Marple's status as "spinster" results in other characters "mocking" the sleuth because she falls outside of social norms, which then only helps to hide her cleverness (32). A widow, Laurel might seem to be in a different category, but throughout the novel, the other characters remark on her odd separateness, both as a single woman and as an emigrant from their town. They even ask her to stay in Mount Salus because they imagine that she can have "no other life" (951). As single and now as an outsider, Laurel is perfectly positioned to play detective.

In hoping for a legal trajectory, Laurel sees her father's lawyer friends at the gathering at the McKelva house sitting "together on a row of dining room chairs" as "some form of jury" (926). In that confined space, where they are "being egged on a little bit," as Adele notices, by the "rivalry" with the Chisom family, those friends tell stories about the judge's life that Laurel knows are not true (932). Unlike the courtroom's exposure of fact, the funeral setting elicits exaggeration, as the townspeople aim to honor the judge's life. Major Bullock, for example, tells a story of the judge standing up to the "White Caps" (the KKK) and telling them, "Back to your holes, rats" (931). Laurel responds that they are making him into "a crusader. And an angel on the face of the earth" and in the process "misrepresenting him—falsifying" (932, 933). In response, Laurel "might have been trying to testify now for her father's life" (83). If she is alone in wanting to tell a more honest version of his life, she becomes even more isolated in her knowledge of his death. She considers revealing what she already knows: "I saw Fay come out into the open. Why, it would stand up in court!" (963). Though she thinks that she "had the proof, the damnable evidence," she guesses that Fay would deny the incident and simply respond, "I don't even know what you're talking about" (963). In fact, all that Laurel has is her own eyewitness testimony. She needs more evidence.

Laurel looks in the prime place for clues in mystery novels: the victim's desk. Often among the papers and letters hidden in drawers or cubby holes is the key to solving a murder. In Christie's *The Mysterious Affair at Styles* (1920), for example, Hercule Poirot finds a writing case with letters and the fragments of a will, suggesting that a potential change of someone's fortune was the motive for murder. Laurel examines her father's desk only to find it is empty and that someone has "been here ahead of her" (957). Instead of letters and documents, she finds "vermillion drops of hardened stuff on the dark wood—not sealing wax; nail polish" (957). She knows, of course, that these drops are evidence of Fay's presence and her disregard for the family's heirlooms. The drops of polish, however, further signify fingerprints: "They made a little track toward the chair, as if Fay had walked her fingers over the desk from where she'd sat perched on its corner, doing her nails" (957). Fay blatantly leaves her mark in the very place where clues live.

Despite these clues, Laurel decides not to be a Poirot or Marple. She realizes that she has her father's "memory to protect," and asserting that his wife killed him would highlight the judge's faulty judgment (962). His marriage to the younger woman has already made her family the subject of town gossip. If Laurel is to protect her father's poor judgment from even more exposure, she has to stay quiet about Fay's violent act. After the funeral while Laurel is tending to her mother's garden, her friends discuss Fay's scene at the funeral, questioning yet again the Judge's discernment. Laurel remains silent during the entire conversation, refusing to take part until finally commanded to by the bossy Miss Tennyson, "Well, answer!" (950). Laurel exclaims, "I hope I never see [Fay] again" (950). Wishing Fay out of her life is the most that Laurel can do and remain loyal to her father. And to her mother as well, since acknowledging Fay may have abused her father would also confirm the harm the judge did to her mother's memory in remarrying such an inappropriate person. Laurel furthermore realizes that revealing her suspicions about Fay would probably not have the effect she desires anyway. In concert with the other characters, she reads Fay as too ignorant to understand her actions; she thinks that Fay "never dreamed" she had done something wrong (963). Although Laurel does not want "punishment" for Fay, only an "admission," she knows that she will never get it.

Laurel's guilt, however, for keeping Fay's crime secret remains, and Laurel knows that "to be released is to tell, unburden it" (963). The only person Laurel wants to tell is her mother because only her mother would understand Laurel's devastation in the face of Fay's crime: "She had the proof, the damnable evidence ready for her mother, and was in anguish because she could not give it to her, and so be herself consoled" (963). But then Laurel imagines what horror she would be giving her mother by exposing the true nature of the judge's second marriage. In confronting her own selfishness, Laurel realizes, "The scene she had just imagined, herself confiding the abuse to her mother, and confiding it in all tenderness, was a more devastating one than all Fay had acted out in the hospital" (963). Laurel gives up her investigation into her father's death, and the text drops its murder mystery scaffolding.

Welty thus borrows the closed-circle setting, provides possible motives, and dangles clues such as the drops of nail polish, only to alter the narrative line, eschewing the expected grand revelation. Without a "*j'accuse*" moment, the text forgoes the particular pleasure provided by the classic detective story. Edmund Wilson describes the typical reaction: "Nobody seems guilt-less, nobody seems safe; and then, suddenly, the murderer is spotted, and—relief!—he is not, after all, a person like you or me. He is a villain—known to the trade as George Gruesome—and he has been caught by an infallible Power, the supercilious and omniscient detective, who knows exactly how to fix the guilt." Although Laurel wants to blame Fay, she resists the tempta-tion of pointing to a clear and easy villain. In contrast, Miss Marple in *The Body in the Library* discovers a villain by figuring out that the body in that library is only disguised as Mr. Jefferson's ward but is another girl altogether, a discovery she makes because of the girl's bitten-off fingernails. Once the timelines of both girls' deaths are corrected, Miss Marple asserts the correct killer as Mr. Jefferson's son-in-law, who wanted the ward out of the way so that he would inherit all of the family money. The crime is solved, Miss Marple saves the day, and order is restored. No such luck for Welty's characters. Although Laurel asks, "What would I not do, perpetrate, she wondered, for consolation," she will not pursue the answer to her father's death, even if that answer would provide much-needed relief (963).

GENRE BENDING: WHAT STORY TO TELL?

With Laurel's decision to stop playing detective, the novel engages in genre bending, as Welty subverts the murder mystery genre by bending its line to go another direction. This turn is indicated by a question that eventually supersedes the question of the judge's death: what book should Laurel read? To understand how reading becomes the primary concern, we need to attend once again to that trope of the body in the library. In murder mystery nar-ratives, the library setting is a metafictional wink to the reader, as bodies are "killed" by authors through the words in their books. As Michael Cook observes, the reader of detective fiction parallels the detective in "reading the clues" (44). Cook explains that this "self-reflexive" bent to the murder mystery had its beginning in the work of the nineteenth-century American writer Anna Katharine Green, a favorite of Christie's (44). The metafictional play then extends all the way to contemporary works, such as Umberto Eco's 1980 novel, *The Name of the Rose*, and Elizabeth Kostova's 2005 novel, *The*

Historian. In *The Optimist's Daughter*, however, the metafiction turns on itself, as the question becomes whether the mystery genre proves adequate in shaping the experience of death. When Laurel reads the clues to ascertain a definitive answer, she realizes that she is attempting to put a too-neat narrative frame on the messiness of her experience. In ceasing to build upon the initial mystery genre scaffolding, *The Optimist's Daughter* thus offers a doubling: the story itself and the story of how to tell the story.

That all-important question of what to read begins at the hospital. With her father unable to move for days, Laurel tries to entertain him: "He'd loved being read to, once. With good hopes, she brought in a stack of paperbacks and began on the newest of his favorite detective novelist. He listened without much comment. She went back to one of the old ones they'd both admired, and he listened with greater quiet. Pity stabbed her. Did they *move too fast* for him now?" (893). Even before witnessing Fay's abuse and Judge McKelva's resulting death, Laurel injects the genre of the detective novel into the atmosphere of the hospital room; she is therefore primed to shape Fay's actions as part of some murder mystery. She does not understand, however, her father's denial of that genre, guessing that his lack of attention derives from his infirmity. She next tries to read him *Nicholas Nickleby,* a book "she had the luck to detect" in a store. In having to "detect" the novel, she is already playing the role of Miss Marple. Judge McKelva, though, still does not seem to listen, so Laurel begins reading the book silently beside him during her watch, an agreement she imagines "arranged between them, without words" (897). Thus added to Laurel's angst about what book would appeal to her father is this silence, which strikes against the heart of her identity as a daughter because she remembers her parents at night "reading to each other where she could hear them, never letting a silence divide or interrupt them, combined into one unceasing voice, and wrapped her around as she listened" (916). It is as if the words they read together construct their family as well as Laurel's dreams: "She was sent to sleep under a velvety cloak of words, richly patterned and stitched with gold, straight out of a fairy tale, while they went reading on into her dreams" (917).

Laurel does not rethink her presumption about her father's silence until the funeral. When Adele tries to tell her that Judge McKelva would understand the community's need to exaggerate in their tales about him, Laurel answers, "I'm his daughter. I want what people say now to be the truth" (933). At this moment, though, she looks at her father's library, the "two loaded bookcases" and the "shelf-load of Gibbon stretched like a sagging sash across one of them," and has an epiphany: "She had not read her father the book he'd wanted after all. The wrong book! The wrong book!" (933).

Laurel's exclamation that she has read the "wrong book" has led several critics to wonder about the problem of reading *Nicholas Nickleby*.[14] Leslie Harris argues that Laurel's "realization that she should have read Gibbon rather than Dickens to her father during his last illness illustrates her preference for the factual order of history to the fluidity of fiction, whether Dickens' fiction or Mt. Salus' fictionalized biography" (35). Although Harris's argument benefits from the context of the community's falsehoods, I read the reference to Edward Gibbon's *The History of the Decline and Fall of the Roman Empire* not as the correct answer to what Laurel should have read, but as simply more of the same problem: "She was looking at her own mistake, and its long shadow reaching back to join the others" (933). "The others" suggests that all of the books on the shelves are wrong, including Gibbon's.

What is wrong with these books becomes clearer the day after the funeral, when everyone but Laurel has gone, and she "faced the library" (954). As she sees individual titles next to each other on the bookshelves, she again thinks of reading as constructing her family: "Shoulder to shoulder, they had long since made their own family. For every book here she had heard their voices, father's and mother's" (955). She sees Tennyson, *Jane Eyre*, the Webster's dictionary and the Bible along with an entire set of Dickens, the aforementioned Gibbon, and the Mississippi Law Code.[15] Many of the books are canonical works from fiction or history, but the problem with all of them is that they do not give her an adequate way of constructing her father's death. Even the ones that offer "truth" in objective form do not give her the truth she seeks. In examining the Gibbon's history of Rome, Laurel realizes that it "was not sacrosanct: *The Adventures of Sherlock Holmes* looked out from between two volumes" (955). This amusing image of Holmes interrupting history at first appears to augment Welty's use of the murder mystery to frame her novel, as the fellow detective's appearance indicates that there is indeed something to detect. Laurel's response, though, reveals her growing suspicion of concrete answers, the kind a history like Gibbon's offers or that a master detective like Sherlock Holmes always presumes to provide. Instead of opening these books to read them, she dusts them off and puts them back "in the same order," thus keeping Holmes in his spot, suggesting that his narrative belongs with those of history. None of these books are what she needs to read. Dismissing these genres, she moves on in search of other possibilities.

Although Laurel had never "thought of opening [her father's desk] in her life," now that he is dead, she needs to find traces of him; she is looking specifically for texts. Her search, though, is in vain: "She opened the drawers one after the other on both sides of the huge desk: they had been cleaned out. Someone had, after all, been here ahead of her" (957). Still in detective mode,

Laurel suggests that "someone" had been careful to discard all evidence of wrongdoing, and when she consequently notices the drops of nail polish, Laurel can place the blame on her preferred target of Fay. Twice Laurel asks, "Where were the letters?" (957). She knows that her mother had written to her father every day that they were apart, and Laurel thinks through the various times that this was the case, from her father's business trips to her mother's trips back home to Virginia. Although Laurel does concede that they could have just been "put away somewhere," she is still momentarily suspicious about their absence.

Missing letters are yet another cliché of the mystery genre, originating in one of the first detective stories, Edgar Allan Poe's "The Purloined Letter" (1844). In Poe's foundational story, the Paris police request the assistance of C. Auguste Dupin in locating a letter stolen by Minister D from the apartment of a royal lady. Dupin famously finds the letter when the police are unable to do so because he looks for it "hidden" in plain sight. This story not only helped launch the detective genre; it became a favorite target of twentieth-century literary theorists, particularly Jacques Lacan, who in his "Seminar on 'The Purloined Letter'" (1952) uses Poe's text to forward his theories of psychoanalysis. In focusing on the power relationships between the characters in the story, Lacan argues that the letter is a "pure signifier," meaning that it exists only to point to meaning outside itself (the "signified") (32). Joel Black further explains this reasoning: "The mystery has nothing to do with the letter's content, which is not disclosed in the story, remains unknown to the reader, and must therefore be assumed to be irrelevant to the tale" (75). I have argued elsewhere that in a subsequent scene of *The Optimist's Daughter*, Welty rewrites Poe's poem "The Raven" by having Laurel trapped in a house late at night in a storm with a bird tapping on the door. Although Welty may not be specifically rewriting "The Purloined Letter" in this scene with her father's desk, the novel certainly plays with the trope that Poe's story initiates.

In Welty's genre bending, however, the detective narrative overlay fails in *The Optimist's Daughter* for two reasons. On a basic level, Laurel remembers that her father did not keep letters: "He'd never kept them: Laurel knew it and should have known it to start with" (957). Laurel does not think of this immediately because she still has those detective lenses on, positing her father's death as a murder and Fay as culprit. But Laurel "had seen him" drop letters into the trash as soon as he read them, so there is in fact no mystery. A second reason proves more significant. Unlike Dupin in Poe's story, Laurel does not imagine letters as empty signifiers whose possession will give her power. Welty's novel thus reveals a different trajectory of significance than

Lacan's for language that is lost and found. Laurel actually wants to read the letters, and it is the move from her father's desk bereft of texts to her mother's desk full of papers that allows her to discover what she should read to make sense of death.[16]

Becky McKelva's desk has twenty-six pigeonholes like a "country post office" full of pages. By imagining the desk as a kind of post office, Laurel sees all of these texts as letters she can read. She finds the letters her father had written her mother, starting with those addressed to her as "Miss Becky Thurston" (965). She finds the letters that her grandmother wrote when she was "widowed, her health failing, lonely and sometimes bedridden" (977). She finds address books, correspondence records, garden diaries, photographs of her parents, and notebooks full of recipes and old class notes. Together, all of these texts start an avalanche of memories for Laurel in which she hears her mother's voice telling stories. She hears how "darling and vain" her mother was when she was young: "The most beautiful blouse I ever owned in my life—I made it" (966). She hears how her mother was "brave": "Up home, we loved a good storm coming, we'd fly outdoors and run up and down to meet it" (971). Laurel also, however, hears the darker memories, such as how anxious her mother was about surgery: "Don't let them tie me down" (970). With the good and bad mixed, the texts allow her mother's voice to speak again. Instead of death, the texts bring life, even the last difficult days of life. Unlike the detective novels and the histories that do not help Laurel, these texts give her what she has been looking for in trying to "solve" her father's death: a meaningful, though complicated, narrative about her parents' lives.

The swerve from the mystery genre to the personal narrative provided by her mother's papers reveals the novel's valuing of character over plot. Just as Lacan describes the letter as only a signifier, the dead body in murder mysteries only exists to get the plot started. The character of the person, like the letter's contents, is not important because the genre relies on the intricacies of plot design to produce a puzzle for readers. As Raymond Chandler famously complains of characters in mystery novels, they are "puppets and cardboard lovers and papier maché villains" (215). In Christie's novel, in fact, when another character remarks that the dead girl "may, of course, have had some remarkable qualities," Miss Marple "placidly" answers, "Probably not" and "I don't think her qualities entered into it" (95). As the dead body, the girl is there only to show off the reasoning skills of the detective, not to be mourned as a human whose life has been cut short.

Laurel drops her role as detective, therefore, not just because she believes Fay incapable of murdering the judge; Laurel also does not want to bury her father or her mother in simple plot devices that make them flat characters.

The move to value complex characterization may derive in part from how much of the novel is autobiographical. Welty's own father had died decades before her mother, so the betrayal Becky feels that the judge committed is not a mark of Welty's experience, but the guilt felt by a daughter watching her mother die certainly was. Suzanne Marrs explains that "Eudora confronted the long years of her mother's illness and the emptiness left by her death. Chestina Welty had been self-reliant for most of her life, and she hated finding herself old and weak and blind" (331). Welty's experience then informed her writing: "a sense of betrayal deepened Eudora's investigation of love and separateness, an investigation that went beyond the bounds of individual experience but that also drew upon the helplessness Eudora herself felt when, despite the ability to recognize and consider her mother's desperation, she was unable to assuage it" (Marrs 332).[17]

Betrayal, guilt, and forgiveness are all intense emotions, but Joan Acocella identifies one of the cardinal rules of Christie's books as the "absolutely central role of ratiocination. The detective, when he is working, shows almost no emotion. What he shows—and what constitutes the main pleasure of the stories—is inductive reasoning" (82). That reasoning must end with a resolution to the plot. By bending the genre to value character over plot, Welty's narrative focuses on a different variety of "mystery": not the "mystery" of plot that can be solved by the detective's rational mind but the "mystery" of character that becomes more complex with investigation instead of less. In her essay "Must the Novelist Crusade?" (1965), Welty writes,

> Great fiction, we very much fear, abounds in what makes for confusion; it generates it, being on a scale which copies life, which it confronts. It is very seldom near, is given to sprawling and escaping from bounds, is capable of contradicting itself, and is not impervious to humor. There is absolutely everything in great fiction but a clear answer. Humanity itself seems to matter more to the novelist than what humanity thinks it can prove. (806)

Although Welty is speaking to a different context here—whether a writer should produce works with immediate, explicit political messages—her preference for "confusion" over a "clear answer" has implications for *The Optimist's Daughter* and for her underlying attitude toward the detective genre. In examining Welty's unpublished crime narrative entitled "The Shadow Club," Harriet Pollack argues that "a strategy of secrets is clear across her career. Welty characteristically adapts mystery conventions without bringing easy resolution, thickening rather than solving mystery" ("Evolving"

142). Pollack's exploration of Welty's friendship with mystery novelist Ross Macdonald (aka Kenneth Millar) provides an additional biographical clue to the presence of the detective genre in the novel: "Their influence on one another's work is apparent in the record of their exchanged letters. Millar's words seep into Welty's *The Optimist's Daughter* and Welty's *The Optimist's Daughter* seeps into his *Sleeping Beauty*" ("Evolving" 145). As much as Welty loved reading mystery novels and as much as she borrows from the genre in this text, her depiction of Laurel's finding the right narrative in her mother's texts reveals Welty's choice of "great fiction" with its exploration of humanity over the mystery genre with its focus on plot to help Laurel explore her parents' deaths. What is important is not what Laurel can prove about her parents' deaths, but the confusing humanity of their lives.

Her father's death thus becomes no longer a murder to solve but an experience to understand. Earlier when she wanted to blame the outsider Fay for her father's demise, Laurel had dismissed all the clues that suggest that her father simply gave up on life, committing a passive suicide. After his eye surgery, he ceases to speak and withdraws from everyone, seemingly ignoring not just the books Laurel reads but also almost any conversation. When Laurel rushes into the room after Fay attacks him, she sees that "his whole, pillowless head went dusky, as if he laid it under the surface of dark, pouring water and held it there" (902). The syntax is telling in that "he laid" suggests an action he takes and not something that happens to him; he drowns himself. The doctor then affirms, "I believe he's just plain sneaked out on us" (903). That Judge McKelva gives Major Bullock the contact information for Fay's family suggests that he had been planning or at least expecting to die. Although Laurel remembers the wonderful stories of her parents courting as she digs through her mother's desk, she also has to confront what her mother's illness did to her father: "What he could not control was his belief that all his wife's troubles would turn out all right because there was nothing he would not have given her" (972). Becky calls him a "coward" for not facing her death; ironically his unfailing optimism prevents him from being the husband that Becky needed in her illness and dying. Laurel now understands what all of her detecting could not uncover: "He died worn out with both wives" (976). In the genre bending, she must contemplate her father's failings, including his giving up on life.[18]

Likewise hidden under the mystery genre's hunt for clues about whether Fay murdered her father is Laurel's guilt for her mother's death, echoing the guilt Welty had felt. Laurel's mother directly blamed her: "You could have saved your mother's life. But you stood by and wouldn't intervene. I despair for you" (975). Becky wanted Laurel to acknowledge her suffering and despair, but as that "optimist's daughter," Laurel had not, thus committing a sin of omission instead of commission but a fault nonetheless. Laurel has thought of herself as culpable, which makes her perhaps too much like Fay. Harriet Pollack points out that "perhaps Laurel judges Fay with such aggravated aggression in order to assert and to show that she knows selfishness when she sees it" (*Eudora* 63, 65).[19] Becky's accusation suggests that Laurel selfishly chose the reaction easiest for her instead of the one her mother desired. Laurel's move to posit Fay as a kind of femme fatale initially distances Laurel from responsibility in that Fay with her overt sexuality, uncaring demeanor, and thirst for money, seems glaringly the culprit. But Fay's culpability only temporarily hides Laurel's conviction of guilt for her mother's suffering. Further complicating Laurel's remorse are her feelings about her husband's death. Although Phil died years earlier in World War II, memories of their time together resurface in Laurel's mourning of her parents. She remembers how she naively thought "we're going to live forever," but that in his death Phil was "left bodiless and graveless" (979). Even now, Laurel realizes that the guilt of "outliving those you love is justly to be borne" (981). Bearing the guilt of three deaths is a more challenging narrative than a murder mystery because for Laurel there is no resolution.

Hence, in reading her mother's letters, Laurel confronts the confusion of delving into humanity in a way that Fay never does. Fay remains in the mode of the mystery genre in that she does not care about the dead; in her narrative, the corpse is just a means to an end. When Laurel tries to explain to Fay the significance of the breadboard, lovingly crafted by Phil and used by her mother to make bread. Fay answers, "Who cares? She's not making it now" (987). Although Becky and Phil still exist for Laurel as "ghosts," Fay claims, "The past isn't a thing to me" (991). Fay is not dwelling on the complex humanity of her late husband; she is concerned rather with her ownership of his property: "But I'll have you remember it's my house now, and I can do what I want to with it. With everything in it. And that goes for that breadboard too" (988). Fay fittingly claims the house that signifies the murder mystery narrative. Laurel, however, rejects the dead end of that genre. She may not have "saved her mother's life," but she reads her texts, hearing her voice again and bringing her back to life.

Given that the papers Laurel finds in her mother's desk are the answer to what she needs all along to comprehend both of her parents' deaths, her subsequent decision to burn them seems odd. She could be saving them from coming into Fay's hands with the rest of the belongings or she could be saving herself from clinging to property the way Fay does. However, given the importance of the complicated but human narrative the texts have given her, Laurel does not abandon the texts as much as internalize them. Just as Laurel turns away from the concrete answers seemingly offered by the genres of murder mystery and history in leaving her father's books on the shelf, she lets go of the "signifier" found in the personal texts as well because the solution for Laurel is not a clue located in a tangible object that imbues power. As the papers burn, Laurel spies one little scrap with her mother's handwriting, asking "this morning?" (985). If Christie were writing this as a true murder mystery, that scrap of paper would be evidence pointing to a killer and providing a resolution that located crime, violence, and loss in some other person.[20] Instead, Laurel has moved from detecting texts to destroying them because she no longer needs to search externally for clues to solve a plot. She has delved into character and has thus become her mother's text, her parents' daughter, and the product of their story, just as their reading aloud constructed their family.[21]

By borrowing from Christie's recipe, Welty's novel exposes connections between class, gender, and marriage, as Fay plays the roles of gold-digger, femme fatale, and suspect. However, by bending the narrative away from the murder mystery genre's satisfying solution to a valuing of flawed, confusing characters, Welty depicts Laurel finding an answer, not to the question of whodunit as in an Agatha Christie novel, but to the question of what and how to read. When confronted with the false stories about her father, Laurel realizes, "The mystery in how little we know of other people is no greater than the mystery of how much" (931). In The Optimist's Daughter, mystery is not a puzzle to be solved. Mystery is to be valued as an indication of the complexity and richness of life.

Notes

1. See Appendix for the specific Christie titles in Welty's library.

2. Carson finds Fay, whose name echoes "fairy," to be simply "childish" (108).

3. Traber likewise finds Fay to have a "subversive role" in the text but argues that Fay's "resistant spirit" comes through seemingly against Welty's intentions to silence her character (185, 188).

4. Eichelberger argues that Fay's selfishness is echoed by the community in the novel: Welty "presents ample evidence to readers that the town is an unjust and artificial hierarchy, and she portrays Fay's egotism, or individualism, as much more typical of Mount Salus than deviant from it" (132). Akins argues that Welty critiques characters including Fay but also Miss Tennyson Bullock, Mrs. Bolt, old Mrs. Pease, and Mrs. Chisom who reveal a "lack of both compassion and comprehension" (90).

5. When asked directly in an interview whether Judge McKelva died from the retina problem, Welty is a bit cagey, explaining that it is "complicated" and that "the way Fay

treated him also had something to do with it. She came in and tried to jerk him off the bed. And in those days, when you operated for cataracts, you couldn't move the head for a long time," but when pressured by the interviewer, she backs off: "Fay didn't intend to kill him in her selfishness. I didn't think the novel said *that*" (*More* 97). That the story has its origin in an event that happened in her family might also explain her hesitancy about this scene. In a letter to William Maxwell, Welty writes, "The fact about the hospital is that before my brother [Edward] died last January, his frantic wife [Elinor] came to the hospital where he was stretched in a harness with a broken neck and hit him, according to the nurse" (*What* 225).

6. Weston calls Fay in this moment a "Gothic vampire" (164).

7. See Agner for a reading of noir in Welty's "The Demonstrators."

8. See Bargainnier for more information on the closed circle.

9. The closed circle in Christie's works is often an iconic English country house. Welty is able to replicate Christie's dynamics in an America setting because, as Žaneta Stýblová explains, the country house's value was that it was ordinary (116); Christie borrowed places easily recognizable to her readers. The McKelva house fits the need for a familiar environment as a container for the action.

10. See Rozier for a reading of how "Fay represents the new consumer culture that puts less emphasis on lineage and social standing than on what one can buy and own" (139).

11. See Patterson for a reading of funerals and social boundaries.

12. The language here is almost identical to that describing the evil character of Judge Pyncheon in Nathaniel Hawthorne's *The House of Seven Gables* as having a smile that conceals a scowl.

13. See Mark for a reading of Becky as one possibility of what kills the judge (335).

14. In contrast, Blair argues that the fictionality of Dickens's novel is not the problem. Rather the issue is that Nicholas Nickleby is "a genuine optimist in a way that Judge McKelva is not" because "The judge's optimism is no more than forbearance; and by ignoring his wife's pain to protect himself, he only exacerbates her despair" (27, 28).

15. Neckles, in taking an intertextual approach to the novel, observes that the Dickens's novel, along with most of the other books mentioned, are "quintessentially British texts" that "pointedly position Britain as America's literary memory" (161).

16. See Fuller, Gygax, and Mark for readings of the gender dynamics as Laurel shifts from focusing on her father to focusing on her mother.

17. For the autobiographical connections, see also Wolff.

18. The suggestions that the judge may have willed his own death further indicate that Welty veers away from the mystery genre by breaking one of S. S. Van Dine's 1928 "20 Rules for Writing Detective Fiction": "A crime in a detective story must never turn out to be an accident or a suicide. To end an odyssey of sleuthing with such an anti-climax is to hoodwink the trusting and kind-hearted reader" (Jones).

19. See also Brinkmeyer and Carson.

20. For example, a scrap of paper left from papers burned in a fireplace becomes a central clue in Christie's *The Mysterious Affair at Styles*.

21. Although I am reading Laurel's burning of the papers as a positive way of helping her learn to address the complexity of the past, Pickard points out that many of the items

Welty has Laurel leaving behind in *The Optimist's Daughter* match items Welty herself kept: "several of the objects Laurel leaves behind or seeks to leave behind, from the plantation desk to the soapstone boat, appear in the Welty House, which everywhere testifies to the capacity of things to spark as well as to anchor memories, forming communities of recollection across time" (64).

Works Cited

Acocella, Joan. "Queen of Crime: How Agatha Christie created the modern murder mystery." *New Yorker*, 16 Aug. 2010, pp. 82–88.

Agner, Jacob. "Welty's Moonlighting Detective: Whiteness and Eudora Welty's Subversion of the American Noir Tradition in 'The Demonstrators.'" *New Essays on Eudora Welty, Class, and Race*, edited by Harriet Pollack, UP of Mississippi, 2020, pp. 189–213.

Akins, Adrienne V. "'We Weren't Laughing at Them . . . We're Grieving with You': Empathy and Comic Vision in Welty's *The Optimist's Daughter*." *Southern Literary Journal*, vol. 43, no. 2, 2011, pp. 87–104.

Auden, W. H. "The Guilty Vicarage: Notes on the Detective Story." *Harper's Magazine*, May 1948, pp. 406–12.

Bargainnier, Earl F. *The Gentle Art of Murder: The Detective Fiction of Agatha Christie.* Bowling Green UP, 1980.

Black, Joel. "(De)feats of Detection: The Spurious Key Text from Poe to Eco." *Detecting Texts: The Metaphysical Detective Story from Poe to Postmodernism*, edited by Patricia Merivale and Susan Elizabeth Sweeney, U of Pennsylvania P, 1999, pp. 75–98.

Blair, John. "Nicholas and the Judge: The 'Wrong Book' in Eudora Welty's *The Optimist's Daughter*." *Notes on Mississippi Writers*, vol. 24, no. 1, 1992, pp. 25–33.

Brinkmeyer, Robert H., Jr. "New Orleans, Mardi Gras, and Eudora Welty's *The Optimist's Daughter*." *Mississippi Quarterly*, vol. 44, no. 4, 1991, pp. 429–41.

Brockman, Beatrix M. "The Genealogy of the Spinster Sleuth in Detective Stories." *Tennessee Philological Bulletin: Proceedings of the Annual Meeting of the Tennessee Philological Association*, vol. 52, 2015, pp. 30–39.

Brooks, Cleanth. "The Past Reexamined: *The Optimist's Daughter*." *The Critical Response to Eudora Welty's Fiction*, edited by Laurie Champion, Greenwood P, 1994, pp. 226–34.

Carson, Barbara Harrell. "Eudora Welty's Heart of Darkness, Heart of Light." *South Central Review*, vol. 4, no. 1, 1987. pp. 106–22.

Chandler, Raymond. "The Simple Art of Murder." *Raymond Chandler: Later Novels and Other Writings*. Library of America, 1995.

Christie, Agatha. *The Body in the Library*. 1942. Harper, 2011.

Cook, Michael. *Narratives of Enclosure in Detective Fiction: The Locked Room Mystery.* Palgrave Macmillan, 2011.

Doane, Mary Ann. *Femmes Fatales: Feminism, Film Theory, Psychoanalysis*. Routledge, 1991.

Eichelberger, Julia. *Prophets of Recognition: Ideology and the Individual in Novels by Ralph Ellison, Toni Morrison, Saul Bellow, and Eudora Welty*. Louisiana State UP, 1999.

Fuller, Danielle. "'Making a Scene': Some Thoughts on Female Sexuality and Marriage in Eudora Welty's *Delta Wedding* and *The Optimist's Daughter.*" *Mississippi Quarterly*, vol. 48, no. 2, 1995, pp. 291–318.

Grimstad, Paul. "What Makes Great Detective Fiction, According to T. S. Eliot" *New Yorker*, 2 Feb. 2016, www.newyorker.com/books/page-turner/what-makes-great-detective -fiction-according-to-t-s-eliot.

Gygax, Franziska. *Serious Daring from Within: Female Narrative Strategies in Eudora Welty's Novels.* Greenwood Publishing Group, 1990.

Hanson, Helen, and Catherine O'Rawe. *The Femme Fatale: Images, Histories, Contexts.* Palgrave Macmillan, 2010.

Harris, Leslie. "The Mystic Vision in *The Optimist's Daughter*" *Studies in the Humanities*, vol. 13, no.1, 1986, pp. 31–41.

Jones, Josh. "'20 Rules for Writing Detective Stories' by S. S. Van Dyne, One of T. S. Eliot's Favorite Genre Writers (1928)." *Open Culture*, 5 Feb. 2016, www.openculture.com /2016/02/20-rules-for-writing-detective-stories.html.

Lacan, Jacques. "Seminar on 'The Purloined Letter.'" Translated by Jeffrey Mehlman. *The Purloined Poe: Lacan, Derrida, & Psychoanalytic Reading*, edited by John P. Muller and William J. Richardson, The Johns Hopkins UP, 1988, pp. 28–54.

Landess, Thomas H. "The Function of Taste in the Fiction of Eudora Welty." *Mississippi Quarterly*, vol. 26, 1973, pp. 543–57.

Mark, Rebecca. "Wild Strawberries, Cataracts, and Climbing Roses: Clitoral and Seminal Imagery in *The Optimist's Daughter.*" *Mississippi Quarterly*, vol. 56, no. 2, 2003, pp. 331–50.

Marrs, Suzanne. *One Writer's Imagination: The Fiction of Eudora Welty.* Louisiana State UP, 2002.

Neckles, Christina. "Revaluative Reading and Literary Memory in Welty's *The Optimist's Daughter.*" *Mississippi Quarterly*, Supplement, 2009, pp. 159–78.

Patterson, Laura. "'The Thing They Knew': Social Exclusion at Southern Wakes in Eudora Welty's 'The Wanderers' and *The Optimist's Daughter.*" *Women and the Material Culture of Death*, edited by Maureen Daly Goggin and Beth Fowkes Tobin, Ashgate, 2013, pp. 91–101.

Pickard, Michael. "Eudora Welty and the House of Fiction." *Eudora Welty Review*, 2020, pp. 53–68.

Poe, Edgar Allan. "The Purloined Letter." 1845. *The Selected Writings of Edgar Allan Poe*, edited by G. R. Thompson, W. W. Norton & Company, 2004, pp. 367–82.

Pollack, Harriet. *Eudora Welty's Fiction and Photography: The Body of the Other Woman.* U of Georgia P, 2016.

Pollack, Harriet. "Evolving Secrets: Eudora Welty and the Mystery Genre." *Detecting the South in Fiction, Film, and Television*, edited by Deborah E. Barker and Theresa Starkey, Louisiana UP, 2019, pp. 142–58.

Rozier, Travis. "'The Whole Solid Past': Memorial Objects and Consumer Culture in Eudora Welty's *The Optimist's Daughter.*" *The Southern Quarterly*, vol. 53, no. 1, 2015, pp. 137–51.

Stýblová, Žaneta. "The Role of Setting in the Golden Age Detective Novel." *American and British Studies Annual*, vol. 11, 2018, pp. 115–26.

Traber, Daniel S. "(Silenced) Transgression in Eudora Welty's *The Optimist's Daughter*." *Critique*, vol. 48, no. 2, 2007, pp. 184–96.

Trouard, Dawn. "Burying Below Sea Level: The Erotics of Sex and Death in *The Optimist's Daughter*." *Mississippi Quarterly*, vol. 56, no. 2, 2003, pp. 231–50.

Welty, Eudora. *Conversations with Eudora Welty*, edited by Peggy Whitman Prenshaw, UP of Mississippi, 1984.

Welty, Eudora. *Meanwhile There Are Letters: The Correspondence of Eudora Welty and Ross Macdonald*, edited by Suzanne Marrs and Tom Nolan, Arcade Publishing, 2015.

Welty, Eudora. *More Conversations with Eudora Welty*, edited by Peggy Whitman Prenshaw, UP of Mississippi, 1996.

Welty, Eudora. "Must the Novelist Crusade?" 1965. *Eudora Welty: Stories, Essays, & Memoir*, edited by Richard Ford and Michael Kreyling, Library of America, 1998, pp. 803–14.

Welty, Eudora. *Occasions: Selected Writings*, edited by Pearl Amelia McHaney. UP of Mississippi, 2009.

Welty, Eudora. *The Optimist's Daughter*. 1972. *Eudora Welty: Complete Novels*, edited by Richard Ford and Michael Kreyling, Library of America, 1998, pp. 881–992.

Welty, Eudora. *What There is to Say We Have Said: The Correspondence of Eudora Welty and William Maxwell*, edited by Suzanne Marrs, Mariner Books, 2012.

Weston, Ruth D. *Gothic Traditions and Narrative Techniques in the Fiction of Eudora Welty*. Louisiana State UP, 1994.

Wilson, Edmund. "Why Do People Read Detective Stories?" *New Yorker*, 14 Oct. 1944, www.newyorker.com/magazine/1944/10/14/why-do-people-read-detective-stories.

Wolff, Sally. "Eudora Welty's Autobiographical Duet: *The Optimist's Daughter* and *One Writer's Beginnings*." *Located Lives: Place and Idea in Southern Autobiography*, edited by J. Bill Berry, U of Georgia P, 1990, pp. 78–92.

CONFLUENCE

The Fiction of Eudora Welty and Ross Macdonald

SUZANNE MARRS

Even before Eudora Welty, the distinguished writer of literary fiction, met Kenneth Millar, aka Ross Macdonald, a master of the mystery genre, they began to correspond, both regularly and frequently. In an early letter (May 11, 1971), Welty wrote to describe a notable journey she had made as a young woman:

> I was going north on the train and it was running away off schedule so that we went through Cairo [Illinois] by daylight, the one time for me, and I could see from the bridge. It's the high railroad bridge and long trestle over a wide reach where the Ohio and the Mississippi and (I believe) a little local river too all come together. It took a long time to cross it and the train went slowly, and while we were still on it I saw high up in the light a long ragged V of birds flying south with the river. I kept hearing in my head all the way that beautiful word "confluence"—"the confluence of the waters"—everything the eyes could see was like the word happening. I don't remember that there were any houses or roads or people anywhere, just treetops and water and distance and sky and birds and confluence. It may not be so rare but I thought so then and I do now—it's all so rarely the blessing falls. (*Meanwhile* 20)

Six days later the two writers met in the lobby of the Algonquin Hotel in New York City, a convergence arranged by friends of both. And not long afterwards, Millar urged Welty to write a story about the "Cairo convergence" detailed in her letter (*Meanwhile* 35). No such story was forthcoming, but a novel was. Seeing the "confluence of the waters" became a memorable experience and symbol for Laurel Hand, the protagonist in Welty's Pulitzer Prize-winning novel, *The Optimist's Daughter*.

Welty and Millar would spend only six weeks or so in each other's company after that first meeting, but the ongoing confluence of their lives and spirits through letters proved an enduring blessing to both, though for many years their relationship was largely unknown to readers of their work. Only after Millar's death in 1983 did his friend Ralph Sipper come into possession of Welty's missives to Millar; he returned them to the Mississippi writer. And only after her death in 2001 were their letters to each other available for research; in her will Welty donated them all to the Mississippi Department of Archives and History. Tom Nolan and I were privileged to transcribe and publish them in *Meanwhile There Are Letters: The Correspondence of Eudora Welty and Ross Macdonald* (2015).

This correspondence reveals a meeting of the minds on matters professional and private. In 1973, for instance, when Millar/Macdonald was asked to compile an anthology of mystery and suspense fiction, which would include novels, novellas, and stories, he wrote to ask for recommendations from Welty, and the two shared their thoughts on the best possible choices for his book. Letters of a literary bent, however, are not the only ones in which they felt their lives converge. Many more are personal in nature. Indeed, these letters tell the story of a deep and abiding love, not a love affair, that united individuals living half a continent apart: she a single woman in Jackson, Mississippi; he a married man in Santa Barbara, California. And when each writer sought to translate this love into fiction, the chosen genre was mystery fiction.

While crime writing is often dismissed as popular rather than serious fiction, Welty and Millar believed that distinctions between literary and mystery fiction were artificial and destructive; they felt that intersections between the genres had been key to works by many writers, including themselves. In addition, each felt that the novel of detection was well suited to the complex investigation of heart-felt, autobiographical concerns, perhaps at times more suited than literary fiction; neither saw it as inevitably escapist in nature. The word "confluence," which Welty believed "exists as a reality and a symbol in one," thus defines a pattern of experience not only for two individuals but also for these two writers (*One Writer's Beginnings* 947). Just as Eudora Welty and Kenneth Millar were united and sustained by the flow of letters written exclusively for themselves, Eudora Welty and Ross Macdonald in their careers jointly realized the power and potential of merging one genre with another, of transforming their personal experience into boundary-crossing fiction, and of drawing upon each other's work in doing so.

I: LITERARY FICTION AND THE MYSTERY GENRE

The mystery genre was an important topic for epistolary discussion between Macdonald and Welty: both had been lifelong readers of the genre, and in their respective ways, whether explicit or implicit, both were at once mystery writers and authors of literary fiction. When Macdonald asked Welty to recommend texts for an anthology of mystery and suspense fiction he was compiling, he knew she would advance knowledgeable suggestions.[1] And her first suggestion proved his wisdom: she recommended a Patrick O'Brian story called "The Walker" (1953), a story so "powerful & terrible—It has stayed with me for years," she recalled (*Meanwhile* 162). But, she later added, "It's so sad to think that [O'Brian's] never realized his powers, apparently— just writes run-of-the-mill historical or adventure books, or according to the reviews that's what they are" (*Meanwhile* 177).

For Welty, who was so opposed to judging a book by its genre, especially if the book were a mystery novel, this was an unusual statement, and she clearly recognized the danger of generalization when she qualified her assertion with the phrase "according to the reviews that's what they are." I feel certain she would have admired the O'Brian novels had she read them. She certainly admired "The Walker," which had lent its title to a book of stories published by Harcourt Brace in 1955. And one key purpose behind Macdonald's anthol- ogy was to show how blurred are the lines between serious fiction and genre fiction. This book includes stories or novels by Dashiell Hammett *and* John Cheever, Dick Francis *and* Flannery O'Connor, Agatha Christie *and* Graham Greene. But it does not contain a story by Patrick O'Brian. Macdonald was ultimately forced to cut O'Brian's piece and two others because the Book-of- the-Month Club feared they might make the anthology seem "too literary" in nature (*Meanwhile* 187). Such a stance was anathema to both Macdonald and Welty, who in their admiration for "The Walker" and in their own deci- sions as writers refused to abide by proscriptive standards.

Certainly, the O'Brian story qualifies as both literary fiction and a mystery story. Set in Ireland, it is narrated by a walker, who describes his philosophy of walking—he tells us that he walks not to view spectacular scenery or to prove his physical prowess, but to enhance his time for reflection. Gradually, the narrator describes his landlords, a couple who, he ultimately discovers, have a dark past to conceal. It seems that the husband, while serving on a packet boat running between France and North Africa, had been party to a murder and robbery. His two accomplices had subsequently met horrible deaths, and now he and his wife fear the worst for themselves. The narrator concludes they keep him as a tenant as a form of protection against some dire end: they see him as an innocent who will not be made to perish with the guilty. And this philosophical narrator agrees with that assessment, even as his line of reasoning departs from theirs. We readers are stunned to learn that the walker believes he has administered God's retribution once before and that he sees himself being given a second chance to act in this role: he will punish his landlords for their inability to trust in divine forgiveness. "I was the hand of God again"; he proclaims, "the wrath of a jealous God Who spoke through the prophet and ploughed the Amalekites into the ground" (242–43). Wrath in the name of God comes to the old couple one night as they inspect their dark house for intruders. The narrator springs upon them, howling, and ultimately causes them to plunge down the stairs and be killed upon a stone floor. Though he evidently escapes detection, he is not satisfied with the event. "It was finished almost before it had begun," he tells readers. "I had meant a full night's inspired, enormous ecstasy, and I had wasted it in half an hour" (243–44).

This is a mystery filled with mysteries: what are the circumstances of the narrator's past? How has he escaped detection, not once but twice? Will he cause a murderous accident yet again? How does an individual convince himself to murder in the name of God? And how have we as readers been so deceived about the narrator's true nature? Why have we failed to recognize O'Brian's use of an unreliable narrator? As Millar wrote to Welty, "That story you sent me, 'The Walker,' is just about the most frightening thing I've ever read, the more so that its ending has a dreadful subjective quality, the reader having been gradually betrayed into complicity" (*Meanwhile* 160).

Millar's own novels may not be as frightening as "The Walker," but they too leave the reader feeling that he has been, if not betrayed, led to recognize that even efforts of good will may well involve complicity with destructive forces. This impact ironically caused novelist/critic Wilfrid Sheed to disparage Macdonald's work and implicitly to denigrate Welty's publicly expressed esteem for it. "The hack's first duty," Sheed wrote in his September 5, 1971, *New York Times Book Review* column, "whatever the highbrows may think he's up to, is to his middlebrow client: to do the job he was paid for, tie up the loose ends and wipe off his own fingerprints. Macdonald, like his alter ego Archer, increasingly takes the risk of offering the client something sloppier and more complicated" (2). For Sheed, the mystery writer should not become uppity, should not dare to encroach on the serious writer's territory.[2] But such encroachment is precisely what makes Macdonald so fine a mystery writer that he can also be called a writer of literary fiction. As Welty has argued, "Great fiction, we very much fear, abounds in what makes for confusion. . . . It is very seldom neat, is given to sprawling and escaping from bounds, is

capable of contradicting itself. . . . There is absolutely everything in great fiction but a clear answer. Humanity itself seems to matter more to the novelist
than what humanity thinks it can prove" ("Must the Novelist Crusade?" 149).

Case in point: *The Underground Man*, which Welty had praised on the
front page of the *New York Times Book Review* early in 1971, less than a year
before Sheed's attack. In this novel, private detective Lew Archer sets out
to bring the young boy Ronny back to his mother, Jean Broadhurst, whose
husband Stanley, she fears, may have abducted the boy. But Archer's brief
encounter with Stanley early in the novel is his last view of the man alive.
Instead he finds Stanley murdered and buried in the forest outside Santa
Teresa, California (aka Santa Barbara), where Stanley's dropped cigarillo has
started a rampaging forest fire. Ronny has disappeared, and Archer must try
to solve the murder in order to find and save the child. In the process, Archer
discovers another murder, two blackmail plots, the ecologically ruinous
development of Santa Teresa, and a series of dysfunctional families, all linked
to a disappearance that had taken place fifteen years earlier. This is not a tidy,
reassuring plot to be solved by a transcendent detective. To the contrary, its
many strands reveal the complex humanity of Macdonald's detective.

Archer's attempts to crack this case (or these cases) are all grounded in a
genuine concern for the individuals involved. As Welty wrote in her review
of the novel:

> It is [the] character of Archer, whose first-person narrative forms the
> novels, that makes [this case] matter to us. Archer from the start has
> been a distinguished creation; he was always an attractive figure, and
> in the course of the last several books has matured and deepened in
> substance to our still greater pleasure. Possessed even when young of
> an endless backlog of stored information, most of it sad, on human
> nature, he tended once, unless I'm mistaken, to be a bit cynical. Now
> he is something much more, he is vulnerable. As a detective and as
> a man he takes the human situation with full seriousness. He cares.
> And good and evil both are real to him. (258)

But as attractive a character as he is, Archer himself recognizes that he
"sometimes served as a catalyst for trouble, not unwillingly" (86). In *The
Underground Man*, his investigation prompts two teenagers to flee with
Ronny and endanger all their lives, and it leaves the young people with
uncertain futures; it prompts the murderous Mrs. Snow to strike again; it
leads to the suicide of a real estate developer/blackmailer; and it leaves the
mentally compromised Fritz Snow free of his deranged mother but alone to

face a threatening world.[3] Archer cares about humanity, but he knows that his unraveling of mysteries is not without destructive consequences that portend future mysteries. In our affection for and trust in Archer, in our desire to see the mystery solved, we readers recognize our own tendencies to serve as "catalyst[s] for trouble," we recognize our own leanings toward complicity. Ross Macdonald's novels do not absolve us; they indict us. They are not escapist in impact. They are the reverse. For Sheed, they violate the demands of genre; for less hidebound readers they embrace the genre's potential. Macdonald modestly avowed that his own reach for this potential exceeded his grasp, but he was not modest in assessing his chosen genre: "*The Brothers Karamazov*," he contended, "*is* a detective story. I don't mean to say that it's that in a limited way; it's prime example of detective fiction—what it *can* become in the hands of a world genius. I regard Dostoyevsky as probably the greatest of all fiction writers" (Nelson, Avery, and Wong 55).[4]

Of course, Wilfrid Sheed, who branded Ross Macdonald as a hack refusing to accept the boundaries of his genre, would never have seen Fyodor Dostoevsky in these terms. Nor would he have thought of Welty in such a way. Her status as a "highbrow" writer of literary fiction had been secure from the time she published her first book. She was not in the business, as conventional mystery writers typically were, of tying up loose ends and assigning guilt. "No," she wrote, "I think we [literary fiction writers] take hold of the other end of the stick. In very practical ways, we rediscover the mystery. We even, I might say, take advantage of it" ("Words into Fiction" 137). Yet Welty's assertion makes clear what Sheed failed to appreciate: how effectively a major writer can take advantage of crime fiction while resisting its stereotypical character development and plot resolution. A self-confessed devotee of the genre—Welty told Millar, "I have a lifetime habit of reading [mysteries]" (*Meanwhile* 170)—she also had a lifetime habit of drawing upon those mysteries, though always doing so with a twist. In "Petrified Man" (first published in 1939), Mrs. Pike plays the role of detective and her sleuthing leads to the arrest of the serial rapist Mr. Petrie, but Mrs. Pike's delight in learning that Petrie's victims are worth $250 apiece in reward money (and fellow beautician Leota sees her point) makes her seem almost as horrifying as Mr. Petrie. In "The Hitch-Hikers" (first published in 1939), traveling salesman Tom Harris picks up two hitchhikers and briefly leaves them alone in his car, unwittingly providing an opportunity for one of the tramps to kill the other. Tom then half-heartedly attempts to ascertain what has led to the murder, but he refuses to linger at the murder site or to play the role of dogged amateur detective. Instead, he has his bloodstained car cleaned and drives away. In *The Robber Bridegroom* (1942), Clement Musgrove enlists Jamie Lockhart to investigate his daughter's disappearance and thereby becomes complicit with a man who is both hero and robber, whose dirk is "not unstained with blood," and who is involved in the destruction of native peoples and the commercialization of America (54). In "The Whole World Knows" (first published 1947), "Where Is the Voice Coming From?" (1963), and *Losing Battles* (1970), a rapist and two murderers confess their crimes much as the narrator of "The Walker" does, and issues of the reader's complicity arise again.

But what about Welty's phrase "rediscover the mystery"? These three words, it seems to me, describe what happens when a serious writer draws upon genre fiction and what attentive readers do as they encounter such stories. Analyzing "A Still Moment" (first published 1942) as a cross-genre piece reveals just such an effect. This work of historical fiction is about a murderer (James Murrell) and a bird murderer (John James Audubon), but the mystery here is not "who done it." We know that Murrell intends to kill Lorenzo Dow, though he does not. The appearance of Audubon forestalls the murder. We further know that Audubon, who is a sort of detective, a man who examines in detail the world around him, nevertheless shoots the snowy heron. There is no mystery here. The story's mystery lies somewhere else. It lies in Dow's questions about love and separateness. It lies in Murrell's attempts to plumb the "mystery of being." It lies in Audubon's unceasing and unsatisfying quest to discover his own identity and to discover "what a man had to seize beyond that" (232, 237). Ultimately the strands of mystery in the story coalesce in the appearance of the beautiful snowy heron and in the still moment, removed from time, that the bird brings to three men obsessed with time's movement. What is the bird's metaphysical significance? What is the nature of the artist in our fallen world? Are paintings like Audubon's worth the death of the birds he must kill to paint? Are we as readers and lovers of Audubon's work complicit in the morally ambiguous decision he makes in the story? And does storytelling like Murrell's suggest he is also an artist figure but a far less appealing one? These questions are not answered. The story is, as Millar told Welty, both haunting and baffling (*Meanwhile* 35). What Maynard Mack said of *Hamlet*, we can say of "A Still Moment" and many another Welty story: they are written in the interrogative mood (49). They invoke even as they abandon the conventional and solvable mystery of crime fiction in order to rediscover the mystery of being.

Long ago in his famous essay "The Art of Fiction," Henry James rejected any endeavor to establish *a priori* "what sort of affair a good novel will be" or to determine "by prescription" what a novelist should attempt. "We must grant the artist his subject, his idea, his *donnée*," James wrote; "our criticism is applied only to what he makes of it" (49, 56). Almost one hundred years

later, Macdonald and Welty adopted a Jamesian stance in both precept and
example. Branded a hack and told his duty was merely to please a middlebrow audience, Ross Macdonald demurred. Expected to be a highbrow and
disdain mystery fiction, Eudora Welty declined. "Personal judgment however
imperfect and a sense of freedom however illusory are the source of creative
energy," Macdonald wrote to Alfred Knopf (861). And in her essay "Place in
Fiction," Welty made the same assertion in a different, but fully applicable
context: "One can no more say, 'To write stay home,' than one can say, 'To
write leave home.' It is the writing that makes its own rules and conditions
for each person" (129). By hewing to their faith in the artist's freedom, Ross
Macdonald and Eudora Welty added their work to the confluence of literary
fiction and detective stories. They fulfilled the genre of mystery fiction, and
they rediscovered its true mystery.

II: THE MYSTERY NOVEL AND
IMAGINATIVE AUTOBIOGRAPHY

For Eudora Welty and Kenneth Millar, the confluence of their lives, which
began with an exchange of letters in 1970, led to a new and quite personal
confluence in their work. As they grew close together, each translated aspects
of their relationship into the literary-mystery genre they so valued, a genre
that seemed particularly well suited for this purpose. Indeed, for Millar himself, the mystery novel was a form of "imaginative autobiography." In an
interview with *Rolling Stone* critic Paul Nelson, he cited *The Galton Case*
(1959) as an example of self-detection, but he might well have cited his novel
Sleeping Beauty (Nelson, Avery, and Wong 120). In 1972, when he wrote to
Welty, asking if he might dedicate *Sleeping Beauty* to her, he called her attention to the title character's name—Laurel—which he may or may not have
consciously drawn from her Pulitzer Prize winner, *The Optimist's Daughter*,
and he also pointed to a book his Laurel is reading—*Permanent Errors*,
the 1970 story collection Reynolds Price had dedicated to Eudora. Millar's
sleeping beauty, gentle and generous of spirit, but psychologically wounded
by her family's permanent errors, surely is based to a considerable extent
on his daughter Linda, who had only recently died at age thirty-one after a
troubled youth, and detective Lew Archer's heroic and successful effort to
save her is Ken's wish-fulfillment.[5] Still, the title *Sleeping Beauty* may have
been inspired by Eudora and by his gratitude for the relationship they shared.
He told her that seeing this phrase used by Henry Green, a British novelist
he and Eudora had both praised in their correspondence, validated the title

for him: "I mean the use of the phrase," he added, "as a generalized abstract noun. Well, the beauty is sleeping indeed but your sweet and penetrating thoughts, Eudora, awaken her continually, indeed become her" (*Meanwhile* 96). To Ken, Eudora embodied the abstract concept at the heart of his novel, the concept of beauty revived and reviving, beauty of empathy and intellect, a life-giving force.

In 1973, Ken traveled to Jackson, Mississippi for the state's celebration of Eudora Welty Day, and in 1975, Eudora made the first of three visits to speak at the Santa Barbara Writers Conference and spend time with Ken. The powerful bond between them was marked in 1976 by Ken's decision to confide in Eudora what he had not yet put in a letter to anyone else: he had begun to experience lapses of memory (*Meanwhile* 306). In 1977, Eudora asked if she might dedicate her book of nonfiction (*The Eye of the Story*) to him, and he quickly accepted, replying that their "love and friendship" would now "persist beyond life, as we want them to" (*Meanwhile* 344). A year later, when Alzheimer's disease, not yet diagnosed, was seriously threatening Ken and its symptoms deeply concerning Eudora, he even more movingly expressed his devotion to her: "The best thing that can happen to a man," he declared, "is to be known, and by a woman of your great kindness and light and depth" (*Meanwhile* 405). Eudora's response to this letter revealed a similar devotion: "Our friendship blesses my life," she wrote, "and I wish life could be longer for it" (*Meanwhile* 408). When in the course of their ardent correspondence Welty turned anew to writing fiction, she did so within the mystery form to which Ken had given his life and through a plot and a motif that parallel ones in the novel he had dedicated to her. It would prove a difficult endeavor.

"The Shadow Club," likely begun in 1975, was under construction for the next six years. Never completed or published, it drew upon a story she had tried to write in the 1940s, then resurrected and reframed in the 1960s. Recognizing that her work from the past reverberated with connections to the present, and that newly minted material could build upon those confluences, she selected or reshaped previously written scenes, invented others, and put her unsettled text in conversation with *Sleeping Beauty*. Of course, the two works are set in contrasting worlds—a quiet southern town, on the one hand, and southern California in the wake of a major oil spill, on the other—but their key plot lines are remarkably similar.[6] In *Sleeping Beauty*, a past that has been repressed haunts a married couple, Laurel and Tom Russo, who as children may or may not have witnessed an affair between his mother and her father as well as the murder of his mother by hers. In "The Shadow Club," a repressed past similarly haunts Justine and Ralph, two

lifelong friends, who at an early age have seen his father and her mother making love; subsequently, nine-year-old Justine is further scarred by witnessing the immediate aftermath of her parents' murder/suicide. The children
in both narratives have been encouraged by family members and/or neighbors to forget the past. And in both narratives, only when memory of the
distant past is allowed to emerge is there a possibility that the lives of the
now adult children can become whole.

Lurid though it be, Welty's plot, like Macdonald's before hers and like
that of many another crime novel, proved well suited to developing autobiographical concerns, providing ample opportunity for both self-examination
(in its focus on detection) and self-disguise (in its reliance on extraordinary
situations). Welty had previously taken advantage of such generic virtues. In
an early story about murder—"The Hitch-Hikers" (1939)—she had drawn
upon worries about a problematic romance with John Robinson, her fellow Mississippian. In "A Curtain of Green" (1938), a story about a grief-
stricken widow who briefly contemplates murder, Eudora had investigated
her mother's grief at the death of her husband and Eudora's father. And she
had once extrapolated upon an account of her hospitalized brother Edward
being struck, according to a nurse, by "his frantic wife" (*What There Is to
Say* 225): in *The Optimist's Daughter*, Laurel believes that Fay's abuse of Judge
McKelva has led to his death; the evidence "would stand up in court," she
concludes (963).[7] Not surprisingly, then, the present action of "The Shadow
Club" became, in the process of being rethought, revised, and reworked, the
sort of imaginative autobiography that *Sleeping Beauty* and Millar's other
detective novels so often were. Though it exists only in fragments that must
be combined, ordered, pieced together by the archival reader, it translates
into crime fiction both the love that Eudora and Ken shared and the evolving
nature of Ken's memory loss.

In a few fragments of text, probably written late in the composition process, Justine (also named Cam, Caroline, or Nell in other fragments, but to
be called Justine throughout this essay) has just returned to her Friar's Bluff,
Mississippi, home from New Orleans, where she, a middle-aged, unmarried
teacher, spent six weeks in a summer class and experienced an incipient
romance with a man named Henry, likely her married professor: "Justine
had told him her worst, her deepest secrets. ~~He had kissed her for letting
him hear all she wanted to tell him~~. Henry had listened and fallen asleep
with his trusting head in her lap. Yes, they had loved each other, and they
loved each other now" (Box 268, folder 5, piece 2).[8] In a second plot line, set
forty or so years earlier, Jacob Ledbetter, another married professor, has an
affair with Hallie, Justine's mother, and seems possibly to be Justine's true

father. Ledbetter's gentleness and his tender care of this rebellious daughter evoke elements of Ken's life, and Eudora may have located elements of herself not only in the child Justine, giving her character memories of events to be recounted in the Welty autobiography *One Writer's Beginnings*, but also in Hallie, not in Hallie's flirtatiousness and infidelity, but in her role as the rival of Ledbetter's wife. That wife, Ollie Ledbetter, may in similarly oblique ways, not in details of characterization, prompt thoughts of Margaret Millar, the mystery novelist whose marriage to Ken was filled with tension and who resented his correspondence with Eudora.

Ken, for his part, may appear not only in the guise of Ledbetter but also of Justine, who must deal with memory loss. Early in the morning of her return to her home on Observatory Street in Friar's Bluff, Justine suffers a blow to the head, is knocked unconscious and raped, and then cannot remember the traumatic event. But Justine is also troubled by an inability to remember the distant past; she has since the age of nine repressed the memory of seeing Ledbetter and her mother in the throes of passion and of being the one to find her mother and father dead from gunshot wounds, a murder-suicide. In fact, she has been encouraged to repress these memories. Ledbetter tells the young girl not to speak of these events so that she may protect her dead mother's reputation. But as Justine's story unfolds (with its point of view shifting between first and third person), she recovers the past and ultimately renounces the need for protection from it:

> I lost them when I began to believe it myself—not only that they hadn't died by Papa's determination—the pistol I saw still in his hand, but that they had been nothing but happy in life—nothing but loving and good. It would not have dishonored them, but honored them, had she tried, only tried, to imagine what her mother felt as she crushed her face into the driving chest of Professor Ledbetter, what her father felt as he aimed the pistol by fallible starlight once and then again, not needing the stars. . . . ~~In accepting my protection from them~~ I lost what they really were, a man and a woman of passion, who were young and foolish, with no easy way out of it. . . . She had rejected them; she had somehow orphaned them, for she had been unable to put herself in their place (Box 260, folder 9, piece 41).

Like Laurel Hand in *The Optimist's Daughter*, Justine realizes that the past cannot be put in a silver frame and idealized; it must be subject to the present moment.

Justine realizes that she has betrayed her parents by refusing to "put herself in their place," to empathize with rather than ignore their torment, and Welty intended to juxtapose this recognition (and the scenes leading to it) with an account of Justine's abortive New Orleans romance, thereby showing the "connection" between the two: Justine knows that her failure to form lasting attachments has resulted from fear that love will bring tragedy to her as it had to her parents (Box 268, folder 2, piece 1). However repressed her memories, she has allowed the past to control her. Only by at last facing the past may she be "pardoned and freed" (Welty, *The Optimist's Daughter* 992). In describing Justine's rueful insight, Eudora may have drawn upon her own regret, a regret that she and Ken had led their lives at such a literal distance from each other, but she also must have been addressing Ken's need to face the tormenting memories still available to him and subject them to the present moment.[9] Late in November 1976, while "working hard" on new material for "The Shadow Club," she gently suggested that he write about memories of a fraught relationship with his father: "We somehow do learn to write our stories out of us, however disguised and given other players who can move and act where possibly we can't—. . . . Of course you have written around and about it—your father's (I know no word—his doing)—and into it and out of it, while you yourself have made a whole life that is good and truly good, aware and *un*hurting and understanding of others, a shining way to have dealt with what was done to you—But it hasn't seemed to have been enough for *you*, to bring you real peace of mind. Would it be any use to you to write about this to me? Trying a new way if it came to you?" (*Meanwhile* 316, 319). Eudora hoped that Ken might find the same catharsis that reemerging and reevaluated memories had brought to Justine, and in this way she seemed to associate Justine with Ken as much as she had with herself—Justine embodies the union of the two writers and the realization that memory is the "treasure most dearly regarded" in their lives (*One Writer's Beginnings* 948).

Plot for Welty had always been a vehicle carrying meaning even if it were not a story's dominant element. It is dominant in "The Shadow Club," and in this manuscript Welty contemplated having Justine's parents die in a car accident or a plane crash, but neither of those incidents could have suggested the overwhelming emotions felt by a passionate couple and a betrayed husband, and neither alternative would have been as convincingly haunting as the murder-suicide. This element of her plot, by being sensational within its narrative context, fills demands Welty deemed essential. In her 1949 essay "Looking at Short Stories," she had written: "It is when the plot, whatever it is, is nearest to becoming the same thing on the outside as it is deep inside, that it is purest. When it is identifiable in every motion and progression of its own with the motions and progressions of the story's feeling and its intensity, then this is plot put to its highest use" (94). In 1972, she suggested that *Sleeping Beauty*, by holding "idea & action & meaning in one," exemplified this very definition (*Meanwhile* 92). And a year later, Welty linked her long-held view of plot to the detective novel more generally. As she wrote in her essay "Some Notes on Time in Fiction," an essay composed in the midst of her corresponding with Kenneth Millar: "The close three-way alliance of time, plot and significance can be seen clearly demonstrated in the well-written detective novel. We can learn from it that plot, by the very strength, spareness and boldness of its construction-in-motion, forms a kind of metaphor. I believe every well-made plot does, and needs to do so" (167).

The plot we can discover amid the myriad bits and pieces of "The Shadow Club" pays specific homage to its bold, intricately designed, metaphoric counterpart in *Sleeping Beauty*, but Welty's plot in this case never became well made. Still, even in the manuscript's unfinished state, the double strands of a detective novel—the infidelity, murder, and suicide of the past and the crime of the present (a middle-aged Justine's rape shortly after she has returned from New Orleans to her home on Observatory Street)—are inextricably bound, one necessarily calling forth the memory of the other. Though Elroy Corum, a hapless, forlorn African American youth, displaced in his family and sadly adrift, impulsively commits the rape, no crime is reported, no suspect identified. Justine's white female friends, indulging in what Harriet Pollack accurately calls "a tendency to profile and mythologize," assume that a rapist would almost inevitably be African American ("Evolving Secrets" 147; Box 263, folder 6, piece 2). Despite this assumption (or perhaps because of it), they support Justine's desire to maintain her privacy. Only the outspoken "Yankee" character Jan thinks in more realistic terms about the event: she challenges their racial stereotypes and asks the white women of Observatory Street: "Wasn't it in fact usually a matter of a white man raping a black wom[a]n? . . . Come on now" (Box 263, folder 6, piece 2). Then Jan insists upon an account from Justine: "I want you to tell me what happened to you, at an early hour this morning. And what you're planning to do about this rapist before he does it again" (Box 265, folder 6, piece 89). Justine does not respond to these demands; a concussion has blocked her short-term memory—she cannot recall the attack—and she proves unable, for the moment at least, to consider the issues of racism and civic responsibility that Jan raises. Instead, the assault drives Justine to think of her tragic childhood and allows the shock and horror of repressed memories to resurface for her. "My visitor, unknown to me," she recalls, "entered my house last night. He succeeded only as far as unlocking my locked-up past for me. While I was lying dead to the world [h]e laid bare my life, and that's what I've had to look at all day" (Box 260, folder 9, piece 42).[10] Justine's rape further brings a repressed past to the fore in the mind of her neighbor and childhood friend Ralph, who complains that "Justine by letting this happen to her had brought back everything he could least bear living with again" (Box 260, folder 8, piece 38). These intersecting plotlines thus serve as a kind of metaphor, harkening back to Macdonald's *Sleeping Beauty* and stressing that memories not obstructed by the need for escape or protection, ones not shaped by others, but ones subject to reinterpretation and honest confrontation, may be intensely painful but can also be restorative.

Just as its metaphoric plot, like that of *Sleeping Beauty*, focuses upon the nature of memory, "The Shadow Club" also echoes the fairy tale motif of that work. Of course, echoes of that sort were nothing new for Welty, but here, it seems clear, she responded to and complicated Macdonald's particular use of that one tale. Justine, knocked unconscious by her rapist, plays the sleeping beauty role that Ross Macdonald granted to the drugged Laurel Russo in his novel. As we have seen, when Welty's Justine comes to, though she does not remember what has just occurred, she begins to recover the distant past and the meaning of its loss. She comes to realize, moreover, that the repression of that distant past has left her unable to form enduring romantic relationships—she has lost the promise of love because she could not credit the passion felt by her mother and Ralph's father. Still, if Justine is literally and figuratively an awakened sleeping beauty, she has not been waked, as was Laurel Russo, by an ardent detective named Lew Archer. By 1981, when Eudora was still at work on "The Shadow Club," she knew that Kenneth Millar's Alzheimer's disease would prevent any enduring relationship between them; he could not reenact a fairy-tale role, nor could he gain access to his own past.

Henceforth, Eudora would have to be the detective in her own life and Ken's; she alone would be able to write fiction that investigated their shared experiences. As her recognition of this new reality evolved, it seems likely that she began to adjust "The Shadow Club," rethinking bits of text about an elderly, retired professor of astronomy and old friend of Justine's parents, a man who has progressive memory loss and at one point has wandered away from home, not knowing how to return. But this one character on the periphery of her plot could not evoke powerfully enough the impact of dementia; no simple revision, no added text, could suffice.[11] As a result, in late 1981, she changed course, abandoning "The Shadow Club," its crime plot, Friar's Bluff setting, and most of its characters, for a story called "Henry,"

one expanding upon Justine's recollection of her relationship with an unhap-
pily married English professor in New Orleans, a man who as the central
character in the new story eventually faces Ken's plight.[12] Eudora, lacking
emotional distance from her text, was just as unable to bring this story to
completion as she had been the earlier one. Yet fragmentary and disjointed
as both "The Shadow Club" and "Henry" are, they nevertheless provide a
compelling portrait of a man and of a relationship. They call to mind words
Ken had penned years earlier. "Sometimes your insight is so dazzling," he
wrote to her in January 1977, "that I have to shut my eyes. But you must not
feel that it has ever hurt me to be touched by it. Your rays are wholly benign
and leave no mark" (*Meanwhile* 325).

Kenneth Millar, recipient of the 1974 Mystery Writers of America Grand
Master Award under his pen name Ross Macdonald, believed that the detective narrator in mystery novels "represented his creator and carried his values
into action in society." He contended that Lew Archer, his alter ego, was "The
Writer as Detective Hero" (866). Eudora Welty had no detective in "The
Shadow Club," but in creating that manuscript she became a sort of detective hero, investigating, bringing to light, and transfiguring elements from
her life and Ken's, confronting the nature of memory in both personal and
cultural contexts. She embraced the crime genre's affinity with "imaginative
autobiography." But ultimately, stricken by anxiety and grief, knowing that
Alzheimer's disease had left Ken without hope for recovery, she could find
no way for "The Shadow Club" to convey the overwhelming concerns of the
present moment.

Eudora could, however, preserve the manuscript, make use of it in subsequent work, and guarantee its availability to scholars. She could also preserve
the letters she and Ken had exchanged, letters both professional and personal. By donating her manuscripts and correspondence to the Mississippi
Department of Archives and History, she continued to play the detective
hero, pointing to an evidentiary record, a record of the confluence of her
life with Ken's and of her admiration for what has been unfairly dismissed
as "genre fiction." Moreover, by ensuring that "The Shadow Club" would be
placed on archival shelves next to drafts of her published work, she pointed
us backward in time toward evidence of what had been hidden in plain
sight—the confluence of literary and crime fiction, not merely in her late
manuscript, but also in her critically acclaimed stories and novels. As one of
Eudora Welty's and Ross Macdonald's devoted readers, I am grateful indeed
for this evidence, evidence that has proved crucial to my career as a biographer, editor, critic, and mystery aficionado.

Notes

1. The anthology Macdonald was compiling would be titled *Great Stories of Suspense* (Alfred A. Knopf, 1974).

2. In his column appropriately titled "It All Depends on Your Genre," Sheed maintained that genre writers were inevitably hacks, "genre-hacks," and he criticized the *New York Times Book Review* for devoting its front page so often in recent months to works by genre-hacks; one of those front pages, he indicated, was devoted to a Macdonald book, though the book (*The Underground Man*) and its reviewer (Eudora Welty) remain unnamed by Sheed. Genre-hacks, Sheed contended, "have it in common that when they are approached as major writers they lose all their strength, and don't even seem as good as they are." For Sheed, genre might not be fate, but it was close. "The detective-story genre," he wrote, "makes a skimpy life-belt" for one who would paddle "into the gloomy depths of the Novel." Sheed's comments about Macdonald, which constituted approximately one-third of his column, centered on *The Zebra-Striped Hearse* (1962). He made no mention of the five mysteries Macdonald published between 1962 and 1969, when *The Goodbye Look* was featured on the *Book Review's* front page. He did acknowledge not having read "the latest Macdonald," though *The Underground Man* had been published six months before his column went to press. Perhaps Sheed felt its genre told him all he needed to know about the new book.

3. In her 1971 review of *The Underground Man*, Welty linked these plot complications to a cast of supporting characters who cannot, as Archer must, tell "the real and the fabricated" apart. She astutely observed: "The plot is intricate, involuted and complicated to the hilt; and this, as I see it, is the novel's point" (255).

4. In this same interview, Macdonald also called *The Great Gatsby* "an example of what the crime novel can be developed into" (39).

5. For a wide-ranging analysis of *Sleeping Beauty*, including the ways in which Millar transformed the life of his daughter into fiction, see Nolan 329–32.

6. For a discussion of Millar's response to the 1969 Santa Barbara oil spill and of the role that spill played in *Sleeping Beauty*, see Nolan 282–84 and 329.

7. *The Optimist's Daughter* was published in the *New Yorker* in 1969, in revised form as a novel in 1972, and received the Pulitzer Prize in 1973.

8. All quotations from "The Shadow Club" are Copyright (c) Eudora Welty, used with permission of Russell & Volkening Agency and The Welty LLC and courtesy of The Eudora Welty Collection—Mississippi Department of Archives and History. Passages from "The Shadow Club" typically include strikeovers, instructions for transpositions, and other signs of being in a state of flux. If information in a passage I am quoting includes strikeovers that are relevant to my argument, they are shown here as lined through. Otherwise, I have noted the omission of Welty's strikeovers by using ellipses. Corrections of typographical errors appear in square brackets. If instructions for transpositions seem clear, I have made them without note. In addition to the mention of Henry in the cited passage, "The Shadow Club" also includes references to the subject of linguistics, to the two characters dancing together, and to Henry's realization that Justine reminds him of another woman,

perhaps his wife (Box 262, folder 1, piece 136). In a later manuscript of a different story, Welty develops each of these references. See "Henry," an appendix in *Meanwhile*, pp. 462–90.

9. The love the two writers shared at long-distance, as each honored his marriage vows, dates from 1973 (or perhaps earlier) until Ken died in July 1983. In May 1973, when he and Reynolds Price were together in Jackson, Mississippi, to celebrate Eudora Welty Day, Ken had told Price: "You love Eudora as a friend. I love her as a woman." Ten years later, Eudora wrote to her friends Sonja and William Jay Smith, reflecting on love and on Ken's loss of memory and of life: "I've been grieving about Ken Millar who died of Alzheimer's Disease, or so it was diagnosed. I went out to see him in December [1982] and we had a good visit—talked together and got to be together every day for a while for about a week—As you know, we loved each other, and what happened to him was so abominable—He hadn't been able to write for two years but a mutual friend in Santa Barbara had kept me in touch. He remained himself—gentle and enduring" (Marrs 387, 483–84).

10. Welty almost certainly drew upon and transformed two actual events in creating the story's rape plot: a 1967 attack upon a retired Jackson woman, who had been a math teacher at Jackson's Central High School when Welty was a student there in the 1920s, and the 1975 murder of Frank Hains, arts editor at the *Jackson Daily News*, director of plays at Jackson's Little Theatre and New Stage Theatre, and Welty's good friend. See Fairly 7 and "Life Term for Attack on Teacher" 9. See *Meanwhile* 257–59 for the Welty/Millar correspondence about Hains's murder. For a fuller discussion of the story's rape plot, including analyses of its sources, intertextual connections, and place in the Welty canon, see Harriet Pollack's essay "Evolving Secrets."

11. In fall 1978, Eudora was seriously concerned about Ken's memory loss (*Meanwhile* 402–08). By August 1980, as Tom Nolan reports, Ken's situation had worsened and would continue to do so. In May 1981, Ken had an operation designed to improve his memory; it did not help, and he was diagnosed with Alzheimer's disease (Nolan 399, 403). It is difficult to determine when Eudora introduced the issue of advanced, debilitating memory loss into "The Shadow Club." Perhaps it had been on the periphery from the start, for it drew upon a scene with different characters from a manuscript of an earlier, never-published story (Box 281, folder 11, piece 9), but the issue must have taken on added resonance as Ken's situation unfolded. Eudora would have been especially aware of its relevance to that situation as her work on "The Shadow Club" was drawing to a close. Mentions of an elderly character with dementia are present in material headed by the notation "Read over Aug. '80" and also in a folder which includes quotations Welty typed from an October 1981 newspaper (Box 258, folder 1; Box 269, folder 11).

12. After drawing upon "The Shadow Club" in the "Henry" manuscript, Welty in turn transformed elements of "Henry" into an even more overtly biographical novella—"The City of Light"—most of which she would go on to burn. Though these late works of fiction were each informed to varying extents by Welty's relationship with Kenneth Millar, only "The Shadow Club" adhered to the genre of which Millar was a master.

Works Cited

Fairly, Kenneth. "Mayor Commends Police for Arrests in Felonies." *Jackson Clarion-Ledger*, August 9, 1967, p. 7.

James, Henry. "The Art of Fiction." *Collected Literary Criticism*, edited by Leon Edel and Mark Wilson. Vol. 1, Library of America, 1984, pp. 44–65.

"Life Term for Attack on Teacher." *Jackson Clarion-Ledger*, March 8, 1968, p. 9.

Macdonald, Ross, editor. *Great Stories of Suspense*. Alfred A. Knopf, 1974.

Macdonald, Ross. "Letter to Alfred A. Knopf." *Ross Macdonald, Four Novels of the 1950s*, edited by Tom Nolan, Library of America, 2015, p. 861.

Macdonald, Ross. *Sleeping Beauty*. 1973. Vintage, 2000.

Macdonald, Ross. *The Underground Man*. 1971. Vintage, 1996.

Macdonald, Ross. "The Writer as Detective Hero." *Ross Macdonald, Four Novels of the 1950s*, edited by Tom Nolan, Library of America, 2015, pp. 866–74.

Mack, Maynard. "The World of Hamlet." *Tragic Themes in Western Literature*, edited by Cleanth Brooks, Yale UP, 1955, pp. 47–63.

Marrs, Suzanne. *Eudora Welty, A Biography*. Harcourt, 2005.

Marrs, Suzanne, editor. *What There Is to Say We Have Said: The Correspondence of Eudora Welty and William Maxwell*. Houghton Mifflin Harcourt, 2011.

Marrs, Suzanne, and Tom Nolan, editors. *Meanwhile There Are Letters: The Correspondence of Eudora Welty and Ross Macdonald*. Arcade, 2015.

Nelson, Paul and Kevin Avery, with Jeff Wong. *The Illustrated Ross Macdonald Archives*. Fantagraphics Books, 2016.

Nolan, Tom. *Ross Macdonald, A Biography*. Scribner, 1999.

O'Brian, Patrick. "The Walker." *The Walker and Other Stories*. Harcourt, Brace and Company, 1955, pp. 232–44.

Pollack, Harriet. "Evolving Secrets: Eudora Welty and the Mystery Genre." *Detecting the South in Fiction, Film, and Television*, edited by Deborah E. Barker and Theresa Starkey, Louisiana State UP, 2019, pp. 142–58.

Sheed, Wilfrid. "The Good Word: It All Depends on Your Genre." *New York Times Book Review*, September 5, 1971, pp. 2+.

Welty, Eudora. "Looking at Short Stories." *The Eye of the Story*. Random House, 1978, pp. 85–106.

Welty, Eudora. "Must the Novelist Crusade?" *The Eye of the Story*. Random House, 1978, pp. 146–58.

Welty, Eudora. *One Writer's Beginnings. Stories, Essays, Memoir*. Library of America, 1998, pp. 831–948.

Welty, Eudora. "Place in Fiction." *The Eye of the Story*. Random House, 1978, pp. 116–33.

Welty, Eudora. Review of *The Underground Man* by Ross Macdonald. *The Eye of the Story*. Random House, 1978. 251–60.

Welty, Eudora. *The Robber Bridegroom. Complete Novels*. Library of America, 1998, pp. 1–88.

Welty, Eudora. "The Shadow Club." Eudora Welty Collection, Mississippi Department of Archives and History, Jackson, MS.

Welty, Eudora. "Some Notes on River Country." *The Eye of the Story*. Random House,
    1978, pp. 286–99.
Welty, Eudora. "Some Notes on Time in Fiction." *The Eye of the Story*. Random House,
    1978, pp. 163–73.
Welty, Eudora. "A Still Moment." *Stories, Essays, Memoir*, Library of America, 1998,
    pp. 228–40.
Welty, Eudora. "Words into Fiction." *The Eye of the Story*. Random House, 1978,
    pp. 134–45.

APPENDIX: MYSTERIES ON THE SHELVES IN EUDORA WELTY'S HOUSE

MICHAEL PICKARD AND VICTORIA RICHARD

"There is no frigate like a book," Emily Dickinson wrote, "to take us lands away" (*Poems*, 1896, 29). Even in an age of digital media, Dickinson's metaphor has the power to charm us with its truth. Anyone with an internet connection can surf to almost any place on earth, yet reading remains, for many, the most satisfying method of teleportation. Certainly, it was for Eudora Welty, whose final years coincided with the advent of the World Wide Web. Few authors have written as lovingly about reading as she did. "A sweet devouring," she once called it, and she filled her memoir, *One Writer's Beginnings* (1984), with recollections of this species of joy. Reflecting on her childhood, for example, she observes: "Every book I seized on, from *Bunny Brown and His Sister Sue at Camp Rest-a-While* to *Twenty Thousand Leagues under the Sea*, stood for the devouring wish to read being instantly granted. I knew this was bliss, knew it at the time. Taste isn't nearly so important; it comes in its own time. I wanted to read immediately. The only fear was that of books coming to an end" (*Stories, Essays, and Memoir* 872).

Welty could not often have known that fear. At her death in 2001, she owned more than 5,000 books. Her library is as diverse as it is extensive, and it speaks to the considerable taste that did indeed come in its own time. On her shelves stand enduring names (Homer, Virgil, Chaucer, Cervantes, Shakespeare, Austen, Ibsen, Joyce, Ishiguro); cherished family favorites (Twain, Dickens) and childhood treasures (*Our Wonder World*); forerunners and older contemporaries she learned from and admired (Willa Cather, Anton Chekhov, Isak Dinesen, William Faulkner, E. M. Forster, Henry James, Virginia Woolf, William Butler Yeats); friends in the trade (Elizabeth Bowen, Shelby Foote, Henry Green, Walker Percy, Katherine Anne Porter, V. S. Pritchett, Robert Penn Warren); younger writers she valued and, in several cases, supported (Seamus Heaney, Toni Morrison, Joyce Carol Oates, Reynolds Price, Elizabeth Spencer, Anne Tyler); as well as some unexpected finds (Sir Arthur Eddington's *The Nature of the Physical World*, R. Buckminster Fuller's *Operating Manual for Spaceship Earth*). One would need Welty's ninety-two years as well as her thirst for voyage to sail more than half of the biblio-frigates in her shipyard. No wonder that, according to Suzanne Marrs, Welty's biographer, she often had three or four books in progress, each in a different room.

With one important exception, Welty did not own much genre fiction. Not for her science fiction or Harlequin romance. She did, however, give a significant portion of her reading life to mysteries. Judging by her bookshelves, she traversed the history of this genre, from its nineteenth-century beginnings in Edgar Allan Poe and Wilkie Collins through its Golden Age and beyond. In fact, Welty's library contains more than three hundred books belonging or adjacent to the mystery genre, by nearly a hundred different authors and/or editors. A quick glance at the catalog of these books suggests some favorites. Welty owned nineteen distinct works by Agatha Christie, sixteen by Georges Simenon, fourteen each by Elizabeth Daly and Dick Francis, ten each by Ngaio Marsh and Rex Stout, and eight by Freeman Wills Crofts, among many others. Her library also reflects the deep bond that she developed with Ross Macdonald: she owned almost every book he published. It would appear, in short, that Welty read most mystery writers of consequence from the nineteenth century to the 1990s.

By itself, of course, a list of books can say only so much. The list that follows offers no insight into how many times or with what care Welty read a given book. It reveals nothing about marginalia: Marrs tells us that Welty did not often write in her books, but she sometimes marked passages of interest and, on rare occasions, left notes. This list, moreover, cannot speak of books borrowed from the library; books bought, read, and discarded; or books lent to friends who, for any number of understandable reasons, did not return them. Since most people buy books that they do not read immediately, or sometimes ever, we cannot use such a list to determine—at least not definitively—when Welty read a book or, indeed, if she read it at all. If a book does not appear on the list, this absence means only that it was not in the Welty House in July of 2001. These caveats notwithstanding, the following list offers an index of Welty's knowledge of mystery fiction. Suggesting the horizons of possibility within which she innovated the genre for the purposes of her art, it points the way to future research.

This list also helps to frame the present collection. Mystery or mystery-adjacent books make up about six percent of Welty's library. To put this number in context, consider that Welty owned approximately the same number of works—about three hundred, give or take—either by or about Jane Austen, Willa Cather, Anton Chekhov, Flannery O'Conner, William Faulkner, E. M. Forster, Henry Green, Henry James, Katherine Anne Porter, and Virginia Woolf, combined. The comparison, to be sure, is inexact. Austen and Faulkner appear in the following list, as do other writers of so-called literary fiction, such as Joseph Conrad, Charles Dickens, Fyodor Dostoevsky, and Herman Melville. Although a novel like *Crime and Punishment*, for example, may not belong to the mystery genre in the strict sense, it can help us better understand Welty's own use of mystery tropes. In this sense, including these books in the list gives us a new way to envision her kinship with some of her canonical forebears.

For the most part, though, the list abounds in the kind of genre mysteries whose influence on Welty's fiction most critics have not considered until now. Genre fiction, by and large, favors greater consistencies of pattern than its literary counterpart, which values innovation. Welty, we now know, devoured hundreds of whodunits. Surely, their patterns impressed themselves, along the way, on her imagination. Indeed, the sheer volume of these books in her library reinforces the claim that any study of Welty and mystery must begin in genre.

It remains to say that we have derived the following list from the catalog of Welty's library produced by the Mississippi Department of Archives and History (MDAH). Work on this catalog began in the early 2000s and, though nearly finished, continues to this day. For that reason, this list is comprehensive but not definitive. We do not expect, but cannot rule out, that the final phase of cataloging will identify books we have not included. We want to thank the MDAH for permission to refine and publish a portion of the labor of the many people who have contributed to this catalog. In particular, we want to thank four members of the MDAH staff who offered timely and invaluable support: Nan Prince, Director of Collections, Museum Division; Megan Bankston, Curator of Collections, Museum Division; and Beth Batton, Cataloger, Museum Division; and Lauren Rhoades, Director of the Eudora Welty House & Garden.

MYSTERY AND RELATED BOOKS IN
EUDORA WELTY'S LIBRARY

Allingham, Margery. *Death of a Ghost*. Dell, 1958. (Second copy, Manor, 1973.)
Allingham, Margery. *Pearls Before Swine*. Bantam, 1984.

Ambler, Eric. *A Coffin for Dimitrios*. Blakiston, 1943.

Amis, Kingsley. *The Green Man*. Ballantine Books, 1973.

Asquith, Lady Cynthia. *The Second Ghost Book*. Beagle Books, 1970.

Asquith, Lady Cynthia. *The Third Ghost Book*. Beagle Books, 1970.

Austen, Jane. *Northanger Abbey*. M. Secker, 1923. (Second copy, Zodiac, 1948.)

Barnard, Robert. *Death and the Princess*. Dell, 1983.

Barnard, Robert. *Death of a Mystery Writer*. Dell, 1985.

Barnard, Robert. *The Cherry Blossom Corpse*. Dell, 1988.

Bentley, E. C. *Trent's Own Case*. Knopf, 1936.

Bernard, Robert. *Deadly Meeting*. Harper and Row, 1986.

Bierce, Ambrose. *Ghost and Horror Stories*. Dover, 1964.

Blackwood, Algernon. *John Silence*. Donald C. Vaughan, 1915.

Blackwood, Algernon. *Tales of the Uncanny and the Supernatural*. Peter Nevill, 1954.

Blackwood, Algernon. *The Tales of Algernon Blackwood*. E. P. Dutton & Company, Inc., 1939.

Blake, Nicholas. *A Penknife in My Heart*. Harper and Row, 1980.

Blake, Nicholas. *End of Chapter*. Harper and Row, 1977.

Blake, Nicholas. *Head of a Traveler*. Pocket Books, 1950.

Blake, Nicholas. *Minute for Murder*. Harper and Row, 1985.

Blake, Nicholas. *The Worm of Death*. Harper and Row, 1986.

Braun, Lilian Jackson. *The Cat Who Played Brahms*. Berkley, 1987.

Bruccoli, Matthew J. *Ross Macdonald*. Harcourt Brace Jovanovich, 1984.

Carpenter, Margaret. *Experiment Perilous*. Pyramid Books, 1964.

Carr, John Dickson. *The Burning Court*. International Polygonics, 1985.

Carr, John Dickson. *The Crooked Hinge*. Dell, 1938.

Carr, John Dickson. *The Hollow Man*. Penguin, 1954.

Carr, John Dickson. *The Three Coffins*. Popular Library, 1935.

Cerf, Bennett A., editor. *Three Famous Murder Novels: Before the Fact, Trent's Last Case, The House of the Arrow*. Modern Library, 1945.

Chandler, Raymond. *The Blue Dahlia*. Southern Illinois UP, 1976.

Chandler, Raymond. *Killer in the Rain*. Pocket Books, 1965.

Chandler, Raymond. *The Little Sister*. Pocket Books, 1963.

Chandler, Raymond. *Trouble Is My Business*. Ballantine Books, 1972.

Christie, Agatha. *At Bertram's Hotel*. Pocket Books, 1977.

Christie, Agatha. *The Body in the Library*. Pocket Books, 1976.

Christie, Agatha. *A Caribbean Mystery*. Simon and Schuster, 1966.

Christie, Agatha. *Dead Man's Mirror*. Berkley, 1984.

Christie, Agatha. *Elephants can Remember*. Pocket Books, 1970.

Christie, Agatha. *Funerals are Fatal*. Pocket Books, 1970.

Christie, Agatha. *Halloween Party*. Pocket Books, 1970.

Christie, Agatha. *A Holiday for Murder*. Bantam, 1979.

Christie, Agatha. *Mrs. McGinty's Dead*. Pocket Books, 1970.

Christie, Agatha. *Murder in Three Acts*. Popular Library, 1934.

Christie, Agatha. *A Murder is Announced*. Pocket Books, 1970.

Christie, Agatha. *Murder with Mirrors*. Pocket Books, 1970.

Christie, Agatha. *The Mystery of the Blue Train*. Pocket Books, 1955.

Christie, Agatha. *A Pocket Full of Rye*. Pocket Books, 1970.
    (Second copy, Pocket Books, 1973.)

Christie, Agatha. *Poirot Loses a Client*. Dell, 1980.

Christie, Agatha. *Ten Little Indians*. Pocket Books, 1975.

Christie, Agatha. *Third Girl*. Pocket Books, 1984.

Christie, Agatha. *13 for Luck*. Dell, 1977.

Christie, Agatha. *The Tuesday Club Murders*. Berkley, 1985.

Clinton-Baddeley, V. C. *Death's Bright Dart*. Dell, 1982.

Clinton-Baddeley, V. C. *To Study a Long Silence*. Harper and Row, 1984.

Collins, Wilkie. *Armadale*. Dover, 1977.

Collins, Wilkie. *The Moonstone*, edited by J. I. M. Stewart, Penguin,
    1975. (Second copy, Penguin, 1976.)

Collins, Wilkie. *Tales of Terror and the Supernatural*. Dover, 1972.

Collins, Wilkie. *The Woman in White*. Penguin, 1974.

Conrad, Joseph. *Three Great Tales*. Vintage Books, 1962.

Conrad, Joseph. *The Portable Conrad*. Viking Press, 1947.

Crispin, Edmund. *Frequent Hearses*. Penguin, 1982.

Crofts, Freeman Wills. *The Cheyne Mystery*. Penguin, 1965.

Crofts, Freeman Wills. *Crime at Guildford*. Penguin, 1965.

Crofts, Freeman Wills. *Golden Ashes*. Penguin, 1965. (Second copy,
    Penguin, 1965.)

Crofts, Freeman Wills. *Inspector French's Greatest Case*. Penguin, 1965.

Crofts, Freeman Wills. *The Loss of the Jane Vosper*. Penguin, 1965

Crofts, Freeman Wills. *Mystery in the Channel*. Penguin, 1965.

Crofts, Freeman Wills. *The Pit Prop Syndicate*. Penguin, 1965.

Crofts, Freeman Wills. *The 12:30 from Croydon*. Penguin, 1965.

Dahl, Roald. *Someone Like You*. Knopf, 1953.

Daly, Elizabeth. *And Dangerous to Know*. Bantam, 1984.

Daly, Elizabeth. *Any Shape or Form*. Berkley, 1964. (Second copy,
    Dell, 1981.)

Daly, Elizabeth. *Arrow Pointing Nowhere*. Berkley, 1944.

Daly, Elizabeth. *The Book of the Crime*. Berkley, 1964. (2 additional copies, Berkley, 1964 and Bantam, 1983.)

Daly, Elizabeth. *The Book of the Dead*. Berkley Medallion Books, 1944.

Daly, Elizabeth. *The Book of the Lion*. Bantam, 1985.

Daly, Elizabeth. *Deadly Nightshade*. Berkley, 1963.

Daly, Elizabeth. *Death and Letters*. Berkley, 1963. (Second copy, Berkley, 1963.)

Daly, Elizabeth. *Evidence of Things Seen*. Berkley, 1943.

Daly, Elizabeth. *The House Without the Door*. Military Service Pub. Co, 1945. (Second copy, Bantam, 1984.)

Daly, Elizabeth. *Night Walk*. Dell, 1982.

Daly, Elizabeth. *Nothing Can Rescue Me*. Bantam, 1946.

Daly, Elizabeth. *Unexpected Night*. Berkley, 1964.

Daly, Elizabeth. *The Wrong Way Down*. Berkley, 1963.

De la Mare, Walter. *The Connoisseur and Other Stories*. Knopf, 1926.

Derleth, August. *Sleep No More*. Farrar & Rinehart, Inc., 1944.

Derleth, August. *Who Knocks*. Rinehart & Company, Inc., 1946.

Dickens, Charles. *Bleak House. The Works of Charles Dickens*. P. F. Collier, vols. 17–18. Publication date unknown.

Dickens, Charles. *Edwin Drood. The Works of Charles Dickens*. P. F. Collier, vol. 30. Publication date unknown.

Dostoyevsky, Fyodor. *The Brothers Karamazov*. Modern Library, 1950.

Dostoyevsky, Fyodor. *Crime and Punishment*. Modern Library, 1932.

Dostoyevsky, Fyodor. *The Double*. Collins Harvill, 1989.

Doyle, Arthur Conan. *The Adventure of the Speckled Band and Other Stories of Sherlock Holmes*. The New American Library, 1965.

Doyle, Arthur Conan. *The Adventures and Memoirs of Sherlock Holmes*. Modern Library, 1946.

Doyle, Arthur Conan. *The Case-book of Sherlock Holmes*. Penguin, 1951.

Eustis, Helen. *The Horizontal Man*. Penguin, 1982.

Faulkner, William. *Absalom! Absalom!* Modern Library, 1951.

Faulkner, William. *Intruder in the Dust*, Random House, 1948.

Faulkner, William. *Knight's Gambit*, New American Library, 1950.

Faulkner, William. *Sanctuary*. New American Library, 1948.

Faulkner, William. *Sanctuary: The Original Text*. Random House, 1981.

Ferrars, E. X. *The Shape of a Stain*. Doubleday, Doran and Company, 1942.

Fleming, Joan. *Death of a Sardine*. Ballantine Books, 1967.

Francis, Dick. *Bonecrack*. Harper and Row, 1971.

Francis, Dick. *The Danger*. Ballantine Books, 1989.

Francis, Dick. *Decider*. Jove Books: Berkley Pub. Group, 1995.

Francis, Dick. *Enquiry*. Harper and Row, 1969.

Francis, Dick. *Field of Thirteen*. Putnam, 1998.

Francis, Dick. *High Stakes*. Harper and Row, 1975.

Francis, Dick. *Hot Money*. Ballantine Books, 1989.

Francis, Dick. *In the Frame*. Harper and Row, 1976.

Francis, Dick. *Knockdown*. Harper and Row, 1974.

Francis, Dick. *Proof*. Ballantine Books, 1985.

Francis, Dick. *Reflex*. G. P. Putnam's Sons, 1981.

Francis, Dick. *Risk*. Harper and Row, 1977.

Francis, Dick. *Smokescreen*. Bantam, 1973.

Francis, Dick. *Whip Hand*. Harper and Row, 1979.

Garve, Andrew. *The Cuckoo Line Affair*. Harper and Brothers, 1953.
(Second copy, Lancer Books, 1963.)

Garve, Andrew. *Frame-Up*. Harper and Row, 1964.

Garve, Andrew. *Home to Roost*. Penguin, 1978.

Garve, Andrew. *The Narrow Search*. Harper and Brothers, 1957.

Gash, Jonathan. *The Judas Pair*. Harper and Row, 1977. (Second copy, Dell, 1981.)

Gilbert, Michael. *Be Shot for Six-Pence*. Harper and Brothers, 1956.

Gilbert, Michael. *The Black Seraphim*. Penguin, 1985.

Gilbert, Michael. *Blood and Judgement*. Harper and Brothers, 1959.

Gilbert, Michael. *The Country-House Burglar*. Harper, 1955.

Gilbert, Michael. *The Danger Within*. Harper and Brothers, 1952.

Gilbert, Michael. *The Family Tomb*. Harper and Row, 1969.

Gilbert, Michael. *Fear to Tread*. Harper and Brothers, 1953.

Greene, Graham and Carol Reed. *The Third Man*. Simon and Schuster, 1968.

Greene, Hugh, editor. *Cosmopolitan Crimes: Foreign Rivals of Sherlock Holmes*. Pantheon, 1971.

Grimes, Martha. *The Dirty Duck*. Dell, 1985.

Grimes, Martha. *The Old Fox Deceiv'd*. Little Brown & Company, 1982.

Grose, Shirley E. *Murder, Mayhem, Hydrophobia*. BookCrafters, 1987.

Hammett, Dashiell. *The Thin Man*. Pocket Books, 1945. (Second copy, Vintage Books, 1972.)

Hare, Cyril. *Death Among Friends*. Harper and Row, 1984.

Hare, Cyril. *Death is No Sportsman*. Harper and Row, 1981.

Hare, Cyril. *Death Walks the Woods*. Harper and Row, 1981.
(Second copy, Harper and Row, 1981.)

Hare, Cyril. *An English Murder*. Harper and Row, 1978.

Hare, Cyril. *Suicide Excepted*. Harper and Row, 1983.

Hare, Cyril. *Tenant for Death*. Harper and Row, 1982.

Hare, Cyril. *The Wind Blows Death*. Harper and Row, 1982.

Haycraft, Howard, editor. *14 Great Detective Stories*. Modern Library, 1949.

Heard, H. F. *The Lost Cavern and Other Tales of the Fantastic*. The Vanguard Press, 1948. (Second copy, The Vanguard Press, 1948.)

Heard, H. F. *Reply Paid*. The Vanguard Press, Inc., 1942.

Heard, H. F. *A Taste for Honey*. The Vanguard Press, Inc., 1941.

Hillerman, Tony. *Dance Hall of the Dead*. Harper Paperbacks, 1990.

Hillerman, Tony. *A Thief of Time*. Harper Paperbacks, 1990.

Hodge, Harry, editor. *Famous Trials I*. Penguin, 1954.

Hopkins, Kenneth. *Body Blow*. Holt, Rinehart, and Winston, 1965. (Two additional copies, both Harper and Row, 1985.)

Hopkins, Kenneth. *Dead Against My Principles*. Harper and Row, 1984.

Hopkins, Kenneth. *She Died Because . . . .* Harper and Row, 1984.

Hunter, Alan. *Gently Through the Woods*. Dell, 1982.

Innes, Michael. *The Ampersand Papers*. Penguin, 1984.

Innes, Michael. *The Bloody Wood*. Berkley Medallion, 1967.

Innes, Michael. *The Daffodil Affair*. Berkley, 1964.

Innes, Michael. *Hare Sitting Up*. Harper and Row, 1982.

Innes, Michael. *The Weight of the Evidence*. Harper and Row, 1983.

Kahn, Joan, editor. *Chilling and Killing*. Houghton Mifflin, 1978.

Kahn, Joan, editor. *The Edge of the Chair*. Harper and Row, 1967.

Kahn, Joan, editor. *Handle with Care: Frightening Stories*. Greenwillow Books, 1985.

Kahn, Joan, editor. *Hanging by a Thread*. Houghton Mifflin Company, 1969.

Kahn, Joan, editor. *Open at Your Own Risk*. Houghton Mifflin Company, 1975.

Kahn, Joan, editor. *Some Things Dark and Dangerous*. Harper and Row, 1970.

Kahn, Joan, editor. *Some Things Fierce and Fatal*. Harper and Row, 1971.

Kahn, Joan, editor. *Some Things Strange and Sinister*. Harper and Row, 1973.

Kahn, Joan, editor. *Trial and Terror*. Houghton Mifflin, 1973.

Kellerman, Jonathan. *Self Defense*. Bantam, 1995.

Kiely, Benedict. *Honey Seems Bitter*. Methuen, 1954.

James, M. R. *Casting the Runes and other Ghost Stories.* Oxford UP, 1987.

James, M. R. *The Collected Ghost Stories of M. R. James.* Edward Arnold & Company, 1949.

Jesse, F. Tennyson. *Murder and its Motives.* George G. Harrap & Co. Ltd., 1952.

Landesman, Peter. *The Raven.* Baskerville, 1995.

Langton, Jane. *Divine Inspiration.* Viking, 1993.

Langton, Jane. *Emily Dickinson is Dead.* St. Martin's Press, 1984.

Langton, Jane. *Good and Dead.* Penguin, 1989.

Langton, Jane. *The Memorial Hall Murder.* Harper and Row, 1978.

Lathen, Emma. *Pick Up Sticks.* Pocket Books, 1972.

Lee, Vernon. *Hauntings.* Frank F. Lovell, 1890

Lee, Vernon. *Pope Jacynth.* John Lane, 1907.

Lee, Vernon. *The Snake Lady and Other Stories.* Grove Press, 1954.

Le Fanu, Sheridan. *Best Ghost Stories.* Dover, 1964.

Le Fanu, Sheridan. *Guy Deverell.* Dover, 1984.

Le Fanu, Sheridan. *Madam Crowl's Ghost and Other Tales of Mystery.* G. Bell & Sons, 1923.

Le Fanu, Sheridan. *A Strange Adventure in the Life of Miss Laura Mildmay.* Home and Van Thal, 1947.

Le Fanu, Sheridan. *Uncle Silas.* The Cresset Press, 1947.

Lehrer, Jim. *Blue Hearts.* Random House, 1993.

Lehrer, Jim. *Fine Lines.* Random House, 1994.

Leithauser, Brad, editor. *The Norton Book of Ghost Stories.* W. W. Norton, 1994.

Leroux, Gaston. *The Mystery of the Yellow Room.* Dover, 1977.

Levin, Ira. *A Kiss Before Dying.* Simon & Schuster, 1953.

Lowden, Desmond. *Bellman and True.* Holt, Rinehart, & Winston, 1975.

Macdonald, John. *The Moving Target.* Pocket Books, 1950.

Macdonald, John Ross. *The Drowning Pool.* Pocket Books, 1951.

Macdonald, John Ross. *The Way Some People Die.* Pocket Books, 1952. (Second copy, Bantam, 1971.)

Macdonald, Philip. *The Rasp.* Avon Books, 1970.

Macdonald, Ross. *Archer in Jeopardy: The Doomsters, The Zebra-Striped Hearse, The Instant Enemy.* Knopf, 1979

Macdonald, Ross. *Archer at Large: Three Great Lew Archer Novels of Suspense.* Knopf, 1970.

Macdonald, Ross. *Black Money.* Knopf, 1963 (Second copy, Bantam, 1983.)

Macdonald, Ross. *Blue City*. Bantam, 1958.

Macdonald, Ross. *The Blue Hammer*. Knopf, 1976.

Macdonald, Ross. *The Chill*. Knopf, 1964. (Second copy, Bantam, 1970.)

Macdonald, Ross. *A Collection of Reviews*. Lord John Press, 1979.

Macdonald, Ross. *The Dark Tunnel*. Bantam, 1972.

Macdonald, Ross. *The Drowning Pool*. Knopf, 1970. (Second copy, Bantam, 1975.)

Macdonald, Ross. *The Far Side of the Dollar*. Bantam, 1970. (Second copy Bantam, 1984.)

Macdonald, Ross. *The Far Side of the Dollar. Manuscript Edition*. Bruccoli Clark, 1982.

Macdonald, Ross. *Find a Victim*. Bantam, 1967. (Second copy, Bantam, 1972.)

Macdonald, Ross. *The Galton Case*. Bantam, 1970.

Macdonald, Ross. *The Goodbye Look*. Knopf, 1969. (Two additional copies, Bantam 1970.)

Macdonald, Ross. *The Instant Enemy*. Bantam, 1970. (Two additional copies, Bantam 1973, 1985.)

Macdonald, Ross. *Inward Journey*. Cordelia Editions, 1984. (Two additional copies, Cordelia Editions, 1984; Mysterious Press, 1987.)

Macdonald, Ross. *The Ivory Grin*. Bantam, 1971. (Second copy, Bantam, 1972.)

Macdonald, Ross. *Lew Archer: Private Investigator*. Mysterious Press, 1977.

Macdonald, Ross. *Meet me at the Morgue*. Pocket Books, 1967.

Macdonald, Ross. *The Moving Target*. Bantam, 1970.

Macdonald, Ross. *The Name is Archer*. Bantam, 1971.

Macdonald, Ross. *On Crime Writing*. Capra Press, 1973.

Macdonald, Ross. *Self Portrait: Ceaselessly Into the Past*. Capra Press, 1981. (Eighteen additional copies.)

Macdonald, Ross. *Sleeping Beauty*. Knopf, 1973. (Second copy, Knopf, 1973.)

Macdonald, Ross. *The Underground Man*. Knopf, 1971. (Three additional copies, Bantam, 1971, 1972, 1974.)

Macdonald, Ross. *The Wycherly Woman*. Bantam 1973. (Second copy, Bantam, 1973.)

Macdonald, Ross. *The Zebra-Striped Hearse*. Knopf, 1962. (Second copy, Bantam, 1970.)

Macdonald, Ross, editor. *Great Stories of Suspense*. Knopf, 1974.

Macdonald, Ross and Eudora Welty. *The Faulkner Investigation.* Cordelia Editions, 1985. (Eleven additional copies.)

Macdonald, Ross and Margaret Millar. *Early Millar: The First Stories of Ross Macdonald and Margaret Millar.* Cordelia Editions, 1982.

Margolies, Joseph A., editor. *Strange and Fantastic Stories.* Whittlesey House, 1946.

Marsh, Ngaio. *Death at the Bar.* Jove, 1980.

Marsh, Ngaio. *Death of a Fool.* Jove, 1978.

Marsh, Ngaio. *Death of a Peer.* Jove, 1982.

Marsh, Ngaio. *Grave Mistake.* Jove, 1980.

Marsh, Ngaio. *Hand in Glove.* Jove, 1980.

Marsh, Ngaio. *Killer Dolphin.* Jove, 1983.

Marsh, Ngaio. *Light Thickens.* Little, Brown, 1982. (Second copy, Berkley, Jove, 1983.)

Marsh, Ngaio. *Photo Finish.* Jove, 1981.

Marsh, Ngaio. *Spinsters in Jeopardy.* Berkeley, 1986.

Marsh, Ngaio. *When In Rome.* Fontana, 1971.

MacPherson, John. *The Mystery Chef's Own Cook Book.* Garden City Publishing Co., 1943.

Martini, Steve. *Prime Witness.* Jove, 1994.

McGaughey, Neil. *Otherwise Known as Murder.* Scribner, 1994.

Melville, Herman. *Shorter Novels of Herman Melville.* Liveright Publishing, 1942.

Millar, Margaret. *Beyond this Point are Monsters.* Random House, 1970.

Moyes, Patricia. *Down Among the Dead Men.* Dell, 1961.

Moyes, Patricia. *Many Deadly Returns.* H. Holt, 1987.

Moyes, Patricia. *Who is Simon Warwick?* Holt, Rinehart, and Winston, 1982.

Patterson, James. *Kiss the Girls.* Little, Brown, 1995.

Payne, Peggy. *Sister India.* The Eudora Welty House & Garden. 2001. Typescript.

Pearson, Edmund. *More Studies in Murder.* Smith & Robert Haas, 1936.

Pearson, Edmund. *Studies in Murder.* Doubleday, 1963. (Second copy, Doubleday, 1963.)

Pearson, Edmund. *Trial of Lizzie Borden.* Doubleday, Doran, and Company, 1937.

Perry, Anne. *The Silent Cry.* Fawcett Columbine, 1997.

Poe, Edgar Allan. *Poetry and Tales.* Library of America, 1984.

Poe, Edgar Allan. *Essays and Reviews.* Library of America, 1984.

Poe, Edgar Allan. *The Complete Poems*. Barnes and Noble Books, 1994.

Proctor, Maurice. *The Graveyard Rolls*. Popular Library, 1964.

Rendell, Ruth. *The Veiled One*. Hutchinson, 1998.

Rinehart, Mary Roberts. *The Haunted Lady*. Kensington, 1985.

Roosevelt, Elliott. *A First Class Murder*. Avon, 1993.

Roosevelt, Elliott. *Murder at Midnight*. St. Martin's Paperbacks, 1998.

Roosevelt, Elliott. *Murder in the Blue Room*. Avon, 1992.

Roosevelt, Elliott. *Murder in the Oval Office*. Avon, 1990.

Rohmer, Sax. *The Return of Dr. Fu-Manchu*. Pyramid Books, 1961.

Roughead, William. *Classic Crimes*. Cassell, 1951.

Roughead, William. *Nothing But Murder*. Sheridan House, 1946.

Roughead, William. *Tales of the Criminous*. Cassell & Company Ltd., 1956.

Roughead, William. *The Murderer's Companion*. The Press of the Reader's Club, 1941.

Simenon, Georges. *Lost Moorings*. Penguin, 1952.

Simenon, Georges. *Maigret and the Man on the Bench*. Harcourt Brace Jovanovich, 1979.

Simenon, Georges. *Maigret and the Spinster*. Harcourt Brace Jovanovich, 1982.

Simenon, Georges. *Maigret and the Wine Merchant*. Harcourt Brace Jovanovich, 1980.

Simenon, Georges. *Maigret Bides His Time*. Harcourt Brace Jovanovich, 1985.

Simenon, Georges. *Maigret's Boyhood Friend*. Harcourt Brace Jovanovich, 1981.

Simenon, Georges. *Maigret Hesitates*. Curtis Books, 1970.

Simenon, Georges. *Maigret in Exile*. Harcourt Brace and Co., 1994.

Simenon, Georges. *Maigret in Vichy*. Avon, 1970.

Simenon, Georges. *Maigret Loses His Temper*. Harcourt Brace Jovanovich, 1980.

Simenon, Georges. *Maigret on the Defensive*. Avon, 1987.

Simenon, Georges. *Maigret's Special Murder*. Penguin, 1966.

Simenon, Georges. *Maigret Stonewalled*. Penguin, 1963.

Simenon, Georges. *The Man Who Watched Trains Go By*. Penguin, 1964.

Simenon, Georges. *The Methods of Maigret*. Bantam, 1959.

Simenon, Georges. *The Short Cases of Inspector Maigret*. Doubleday, 1959.

Stevenson, Robert Louis. *Novels and Stories*. Pilot Press, 1946.

Stout, Rex. *A Family Affair*. Bantam, 1976.

Stout, Rex. *Death of a Dude*. Bantam, 1984. (Second copy, Bantam, 1990.)

Stout, Rex. *Gambit*. Bantam, 1962.

Stout, Rex. *Plot it Yourself*. Bantam, 1959.

Stout, Rex. *The Black Mountain*. Bantam, 1988.

Stout, Rex. *The Doorbell Rang*. Bantam, 1971.

Stout, Rex. *The Final Deduction*. Bantam, 1985.

Stout, Rex. *Three at Wolfe's Door*. The Viking Press, 1960.

Stout, Rex. *Three for the Chair*. Bantam, 1989.

Stout, Rex. *Triple Jeopardy*. Bantam, 1993.

Summers, Montague. *The Supernatural Omnibus*. Victor Gollancz, 1950.

Tey, Josephine. *The Man in the Queue*. Macmillan, 1953.

Tey, Josephine. *A Shilling for Candles*. Macmillan, 1954.

Tey, Josephine. *The Singing Sands*. Dell, 1965.

Tey, Josephine. *To Love and Be Wise*. Macmillan, 1951.

Troy, Simon. *Swift to its Close*. Perennial Library, 1981.

Truman, Margaret. *Murder at the National Cathedral*. Random House, 1990.

Truman, Margaret. *Murder in the CIA*. Ballantine Books, 1978.

Truman, Margaret. *Murder in the House*. Random House, 1997. (Second copy, Random House, 1997.)

Truman, Margaret. *Murder on the Potomac*. Ballantine Books, 1995.

Twain, Mark. *Tom Sawyer Abroad, Tom Sawyer, Detective and Other Stories, Etc. The Writings of Mark Twain*, Harper and Brothers, 1910.

Twain, Mark. *Pudd'nhead Wilson*. Book of the Month Club, 1992.

Van Doren Stern, Philip, editor. *The Moonlight Traveler: Great Tales of Fantasy and Imagination*. Doubleday, Doran, and Company, 1943.

Van Allsburg, Chris. *The Mysteries of Harris Burdick*. Houghton Mifflin Company, 1984.

Watson, Collin. *Lonelyheart 4122*. Berkley, 1968.

Wise, Herbert A and Phyliss Fraser, editors. *Great Tales of Horror and the Supernatural*. Random House, 1944.

Wodehouse, P. G. *Wodehouse on Crime: A Dozen Tales of Fiendish Cunning*. Ticknor and Fields 1981. (Second copy, Ticknor and Fields, 1981.)

World's Great Detective Stories, W. J. Black, 1928.

ABOUT THE EDITORS
AND CONTRIBUTORS

EDITORS

Jacob Agner is a PhD candidate in English at the University of Mississippi. His dissertation examines the neglected rural underground of the classic noir fiction and film category, and his scholarship thus far ranges topics such as the fiction of Eudora Welty, Cormac McCarthy, and Appalachian film noir. As a recipient of the Eudora Welty Research Fellowship, funded by the Eudora Welty Foundation and the Mississippi Department of Archives and History, he has examined the writer's correspondence for connections to film history. And his 2013 essay, "A Collision of Visions: Montage and the Concept of Collision in Eudora Welty's 'June Recital,'" won the Ruth Vande Kieft Prize awarded by the Eudora Welty Society for "the best essay on Eudora Welty by a beginning scholar."

Harriet Pollack, emerita, Bucknell University, is now affiliate professor of American literature, College of Charleston, a position from which she inaugurated the University Press of Mississippi series Critical Perspectives on Eudora Welty. She is the author of *Eudora Welty's Fiction and Photography: The Body of The Other Woman.* Her previous edited and coedited volumes include *New Essays on Eudora Welty, Class, and Race; Eudora Welty, Whiteness, and Race; Emmett Till in Literary Memory and Imagination* (with Christopher Metress); *Having Our Way: Women Rewriting Tradition in Twentieth-Century America);* and *Eudora Welty and Politics: Did the Writer Crusade?* (with Suzanne Marrs).

CONTRIBUTORS

Sarah Gilbreath Ford is professor of American literature at Baylor University and serves as the director of Baylor's Beall Poetry Festival. She is the author of *Haunted Property: Slavery and the Gothic* (2020) and *Tracing Southern Storytelling in Black and White* (2014). She serves as an associate editor of the *Eudora Welty Review* and as the web editor of the Eudora Welty Society's website. In 2018 she won the Welty society's Phoenix Award for scholarship and service. In 2019 she was named a Baylor Centennial Professor.

Katie Berry Frye is assistant professor of English at Pepperdine University. Her teaching and research interests focus on the literature of the American South, American modernism, the trope of the grotesque, and the work of Eudora Welty. She has published in such journals as *Mississippi Quarterly, Southern Studies: An Interdisciplinary Journal of the South,* and *Women's Studies: An Interdisciplinary Journal.* In addition to teaching courses in composition, the humanities, and literature, she is the coordinator for the women's studies program.

Michael Kreyling, Gertrude Conaway Vanderbilt Professor of English, Emeritus, at Vanderbilt University, claims he is almost as old as noir, having first published on Welty in *The Mississippi Quarterly* in the 1970s. He has since published eight books: *Eudora Welty's Achievement of Order, Figures of the Hero in Southern Narrative, The Novels of Ross Macdonald, Author and Agent: Eudora Welty and Diarmuid Russell, Understanding Eudora Welty, The South That Wasn't There, A Late Encounter with the Civil War,* and *Inventing Southern Literature,* for which he received the Eudora Welty Prize.

Andrew B. Leiter is professor of English at Lycoming College in Williamsport, Pennsylvania. He is author of *In the Shadow of the Black Beast: African American Masculinity in the Harlem and Southern Renaissances* (2010); editor of *Southerners on Film: Essays on Hollywood Portrayals Since the 1970s;* and coeditor (with Christopher Rieger) of *Faulkner & Hurston, Faulkner & Hemingway,* and *Faulkner & García Márquez.*

Rebecca Mark is director of the Institute for Women's Leadership and a professor in Women's Gender and Sexuality Studies at Rutgers University. Her research addresses US southern women's writing with a focus on Eudora Welty, and twentieth-century US cultural representations of trauma. Her books include *The Dragon's Blood: Feminist Intertextuality in Eudora Welty's*

"The Golden Apples" (1994) and *Ersatz America: Hidden Traces, Graphic Texts and the Mending of Democracy* (2014). She received the Public Humanities Achievement Award from the Mississippi Humanities Council for directing the civil rights conference *Unsettling Memories* (2004), and she was the founding director of the Newcomb College Institute and the Center for Academic Equity at Tulane University.

Suzanne Marrs, professor emerita of English at Millsaps College, is author of *Eudora Welty, A Biography*, for which she won a Mississippi Author Award, and *One Writer's Imagination: The Fiction of Eudora Welty*. She is editor of *What There Is to Say We Have Said: The Correspondence of Eudora Welty and William Maxwell*; coeditor of *Eudora Welty and Politics: Did the Writer Crusade?* (with Harriet Pollack); and coeditor of *Meanwhile There Are Letters: The Correspondence of Eudora Welty and Ross Macdonald* (with Tom Nolan), which was a finalist for Edgar, Anthony, and Macavity Awards. Though she has now retired from the faculty of Millsaps College, Marrs continues to serve as Welty Foundation Scholar-in-Residence at the Eudora Welty House.

Tom Nolan is author of *Ross Macdonald: A Biography* and coeditor (with Suzanne Marrs) of *Meanwhile There Are Letters: The Correspondence of Eudora Welty and Ross Macdonald*. He has edited several other Macdonald books, including three Library of America volumes of Macdonald novels. He has also written a biography of Artie Shaw: *Three Chords for Beauty's Sake*. Nolan has reviewed crime fiction for the *Wall Street Journal* since 1990.

Michael Pickard is the E. B. Stewart Family Professor of Language and Literature and an associate professor of English and creative writing at Millsaps College. With Suzanne Marrs and Lee Anne Bryan, he is cowriting a book to be called *Eudora Welty and the House of Fiction*.

Victoria Richard is a junior studying English and creative writing at Millsaps College. She has recently begun a research project demonstrating the correlations between the writing of Eudora Welty and her longtime friend Elizabeth Bowen.

INDEX

References to figures appear in bold.

mystery fiction, 4–14, 118–19, 127, 178, 221–34; readers' expectation, 4, 7, 12–13, 89, 100, 146, 167, 175; relationship with Macdonald, 14–16, 115–29, 202–18

Welty, Eudora, works of: "The Alterations," 10, 16–19, 150; "At the Landing," 150; *The Bride of the Innisfallen*, 14, 101; "The Burning," 96, 112, 146; "The Cheated," 19–20; "Clytie," 21; *A Curtain of Green*, 10, 11, 13, 14, 19; "A Curtain of Green," 21, 64, 96, 211; *Delta Wedding*, 84, 151; "The Demonstrators," 14, 21, 22, 25, 28, 126, 132–44, 163; "First Love," 132; "Flowers for Marjorie," 13, 21, 96; *The Golden Apples*, 14, 21, 24, 69–92, 151, 167; "The Great Pinnington Solves the Mystery," 8–10, **9**, 51; "Henry," 215–16, 218; "The Hitch-Hikers," 13, 21, 84, 96, 207, 211; "June Recital," 14, 24, 69–90, 132, 156; "The Key," 13, 19–20, 22; "Lily Daw and the Three Ladies," 19, 21; "Looking at Short Stories," 137, 213–14; *Losing Battles*, 14, 21, 26, 96, 107, 126, 146–76, **171**; "Moon Lake," 24, 69–74, 80, 82, 85–86, 89, 90, 156; "Must the Novelist Crusade?," 142, 194, 205–6; "The Night of the Little House," 16, 19–20; "No Place for You, My Love," 21, 23, 43–46, 48; "Old Mr. Grenada," 63–64, 67; "Old Mr. Marblehall," 23, 51–53, 61–66, 67; *One Writer's Beginnings*, 5, 27, 168, 170, 203, 212, 213, 221; *The Optimist's Daughter*, 14, 15, 21, 26–28, 84, 90, 178–99; "Petrified Man," 21, 23, 51–61, 65–67, 207; "A Piece of News," 12, 13, 19, 21, 96; "Place in Fiction," 209; *The Ponder Heart*, 14, 21, 23, 24–25, 38–43, 46, 48, 93–114; "Powerhouse," 4, 13, 96, 146, 148; "The Purple Hat," 14; *The Robber Bridegroom*, 96, 150, 207–8; "The Shadow Club," 14, 16, 27, 28, 128, 194, 210–18; "Shower of Gold," 77; "A Sketching Trip," 120; "Some Notes on River Country," 170; "A Still Moment," 208; "The Wanderers," 87–88; "Where Is the Voice Coming From?," 14, 25, 28, 123–25, 129; "The Whistle," 19, 21, 82; "The Whole World Knows," 208; "Why I Live at the P.O.," 19, 21; *The Wide Net*, 14; "The Wide Net," 96, 132, 146, 175; "The Winds," 132; "Words into Fiction," 3, 137; "A Worn Path," 21, 172

Welty House, 7, 8, 19, 27, 28, 131, 199, 222; library, 4–14, 27, 221–34

West, Mae, 114; *I'm No Angel* (1933), 114

Weston, Ruth, 69, 88, 198

Where Danger Lives (1950), 48

White, Patrick, 16

white supremacy, 12, 55, 59, 64–66

whiteness, 4, 22, 23–24, 25, 26, 46, 52–56, 59–66, 78, 88, 98–100, 104, 108–13, 123, 133–42, 146, 147, 149–50, 168–75, 187, 214

whodunit, 53, 54, 132–34, 147, 197

Wilson, Edmund, 36, 37, 119, 178, 189; "Who Cares Who Killed Roger Ackroyd?," 36–37; "Why Do People Read Detective Stories?," 36–37, 178

women crime writers, 7, 24, 95, 113, 150–51

Woolrich, Cornell (William Irish) 12, 75, 79; *After-Dinner Story*, 75, 89; "It Had to Be Murder," 75

World War I, 34, 54, 168, 178

World War II, 53, 99, 120, 178, 196

Wright, Willard Huntington. *See* Van Dine, S. S.

Yaeger, Patricia, 59, 66, 69, 85, 88, 90

Yale University, 115, 116–17

Yeats, William Butler, 34, 221; "Song of the Wandering Aengus," 81

CPSIA information can be obtained
at www.ICGtesting.com
Printed in the USA
BVHW040735231122
652364BV00010B/7